W9-BZD-336

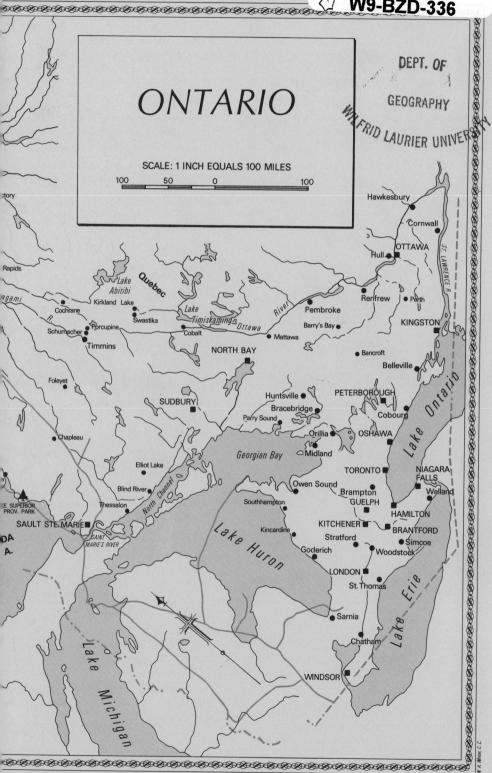

ONTARIO

SCALE: 1 INCH EQUALS 100 MILES

100   50   0   100

DEPT. OF

GEOGRAPHY

WILFRID LAURIER UNIVERSITY

Quebec

Lake Abitibi

Lake Timiskaming

Ottawa River

Hawkesbury

Cornwall

Hull   OTTAWA

ST. LAWRENCE R.

Rapids

Cochrane

Kirkland Lake

Swastika

Porcupine

Schumacher

Cobalt

Timmins

Foleyet

Mattawa

Renfrew   Perth

Pembroke

Barry's Bay

KINGSTON

Bancroft

Belleville

NORTH BAY

SUDBURY

Chapleau

Huntsville

Bracebridge

PETERBOROUGH

Parry Sound

Cobourg

Orillia

OSHAWA

Lake Ontario

Elliot Lake

Midland

Georgian Bay

TORONTO

NIAGARA FALLS

Blind River

Owen Sound

Brampton

Welland

LE. SUPERIOR PROV. PARK

Thessalon

North Channel

Southhampton

GUELPH

HAMILTON

SAULT STE. MARIE

SAINT MARIE'S RIVER

Kincardine

KITCHENER

BRANTFORD

Stratford

Simcoe

ADA A.

Goderich

Woodstock

Lake Huron

LONDON

St. Thomas

Lake Erie

Sarnia

Chatham

Lake Michigan

WINDSOR

tory

agami

R.

ctory

W. A. Weese, C.C.

BOOKS BY MAX BRAITHWAITE

Canada: Wonderland of Surprises
The Cure Searchers
Max Braithwaite's Ontario
The Mystery of the Muffled Man
Never Sleep Three in a Bed
The Night We Stole the Mountie's Car
A Privilege and a Pleasure
Sick Kids, the Story of the Hospital for Sick Children
The Valley of the Vanishing Birds
Voices of the Wild
The Western Plains
Why Shoot the Teacher
The Young Reporter

MAX BRAITHWAITE'S ONTARIO

Max Braithwaite's
ONTA

RIO

J. J. Douglas Ltd.
Vancouver   1974

Copyright © Max Braithwaite, 1974

All rights reserved. No part of this book
may be reproduced or transmitted in any
form by any means without permission in
writing from the publisher, except by a
reviewer, who may quote brief passages in
a review.

ISBN 0-88894-064-5

74 75 76 77 78 5 4 3 2 1

J.J. Douglas Ltd.,
3645 McKechnie Drive
West Vancouver, British Columbia

Designed by Jim Rimmer
Maps by W.A. Winter
Printed and bound in Canada by
The Hunter Rose Company

Cover Photo: Walter Mansfield

Illustrations: Bill Brooks, Metropolitan Toronto Library
Board, Public Archives of Canada, Ontario
Ministry of Industry and Tourism, Buffalo
and Erie County Historical Society, General Motors, Ontario Archives, Ontario
Hydro

Picture section produced by Bill Brooks

To Aileen

Contents

A Completely Biased View

I first saw Ontario when I was 32 years old, and I fell in love with the province immediately. I guess Ontario was in my blood, really. Both my parents had been born there and had emigrated to Saskatchewan while young, and Dad had told us all about the wonders of "Old Ontario," about stump fences, pitching suckers out of the creek with a fork, picking apples, making maple syrup, outings on the lake steamers. It was all wonderful to us who had been born on the southern prairies and who had never seen an apple growing, a creek running, a body of water larger than a slough, or a maple leaf.

Uncles and aunts who came to visit were all from Ontario. They looked a little different from us, somehow, and talked differently, too. One cousin of whom we were particularly fond, I remember, had a beautiful contralto voice and was a soloist at Timothy Eaton Memorial church. Eaton's . . . that was a familiar word, all right, because it was from there we got our long fleece-lined underwear and our shoes and even our kitchen cabinets.

After the Canadian Broadcasting Corporation went on the air in 1936, our house was full of Ontario. Every Saturday night in winter Foster Hewitt's thrilling voice described the action of everybody's favourites, the Toronto Maple Leafs. We hated the Argonauts and Balmy Beach teams that regularly clobbered our western football heroes. We heard the music of Horace Lapp and the comedy of Woodhouse and Hawkins, all from Toronto.

We were literally surrounded by Ontario. *Maclean's* magazine came into the house regularly and in it we read about the problems of Queen's Park, the growth of the mining industry, and the warnings of Grattan O'Leary that high taxes would ruin Canada. *Saturday Night* from Toronto was full of big glossy pictures of the city and portraits of famous Ontarians. Stephen Leacock, whose humour column appeared in the Saskatoon *Star-Phoenix* that I delivered for years, lived somewhere in Ontario, we knew, and the quaint people he wrote about lived there, too.

The book from which I received my most vivid impressions, however, was *The Man From Glengarry* by Ralph Connor. He wrote about all the great Ontario things. Lumber camps along the Ottawa River where sturdy Scotsmen (always the good guys) thrashed conniving, drunken Irishmen and boisterous Canadiens (always the bad guys); and about strange practices such as sugaring off deep in the dusky maple bush, barn raising bees, logging bees, and box socials.

At school we got Ontario from all sides. That was where Champlain fought the Iroquois and made lasting enemies of them so that they burned up missionaries. Toronto was where Mackenzie marched down Yonge Street to fight our battles as well as his. Ottawa was where responsible government was finally granted, then Confederation. And all of it happened in Ontario.

In common with most westerners we had a mental picture of Ontario as fat, prosperous and selfish. When weird things happened to the stock market or the price of grain, Bay Street was to blame. There was sophistication such as didn't yet exist on the plains. Terribly rich people dressed up in fancy clothes and attended horse shows at the Royal Agricultural Winter Fair, and very fancy balls at the Royal York Hotel. There was even a castle called Casa Loma.

Ontario was the place I yearned for. The publishers of magazines and books were there, and the producers of radio shows. People there would actually pay money for writing, and writing had become the focal point of my life. As I sat at my old upright Remington at five o'clock in the morning, indulging in my one-sided love affair with words, I directed my efforts to Toronto.

So, when the Navy transferred me to Toronto in 1944, my wife and I approached the province with the wide-eyed delight of two kids going to their first fair.

Before we crossed the border from Manitoba the fun began. We were in the rock country, the spruce tree country, the lake country of the vast, rugged Canadian Shield that covers nearly all of northern Ontario. As the train rattled over a river bridge or curved along the rocky shore of a beautiful lake we hugged ourselves and each other with pleasure. We were here. This was it. From now on life would be different. And it surely has been.

It took a long time for the train to cross northern Ontario, for it is very wide, as wide as southern Saskatchewan and Manitoba combined. Along the side of the track we saw the swaths of black and white spruce being hewn out of the forest for pulp wood, and streams plugged tight with the floating logs. We saw mine shafts through the trees, too, and at Sudbury the great nickel smelters and the barren waste they have created.

By the time that rock and trees and lakes were becoming monotonous we left them and came into the rolling farmland of southern Ontario. Now we were in Dad's "Old Ontario." We were used to unfenced, flat wheat fields that stretched forever into the horizon. But these little garden plots of fields, neatly fenced, with beef and dairy cattle everywhere, were more like a storybook picture of farms.

The elm trees between the fields, too, were most impressive. Taller than any trees we had been used to and much bigger in diameter, they stood like huge umbrellas spreading their shade over the livestock below. Truly the most striking feature of Ontario farmland.

The barns surprised us, too. On the prairie farms the good farms had immense, domed-roof barns, painted red or black or white. But the Ontario barns were smaller, usually built into the side of a hill so that a hay rack could be driven into the loft and, most surprising of all, unpainted. Those unpainted barns almost offended us. They looked so out of place in the neat farmyards beside the big brick houses with lush fields on all sides, fields that obviously never lacked for rain.

The towns and cities became more numerous and as we continued south, we saw something we never saw in Saskatchewan . . . factories. Huge brick buildings with smoke stacks and names printed on them of familiar products we'd been using all our lives. I think the name that impressed me most was Neilson's Chocolates. I'd gobbled up hundreds of their bars in my day but it felt odd to see an immense factory where they made nothing but chocolate bars.

Then we were in the Toronto area and the track was lined on either side with unbroken rows of dirty brick buildings like Massey

Harris and Westinghouse and General Electric and Steele Briggs seeds. We went underground and pulled into the immensity of Union Station.

We had three children with us on that trip. Beryl was eight and pretty well able to look after herself, but Shari had just turned two and Chris had been with us only a couple of months. So we had a child, a toddler, and an infant in arms, with all the extra gear and paraphernalia they require.

I was clutching a fistful of baggage checks for a baby carriage, a baby's basket and cart, two trunks, a couple of boxes tied with rope and a number of suitcases. We found our way to the the taxi stand. There we stood, unhappy, tired, hungry, and more than a little afraid of this city which, according to all reports, had none of the warmth and hospitality accredited to western communities.

Then a taxi driver came up to me. He was a small, wizened man with a squint and I knew I shouldn't trust strange taxi drivers in a big city, but he asked me where we were going and where our luggage was.

I handed over my tickets and watched as he scanned them.

"I can come back for this stuff. Get your kids into the car and I'll take you to where you are going."

We got into his cab and mighty glad we were to sit down.

"Could you please stop at a confectioner's store?" Aileen asked. "I have to get a bottle of milk for the baby's formula . . . "

"In Toronto! On Sunday! Lady, nothing but the churches are open."

"But I've just got to have milk."

"I'll get you some."

And he did. When we got out to the residential area he spotted a milkman's rig clopping along the street and stopped it. So we had our milk and things looked better. The driver deposited us in front of the furnished house we'd rented on Bain Avenue for the summer and said, "Okay, you go in and get that baby fed. I'll go back for your stuff." He drove away with all my baggage checks and I didn't have his name or the licence number of the cab. Perhaps, I thought, I'll never see him again.

We carried the kids up onto the veranda and I reached into my pocket for the key. It wasn't there. It was, in fact, in the pocket of my uniform which was in one of the suitcases the cabbie had said he would fetch.

There is no way of breaking into a Toronto house. I tried every window and door but they were all tight. A head poked out of the brick house across the street and a man asked me the trouble. Within a few minutes he appeared in his dressing gown with an immense bundle of keys which he fitted and manoeuvred in turn. Finally he woke up another neighbour and it turned out that our landlady had left a key with him years ago. After rummaging through innumerable drawers and boxes he found the key and we were in.

Not long afterwards the taxi pulled up at the curb. Big, bulging boxes stuck out of the open rear trunk and suitcases filled the back seat, while the baby buggy and knocked-down crib were lashed to the top. The grinning driver was enjoying it to the limit. As we unloaded, he told me of his own kids and the exasperating move he'd once made from Kirkland Lake. Finally, after everything was in, I asked him how much I owed him.

He shrugged. "Oh . . . a couple of bucks?"

I gave him five and embarrassed him silly with my fulsome thanks for his services. He was glad to get out of there.

A few years later I wrote an article for *Saturday Night* in which I contended that Torontonians didn't deserve their reputation for aloofness and reserve, that I'd found it as easy to speak to strangers on the streetcar or in restaurants as I'd ever done in a western city. To help prove my point, I described these events of our arrival in Toronto.

Strangely enough the only person to take exception to this article was the late Frank Tumpane, a native Torontonian, who wrote in his newspaper column that I was obviously being more politic than factual. Torontonians, he maintained, were reserved and stand-offish and proud of it. It was one of their better qualities.

During the 25 years we've been in Ontario our enthusiasm for the province hasn't diminished. We still view the landscape with wonder. We've travelled to every part of the province where there are roads. We've camped in most of its provincial parks and swum in many of its lakes. Often on an afternoon we'll just take a drive through the rolling countryside and poke into old churchyards, peer through windows of old farm houses, and inspect old roadside halls of the Orange Lodge that was once the most potent social and political force in the province. There is always something new to see . . . a small waterfall dropping down a limestone cliff, a deep gorge worn down by years of erosion, a drumlin to climb from which we can see for miles, a moraine cut by an old gravel pit where we can find fossils in the limestone, beautiful little rivers that wind through hardwood bush and have names like the Mad and the Noisy and the Pretty.

Or we go hiking along the Bruce Trail. We climb stiles over aged cedar rail fences, fill our bellies with wild apples that grow everywhere, catch glimpses of shy warblers in the trees and listen to the woodpeckers drumming. For the most heavily populated area of Canada, southern Ontario still has plenty of walking room and maple-lined back roads for driving.

Most of all, though, we love the rock country. When we reach the Severn River we are in it. Our kids have a song, "Rock countree . . . rock countree . . . we're getting into rock countree." The words aren't much, but the feeling with which they sing it is tremendous. There we see the big, rounded mounds of granite, pink and black and grey, or cut jagged where the highway has blasted through. And clinging to it with often only inches of topsoil, the evergreen and poplar, white birch and hardwood trees. Fifty feet away from the highway you are in a forest, walking a carpet of leaves, stirring up chipmunks and red squirrels.

And the lakes! There is nothing anywhere like the lakes of the Shield. Their rock bottoms are scarred clean by the glaciers of thousands of years ago, and they are full of water so clear you can see ten feet down, deep and cool and inviting. Although many lakes are lined with cottages and noisy with roaring motor boats, thousands still have no roads to them at all. You have to fight your way through the bush carrying your canoe and gear, slapping at murderous mosquitoes and black flies. But when you get there and come out on a rounded rock and sit looking at the reflection of pines in that clear water, it's worth it all right. The peace and silence seep into your soul and you just want to sit. Some sit in boats pretending to fish, but others just sit and look.

That is Ontario to us. We admit to a tremendous prejudice for the province. We've become as smug and self-satisfied as we used to accuse the visitors from "Old Ontario" of being. We don't mind visiting other parts of Canada and being awed by the Rockies, astounded by the prairies and captivated by the ocean, but we're always glad to get home to Ontario.

That's the place for us.

CHAPTER II

The Essence of Ontario

Since coming to Ontario in 1944 I have been trying to figure out what makes Ontarians tick. How they differ from other Canadians I have known. What, in fact, is the essence of Ontario.

I've lived in the country, in a small town, and in the city. I've been a member of a school board and a town councillor. I've worked with a variety of people and writen dozens of magazine articles and hundreds of radio and television scripts about the people and the land. I've argued with my friends far into the night about whether Ontario is carrying the rest of Canada on its back or the rest of Canada is carrying Ontario.

What characteristics did I think I detected in native Ontarians? Well, to me they always seemed quieter, more reserved, less rambunctious, better mannered, more sophisticated, and outwardly at least, more naive—or was it that they were more devious—than the people I'd known in Saskatchewan.

It is nonsense to maintain that there are no special characteristics of Canadians from different regions of the country. West Coasters *are* different from those who live on the East Coast. Plains dwellers *do* have their own identity, as do the people of Quebec. And these differences are largely due to differences in environment and history.

7

Perhaps a look at the origins of Ontario will help.

Geographically, Ontario is far and away the luckiest province in Canada. First of all it is the most southerly province; Windsor is farther south than half a dozen American states, and Pelee Island is actually farther south than the northern boundary of California. This means that grapes, tobacco, and a number of other crops that have difficulty surviving in other parts of Canada grow in southern Ontario in abundance.

The soil is excellent. Many of the plains are the bottoms of old glacial lakes, and the rich soil which once supported immense forests will grow almost anything.

Then there are the Great Lakes which practically make an island of southern Ontario. Lakes that provide water for drinking, for industry, for transportation, for recreation, for fishing, for sewage disposal, and for hydro-electric power. Fewer than a dozen of the 46 counties of southern Ontario have no Great Lakes shoreline. The lakes also have a tremendous effect on the climate, moderating the weather both in winter and in summer. It is safe to say that the Great Lakes have played a more important role in Ontario's development than any other single factor.

Two major events in Ontario's history have left their mark on the attitudes and mores of the people. The first of these was the coming of the United Empire Loyalists as a consequence of the American Revolution, and the second was the War of 1812. Both are closely connected with the United States, towards which country Ontario's attitude has always been, is now, and likely forever will be ambivalent.

The white man's pre-Loyalist history of Ontario tends to be rather meagre. Because of the terrible rapids on the St. Lawrence River between Montreal and Lake Ontario, the early French traders and explorers almost bypassed what is now southern Ontario.

In 1615 Samuel de Champlain first came to the southern Ontario country by way of the Ottawa River–Lake Nipissing–French River–Georgian Bay route that later became the classic route of the fur traders. Here he found the Huron Indians living contentedly as farmers, fishermen, and hunters. They lived in houses which were made of poles laid over with cedar or elm bark. These houses, some of them 200 feet long, were gathered together in villages surrounded by palisades. Outside the village were the fields in which the Indian women cultivated corn, squash and beans. They also made maple sugar by cutting into the trees, collecting the sap in birch-bark vessels, and boiling it by dropping heated rocks into the sap. When the fields were worked out, the supply of firewood scarce, and the stench from rotting garbage unbearable, the Hurons simply moved their village elsewhere.

To find out more about the Great Lakes, Champlain sent his young friend and lieutenant Etienne Brulé on further exploration trips. Etienne Brulé has been almost entirely neglected by historians and makers of statues (except for a short street near the Humber River in Etobicoke called Brulé Gardens and a belated plaque here and there), because he did not fit the neat, clean-living, God-fearing image we have established for our Canadian heroes. Etienne was a lean, powerful, audacious young man who scorned the establishment and preferred the more natural life and sexual mores of the Indians with whom he travelled. He was the first of the famed *coureurs de bois*; he learned the Indian ways and language, loved the Indian maidens and, inevitably, quarrelled with their menfolk so that they executed him. (But even in death he was useful, for, according to one story, the Indians had him for supper.)

Brulé is given credit for being the first white man to see Georgian Bay, Lake Couchiching, Lake Simcoe, the Holland River, Lake Ontario and the site of Toronto and quite possibly Lake Erie, as well as Lake Superior and the copper mines of its north shore. Not a bad accomplishment for a man whom the history books have shunned.

Apart from the ill-fated Jesuit mission named Ste. Marie near Georgian Bay, which was begun in 1639 and destroyed in 1649, there was little attempt by the French to establish a permanent settlement in the Ontario region. Fur traders came, of course, and explorers. In 1679 a full-sized sailing ship was built at the west end of Lake Erie. This was the 60-ton, 65-foot barque *Griffon*, built by the French explorer and trader the Sieur de la Salle. All the fittings were brought from France and lugged up the St. Lawrence River, around its rapids, across Lake Ontario, past Niagara Falls, and across and up the full length of Lake Erie by birchbark canoe. Then the workmen got busy cutting down oak trees and shaping them for the hull of the ship. Incredible as it is, they finished the job, launched the ship, and in late September set sail into Lake Huron on her maiden trading voyage, during which she was lost with all hands.

The English became involved in the lucrative fur trade when the

Hudson's Bay Company was granted a charter in 1670 giving it control of all the lands draining into Hudson Bay. This set the stage for fierce rivalry between the English and the French for the fur trade. The English made no attempts at colonization, but the Hudson's Bay Company set up a number of trading posts on James Bay and Hudson Bay.

As time went on and the French and English fought over who would control the rich trading country, other vessels were built on the Great Lakes. At Fort Frontenac (now Kingston) the French built the 90-ton, 12-gun schooner *La Hurault*, and then the *Marquis de Vaudreuil* and others with which, on the afternoon of June 26, 1756, they defeated the British ships *Oswego* and *Ontario* in the first naval engagement ever fought on the Great Lakes.

After the Seven Years' War when England took over the province of Quebec (including much of what is now Ontario) from France, nothing much happened in the area until the American Revolutionary War of 1775-81. Many citizens of the thirteen American colonies, although considerably upset by the treatment they were receiving from the British government, still flatly refused to be disloyal to that government or to take up arms against it. Indeed many took up arms on its behalf and joined the British forces fighting the colonists.

These Loyalists were for the most part English, Scottish and, strangely enough, German settlers. Some were wealthy landowners and men holding high positions in civil, military and naval services. Others were lawyers, doctors, teachers and ministers; still others were wealthy men of business. It is estimated that at least one-third of the American population remained loyal to the Crown.

In any case they had to get out. Their property (confiscated during the war) was not returned, their lives were endangered, and most of their civil rights were taken from them. They left their homes, occupations, holdings, and friends in a more or less civilized country to move north into the bush of southern Ontario (many, of course, went to Quebec and the Maritimes). They were able to bring with them only what they could carry on their backs or in crude vehicles to begin life in the forest with an axe and a hoe and a scythe and very little else.

Many came by the Lake Champlain–Richelieu River route to Sorel, and then up the St. Lawrence by canoe or bateau to the Kingston–Bay of Quinte area. Others came across the lake and settled farther west along the north shore of Lake Ontario. Still others crossed at the Niagara Frontier and settled along Lake Erie and in the Niagara Peninsula. But all of them had a most difficult time.

The British government helped them, of course, providing some equipment and livestock and giving grants of land. The pattern of settlement of the first United Empire Loyalists, many of whom were from disbanded regiments that had fought for the British, was along the lines of military hierarchy. The highest ranking officers got the best land along the water front; lesser officers got the land behind them. Then came the sergeants and, finally, the lowly privates, who took up the least attractive land far from easy water transportation.

Also this time came the first wave of what was to be a tide of Scotsmen. They were the officers and men from the King's Royal Regiment of New York who had fought for the British. These hardy Highlanders were Catholics, and when they were granted land on the north shore of the St. Lawrence adjacent to where the Quebec border now is, they named it Glengarry after their homeland.

Many Scots, like the Irishmen who were to follow later, were actually refugees from an intolerable situation at home. The Scots were strong, frugal souls, used to hard work, religious, and determined to succeed. And succeed they did, as witness the Macdonalds and Mackenzies and MacNabs and Thompsons and Mowats and other Scots who have been so prominent in the business and political life of Ontario ever since. It is a rare fair opening or parade or political meeting or official gathering of any kind in Ontario that doesn't feature Scotsmen in kilts blowing lustily on the bagpipes.

The first German settlement in Upper Canada was made up of disbanded mercenaries who settled at Marysburgh on the Bay of Quinte in 1784, and before the end of the 1780s a large number of German-speaking Mennonites were established in the townships west of the Niagara River.

The Constitutional Act of 1791 divided the old province of Quebec into Upper Canada (Ontario) and Lower Canada (Quebec) to deal with the changed conditions resulting from the Loyalist influx. Upper Canada was English-speaking and had English laws and institutions, while Lower Canada remained French-speaking and kept its French laws and seigneurial system.

Even today, travelling the backroads and secondary highways of southern Ontario, one sees evidence of the incredibly hard life endured by these first refugee settlers in Ontario. In many farm-yards the original log house is still there, at a respectable distance from the newer yellow or red brick house. Shored up here and there with bits of iron or concrete, the old one-room structure is usually used as a milkhouse or catch-all shed. It was built by the original settler with nothing more than an axe. Since there were no sawmills in the area, the settler went into the bush, felled the hemlock or white pine, limbed them, chopped them into proper lengths, notched them and fitted them together to form walls. There was no glass for windows, no hinges for doors nor, as often as not, stones for a fireplace. The furniture was all home-made: benches to sit on, crude tables, and a shelf covered with pine or spruce boughs for a bed.

Old split rail fences still snake their crazy way between fields, and here and there are the remains of old stump fences, telling of the back-breaking task of clearing small plots on which to grow crops. For the forest was everywhere. Immense stands of hardwoods and conifers that had to be chopped down and burned before the settler could cultivate the soil. The stumps he left in the ground until he could manage to secure more power in the form of an ox or horse.

This was roughing it with a vengeance. From the Indians the settlers learned to tan hides and make their own buckskin clothing, for in those first hungry years there were no spinning wheels or looms with which to make cloth. Children, we are told, often stayed indoors all winter because they had no shoes.

Much food was obtained indirectly from the forest. Fiddleheads, the succulent first shoots of the forest ferns, made delicious greens. Roots of the water lily and arrowhead were dried and ground into flour. Raspberries, blueberries, and elderberries grew in the forests. Boiled spikenard roots made a good cough syrup, catnip cured the stomach ache, cherry bark made an excellent tonic, and a salve made of black alder, resin and beeswax was soothing for the frequent scalds and burns.

The lakes and streams were full of fish. Salmon spawned in the head waters and lived in the lakes. Speckled trout were plentiful, as were sturgeon and suckers, while Lake Ontario itself had a good supply of pickerel, herring, and other fish.

Edible birds were everywhere. Passenger pigeons, now extinct, came in flocks so huge that it took days for them to pass. Their roosts so burdened the trees as to break off the limbs. They could be taken with musket, net, snare, or by putting lime on the trees and burning their feet. Partridge and quail whirred through the dark woods, ducks nested near the water, and geese were plentiful in fall and spring.

Of four-footed game there was practically no limit. Beaver, muskrat, and raccoon provided not only meat but furs to be sold or used. Deer were plentiful, as were hares, squirrels and other edible mammals. Many stories come from those days of settlers being attacked by wolves, but there is no actual record of anyone ever being killed. Naturalists who study the wolf extensively feel that most stories have grown from some lonely settler's wife or child on a wooded trail hearing the blood-curdling howl of wolves somewhere in the distance.

Luck was with those first settlers in a number of ways. The British navy desperately needed timber and masts for its ships, and special agents of the Crown scoured the province seeking "mast woods." "The trees must be tall ... up to 120 feet ... small of butt and straight of grain." Each tree that fitted the requirements was marked with a broad arrow for the guidance of axemen who followed.

Great care was taken in the felling of the masting giants. So that it would not be injured in the fall, the ground was levelled and cleared of small trees and big rocks. Once down, the giant was treated with extra care. Skilled barkers worked along its length, taking off all the small branches and stripping away the bark. Other axemen squared eight feet of the butt end so that it would fit into the mast block of a ship. Then the mast was carefully winched onto two sets of wheels, one at each end, and as many as 12 teams of oxen were hitched to the load to haul it to the nearest river or lake. Hundreds of masts were formed into huge rafts and floated by professional raftsmen along Lake Ontario and down the St. Lawrence to Montreal for shipment to England.

The squared timber for making lumber took even more work and skill to prepare. Immense white pine trees were felled and squared by experts wielding broadaxes. The straight side of the square was called a "proud edge," while small logs might be squared with a rounded shoulder to produce "waney timber." These squared logs, many of them over a hundred feet long, were like the masts hauled to a river or lake, made into rafts, and floated down to tidewater.

Potash was needed for the making of soap locally and, more

important, for export to Britain where it was used for bleaching linen and cotton. It was produced by gathering the ash after the burning of hardwood and boiling it in immense pots until it became hard. This was usually the woman's job and hour after hour she stood beside the huge pot, piling firewood around it and stirring the mess with a huge paddle until it became pearly white and suitable for sale to the local merchant who sold it to bigger merchants who exported it to England. The price was pitiably low but it did bring in cash, and cash was scarce along the lakes in the first years of the nineteenth century.

Along the shores of Lake Erie, Lake Ontario and the upper St. Lawrence, there are plaques, cairns, monuments, and forts which call to mind the time when Upper and Lower Canada were actually attacked by soldiers from the United States. This was the ill-conceived and badly bungled War of 1812. Although the Americans gained little from the war, Canadians gained a great deal. Not so much in great victories, but in a sense of purpose and the strongest unifying bond that a country can have: the threat of further attack from a powerful neighbour.

The Upper Canada settlers, mostly American-born, had been in the province a bare 25 years or less. They had emerged from the raw pioneer state to a point where they had communities, institutions, and some representative government. At the beginning of hostilities, many seemed to care little one way or the other. However, after General Isaac Brock captured Detroit and repulsed the Americans at Queenston Heights (at the cost of his own life), the resistance stiffened and many a pioneer fought alongside the British regulars. Republicanism became a dirty word.

In fact the War of 1812 is to the Ontarian what the American Revolutionary War is to their southern neighbours. And just as the Americans have never quite forgiven the British or come to trust them wholly, the Ontarian continues to be suspicious of Yankees. Every school boy who is taken by bus to visit old Fort York in Toronto learns that on April 27, 1813, an American fleet under Commodore Chauncey sailed into that very harbour and captured that very fort and then sacked the town of York, burned the public buildings and even the church, and is filled with righteous indignation. And his heart swells with the sweet thrill of revenge as he learns that the next year the British did the same thing to Washington.

A native of western Canada coming to live in Ontario is immediately impressed by this lingering fear and suspicion of the U.S. that exists in Ontario. Oh, he learned about the War of 1812 in his history books all right, but it was something remote. The Americans he knew came up from Minnesota or the Dakotas to take up free homesteads at just about the same time his own parents had come from Ontario. There was a lot of intermarriage and visiting back and forth across the border, and certainly no plaques or monuments to constantly remind the westerner that Americans were after all never to be trusted.

Another important result of the War of 1812 was that it brought more settlers to the province. Britain, having defeated Napoleon and the Yankees, was done with wars for a while and many of the British soldiers who had come to defend the Canadas remained to farm. They were Scots and Englishmen mostly, hardy, proud, adventurous men, rabid in their allegiance to their homelands. They included a goodly number of mercenary soldiers from Germany. The new settlers established homes on farms and in the towns and made a good life, and their descendants have played a leading role in the development of the province.

The next big influx of people to Ontario were of a different breed entirely. They were not soldiers to whom a grateful imperial government doled out land and pensions. They too were refugees, and refugees of the most miserable kind. They came because they were literally starving at home. They brought with them, often, little more than the ragged clothes on their backs, along with their religious and political strifes. But they were rugged, for only the hardiest of them managed to get to the province at all and survive the horrors of their first years. And they made a tremendous contribution to the new province and their political influence was greater, proportionately, than their numbers.

They were the Irish.

Each time the potato crop in Ireland failed through drought or frost or insects, as it did in 1739, 1821, 1831, 1835 and 1839, thousands of Irishmen were forced to emigrate to North America or starve. Never too fond of the English, most of them went to the United States, where they founded large Irish communities in Boston, New York and elsewhere. But a sizeable number also came to Canada.

Then, in the summer of 1845, a new disaster struck in the form of the potato blight, and the potato crop was completely wiped out.

As a consequence, 356,000 of the Irish came to Canada, and the condition of their coming was appalling. Packed in fever-ridden, rat-infested ships, sleeping in tiers like passengers on a slaver, cooking their meagre rations in filthy, foul-smelling holds, bullied by the crews, many never saw the sun or felt the salt sea air during the six weeks of the voyage. Others never left the slabs that served as beds. Thousands were buried at sea.

Many of the ships were wrecked by storms at sea and the passengers drowned before they saw the promised land. Those who did arrive faced a dismal welcome. And they needed all the strength and determination they could muster when they finally managed to get ashore. They were thrust into filthy, over-crowded quarantine stations where many died of fever. The whole process, you might say, was a weeding out of the weak and a survival of the strong and determined. About half of the newcomers braved the trip up the Ottawa and the St. Lawrence to Upper Canada. Many had relatives there who had written them of how much the moraines and drumlins of southern Ontario resembled the hills of northern Ireland. They came up the river in open boats or made their way by oxcart, stagecoach, or on foot, carrying with them all they possessed in the world. And still hunger and misery and disease pursued many of them, as this item from the Kingston *Herald* in June of 1850 reveals:

> What is to be done towards relieving the numbers of immigrants who, having arrived here, are unable to proceed farther for want of means? Every evening numbers are left on our wharves who know not how to provide food for themselves and their families . . . We call upon some wealthy citizens to step forward and take a lead in devising some means of relief for those truly unfortunate people.

The 1851 census shows Kingston to have had 4,396 Irish-born inhabitants out of a total population of 11,585, and Ottawa (then Bytown), Toronto and Hamilton about the same percentage.

A predominance of settlers from a country always noted for political strife and religious upheaval naturally had a tremendous influence on Ontario. Many brought their religious discord with them. About half the immigrants were Protestants from the north of Ireland and about half were Roman Catholics from the south. They opposed each other in everything.

Most of the Protestants joined the already large and powerful Orange Lodge and voted Tory almost to a man. The Catholic Irish usually took the other side. One community in Victoria County was typical of many. Just north of the town of Omemee is a concession road known as "The Orange Line." North of it in Downeyville lived the Catholic Irish while south of the line was solid Orange. It was not too safe for a "papist" to show his nose south of that line unless accompanied by friends well armed with shillelaghs.

On the Glorious Twelfth of July, the Orangemen from Loyal Orange Lodge 646 and other lodges got out their drums, white horse, peaked caps, ribbons and sashes, and paraded through the streets. The boys from the north of the Orange Line naturally came down and tried to break it up. Old timers recall street fights that lasted for days. One story from nearby Peterborough tells how a rash individual snatched the orange ribbons from a pretty lass during the parade. The Orangemen chased him downtown where he took refuge in a hotel. Then they brought a two-wheel cannon, old but still usable, trained it on the hotel, and threatened to blow the place to pieces unless the miscreant was delivered into their hands. He was delivered.

Some historians consider the Orange Lodge to have been the most potent force and the toughest pressure group in Ontario politics and that vital political questions were apt to be decided along strictly religious lines. Orangemen deny this and take credit for keeping Canada loyal to the British crown through trying times. Whatever the political significance of it, certainly between 1845 and some time in the 1890s there were more Irishmen in the country than any other English-speaking group.

But the Irish predominance was short lived. By 1854 economic conditions had improved in Ireland, and the population had shrunk to numbers the land could support. By 1901 there were more Englishmen in Ontario than Irishmen. So the Irish influx was as brief as it was violent. And had it not been for spuds it might never have happened at all. The abundance of spuds produced the surplus Irish; the lack of spuds drove them here. Nobody can say exactly what their influence has been. But one thing is certain—without them our nation would be a lot less melodious, humorous, rugged, and lively. For whatever else the Irish may be, they are rarely dull.

The whole political development of Ontario is far from dull. Rather, the struggle for true democracy is the most robust and heartening part of the Ontario story. The Constitutional Act of 1791 provided for a lieutenant-governor and Executive Council, an appointed Legislative Council, and an elected Legislative Assembly. Unfortunately the Assembly had no control over money and hence no real power.

For some time the settlers were too concerned with establishing homes and towns to concern themselves about government and, in fact, they might never have done so if the ruling clique in the province had not been so blatantly inefficient, corrupt, nepotistic and downright crooked.

The government of Upper Canada was carried on by a small group of Anglicans who were intermarried, rich, and devoted to the idea that the province and its people existed solely for their benefit. They came to be known as the "Family Compact," which in turn became a hated and despised appellation. The most notorious leader of the Compact was Archdeacon John Strachan who, as head of the Anglican Church in Upper Canada, and a member of both the Legislative Council and the Assembly, was a man of great power. Members of the Compact and their toadies got all the good government appointments, pensions, the inside track on land deals, and controlled most of the colony's business. The remainder of the population got along as best they could with what was left.

As always happens when there are glaring wrongs, some determined men arose to try and correct them. One of these was Robert Baldwin, a patient, wise man who worked steadily for reform. Another was the Methodist leader Egerton Ryerson. The Assembly gave them if no real power, at least a meeting place where they could discuss the iniquities of the government.

The man who pressed strongest for reform was an extremely determined and extremely loquacious Scotsman named William Lyon Mackenzie. In his newspapers, the *Colonial Advocate* and the *Constitution*, and at public meetings and in the Assembly (to which he was five times elected and five times expelled, sometimes bodily), he pounded away at the Family Compact and their leader, Archdeacon Strachan.

But of course Strachan always won. Finally the frustration and rage of Mackenzie and his followers became so great that they took up arms against the government in open rebellion in 1837. The rebellion failed, but it had the effect of making the British government do something about the situation, and most of the wrongs were righted. In fact, as a direct result of the rebellion, responsible government or true democracy was established in Ontario.

Mackenzie is certainly part of the essence of Ontario. He has been called many things—fiery, headstrong, irresponsible, treacherous, and even crazy—but I prefer to call him determined, steadfast, and incredibly brave. He did more for Ontario, and Canada, than most of the politicians, business tycoons, and railway builders whose praises our history books proclaim. And still in rural Ontario many farmers have a good healthy suspicion of the motives of "those fellers" in the city.

The Act of Union passed by the British Parliament in 1840 reunited the Canadas, renamed them Canada West (Ontario) and Canada East (Quebec), and provided their joint elected Assembly with more power. In 1849 a wise and fair-minded governor, Lord Elgin, established the principle of responsible government for all time by signing his name to the Rebellion Losses Bill, which was passed by the Assembly but was most unpopular with influential leaders outside the Assembly. Elgin said in effect: "The people's elected representatives have passed it so it must become law." So he signed it. A first-class riot followed, during which the King's representative was pelted with rotten eggs, but ever since then the word of the elected house has been supreme in Canada.

The fight for reform continued in Ontario, led mainly by two other Scots, George Brown and Sir Oliver Mowat. Brown, who was a stern Presbyterian, founded the Toronto *Globe* in 1844 and used it to fight the "French-Catholic domination" and "American leanings," still two of the best vote-getting slogans in Ontario. He was a rabid foe of the Prime Minister, Sir John A. Macdonald, but joined the Conservative leader to bring about Confederation. On May 9, 1880, he was shot and killed by a disgruntled employee.

Mowat, a one-time law partner of Sir John A. Macdonald, became the old chieftain's bitterest opponent. After Sandfield Macdonald (1867-71) and Edward Blake (1871-72), he was premier of Ontario until 1896. Mowat fought Sir John A. on the hustings and in the courts on the issue of provincial rights. His aim was to make Ontario strong politically, and he succeeded. It is still mighty powerful.

One of Mowat's greatest contributions was the introduction of the secret ballot in voting which did more than anything to take the rowdiness, chicanery, bribing and, perhaps, colour out of Ontario elections.

Before this, elections were a combination of a three-ring circus, a full-scale riot, and a grand and glorious drunk. In the first place, the election lasted not one day but rather for as long as there was one voter per hour left, sometimes up to six weeks. Each side hired gangs of toughs to bully voters who opposed them. A man who may have walked or driven 30 miles over abominable roads stepped up before the clerk, stated his name, gave proof of his land ownership, and shouted out the name of the candidate he supported.

Before he did this he had been offered bribes of booze or cash or even land for his vote, and may have been threatened with violence, the loss of his job, or the security of his home.

After the votes were in, considerable manipulation still went on, and the charges and counter charges of corruption went on for months after every election.

Since Confederation, the Liberals and Conservatives have each been in power for over 50 years. Apart from the United Farmers of Ontario who formed the government under Ernest Charles Drury in the early Twenties, none of the new political parties have had much success in Ontario. This is largely due to the fact that Ontario, with its great diversity of natural resources and the West to take up its excess manpower around the turn of the century, has enjoyed almost unbroken prosperity.

The towns and villages of southern Ontario tell their own story. As more settlers came and more goods were brought up the river and over the lakes, settlements grew. First there was a mill on a stream. Farmers brought their grain for miles, often carrying the sacks on their backs, to be ground into flour. Then came sawmills where the great logs were sawn by water-powered "muley" saws into wide, rough boards.

There was the tannery, for instance, a necessary establishment in every town. The farmers, who did all their own butchering, fetched in their bundles of cowhides to be sold for a few cents to the tanner. Since they were sold by weight, the tanner always checked for rocks hidden inside the bundles. The blacksmith and the carriage maker, usually side by side—for one needed the other—were situated near the centre of the town. The carpenter shop provided handles for axes and hoes, and some furniture. The cooper made barrels. Almost everything the settler needed that he could not make at home was made in the small community.

On the main street of Orangeville there is a huge rectangular limestone building that tells another story. It has been renovated many times and is now used as real estate offices, but the row of windows, upstairs and down and along the front, indicate that it was originally an inn. For every village needed overnight accommodation for farmers hauling their produce to market over deep-rutted roads with slow teams of oxen or horses.

In each inn there was a tavern or bar where liquor could be bought for a few cents a glass, and where long into the night men could drink and argue and get so drunk that they would have to be dunked in the horse trough to sober up enough to continue their journey.

Those who complain of what they consider to be ridiculously rigid liquor regulations in the province today often do not realize that liquor was a desperate problem in pioneer times. Every town of any size had its distillery, and every occasion from a wake to a barnraising was a good reason for drinking.

Religious and political differences, both of which aroused much stronger animosities than they do today, were barely kept in control by sober persons. With even a little bit of liquor, the smoldering demons erupted and the fights were on. Free liquor was a common political bribe, which accounts for liquor outlets being closed on election day even now, and political picnics then were robust affairs.

Reaction always follows excess, and the reaction to liquor was strong and stern. Methodist circuit riders who came from the U.S. and who were strong competitors with the established Anglican Church for the souls of the pioneers, led the noble crusade. They went into the backwoods communities where no other clergy were available. They solaced the sad, buried the old, married the young, and promised hellfire and damnation to all sinners . . . and drinkers. The result was oppressively strict liquor laws, the vestiges of which linger to this day.

The old agricultural way of life in Ontario began to change with the advent of electricity. Dams were built and small power stations erected. John M. Deagle was a big name in electrical power in the 1880s. He provided electricity for the farm of David Smith in Caledon Township in 1888, and this is believed to be the first electrified home in Ontario.

In the same year electricity was supplied to the Barber Paper Mill in Georgetown, making it the first manufacturing establishment to be so powered.

A Hydro station at Cataract on the Credit River supplied power for six communities in the area. The remains of the dam are still there, although the Hydro-Electric Power Commission of Ontario had it blown out in 1944.

The H.E.P.C. was, in fact, responsible for the demise of most of the small power stations along the rivers of southern Ontario. Established in 1906, largely through the efforts of Sir Adam Beck, the H.E.P.C. took over all public electrical installations in the province.

The commission's first source of power was Niagara Falls, but later hundreds of other sources were developed. With Beck as chairman the commission was an immediate success. He organized a motorcade, known as "Beck's Circus," to tour the province demonstrating to farmers and townfolk alike how electricity could be used for a great variety of farm and household chores from milking cows to making toast, as well as for running factories.

During the 25 years that he was chairman, Beck developed "Ontario Hydro" into one of the biggest and best known electric power suppliers in the world, and incidentally had a lot to do with changing Ontario from an agricultural province to far and away the most wealthy industrial province in Canada.

So far we have been talking about southern Ontario which is, after all, only a small part of the province. Northern Ontario is as different from southern Ontario as the Yukon is from Prince Edward Island. Not only is the climate different and the land forms, but the people are different, too. There is a spirit of the frontier here, a flamboyance, an openness, that is more akin to the prairies than it is to southern Ontario. This is a newer country, a bigger country, and, as yet, a sparsely settled country. Toronto is a long way off.

This, then, is the heritage of Ontario. Some of the finest and richest land in the world, settled originally by people of strong conviction and purpose. Over the years, these have been joined by people from practically every country of the world. They look upon Ontario as a land of opportunity, a place where governments do not interfere too much with a man's right to work hard and make money.

The latest immigration which has been going on since the end of the Second World War has brought hundreds of thousands of British, Italian, German, Greek, Dutch, and other peoples to Ontario. Whereas before the war it was unusual to hear any language but English spoken in Ontario, there are now areas where it is unusual to hear any English spoken at all. Newcomers are learning the language fast, though, as they are learning to fit into Ontario life.

But it is not the old life. As in every other part of the world, the winds of change are blowing over Ontario. More and more the once satisfied, conservative citizens are asking questions and seeking improvements: the educational system, the church, the municipal governments, the laws . . . all are coming under scrutiny. As well as comparing themselves happily with the United States, they are casting a critical eye over their own condition. A public meeting to protest the building of a freeway through the centre of a city, or an airport that will destroy a suburb, or the commercial destruction of a provincial park or the problem of phosphates in detergents will fill the hall to overflowing. Ontario has changed its ways.

Something else has happened to Ontario. From the provincial government down to the smallest village council, the people have become proud of their land and their heritage and are eager to share it with others. The net is out for more people, both visitors and permanent residents. In the United States and European countries, magazine ads, television commercials, and movies proclaim the glories and riches of Ontario. Town councils vie with each other to attract industries from other countries. Millions are being spent on museums, science centres, parks, historic sites, and monuments. This boasting and self-aggrandizement is something new to "staid old Ontario." Whereas previously they took for granted that theirs was a superior place to live, now they are shouting it loud and clear. The Ontario pavilion at the Osaka World's Fair was one of the most flamboyant and expensive to be found on the grounds. Ontario is the place to stand, and grow, and prosper.

The essence of Ontario? The new, swinging Toronto, noted for its tolerance and understanding and known as a good show town, a city of nightclubs and discotheques? The quarter-million French Canadians who have all but taken over northern Ontario? Italian construction workers in yellow hard hats swarming over new high-rise apartments? The Hungarian Society holding a "gala" in the Royal Ontario Museum? Highways packed with cars pulling boats in summer and snowmobiles in winter into the heart of Ontario's "unspoiled" vacation land? A symphony orchestra playing to a packed house of patrons in evening dress, or rock and roll groups playing outdoors to packed fields of kids in blue jeans and nothing much more at a festival? Bay Street or Main Street? The Canadian National Exhibition, or the Caledon Fall Fair? Industrialists drinking scotch in the York Club, or swingers smoking pot in rooming houses? Indians grubbing out a miserable existence on the shores of James Bay? Over eight million people of dozens of nationalities living in the most favoured area in Canada?

All of these things and many more combine to blast away the old conception of Ontario, and present a paradox that defies classification.

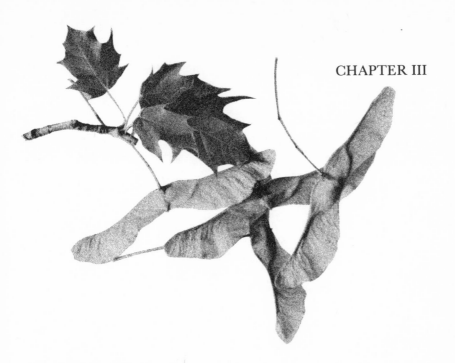

CHAPTER III

The Golden Horseshoe

All my life I had heard about Niagara Falls, honeymoon capital of the world, people going over in barrels, great source of electrical power, and so on. But it was not until 1944 that we actually saw this great marvel, and then under the most bizarre circumstances.

The most exciting way to get to Niagara Falls from Toronto in those days was to take the excursion boat to Port Dalhousie, and then go by streetcar on the radial line to Niagara. By the time we got around to going, the excursion boat was making its final trip for the season and, since we had to be back the next day, it meant that we would be in Niagara only during the hours of darkness.

We went anyway and were the only ones on the radial car as it rattled its way through the dusk of the October evening. When we reached Niagara it was dark and overcast and cold. We checked in at a tourist home near the falls from which we could hear the mighty roar and almost feel the spray, but from our window we couldn't see a thing. Because of war-time power restrictions, the floodlights that usually bathe the cataracts in fire were not on and there were few other lights anywhere.

It was pretty hopeless, but so great was our excitement that, without stopping to eat, we set out to see the spectacle. We found

25

a road that slanted down the side of the limestone cliff of the gorge below the falls and picked our way down it to the very water's edge. The roar was deafening, and we were drenched with spray. Then as if by magic the full moon broke through the clouds and we saw them, the mighty Horseshoe Falls on the right seeming to come right down upon us, and across the river the American Falls, gleaming in the moonlight. It was truly magnificent.

Back in our room at about eleven o'clock we discovered we were starving. So out I went to find food. I walked down every street of Niagara Falls, Ontario, and found not one single establishment open. Finally, in desperation, I entered through a small back door of the Brock Hotel, and wandered down a long corridor into a kitchen where I found a cook still working. He made up two fat ham sandwiches, with dill pickle and mustard, which I took back to the room and saved our lives.

The next time I went to Niagara was with Chris, who was ten, and his older sister Shari. The entire Niagara Falls complex is a great place for lively kids, but not so good for a somewhat overweight parent trying to keep up with them. We did everything: donned rubber suits and went into a tunnel under the falls, crossed the gorge in a cable car, travelled on the *Maid of the Mist* below the falls, wandered through the beautiful park, stood on the very brink of the cataract, shuddered in the wax museum, visited Ontario Hydro's Sir Adam Beck Generating Station and the famous floral clock that contains 24,000 different blooms, and climbed to the top of Brock's monument on Queenston Heights.

This last was a mistake. The kids were lean and nimble and fast. They went up the circular stairway that leads to the inside of the General's head like a couple of mountain goats, while I plodded along behind. At every landing Shari would stop and shout down at me, "Are you having a heart attack, Daddy?"

We've all been back to the falls many times, but those two occasions are by far the most memorable.

Niagara Falls is at the end of an area which stretches around the western end of Lake Ontario from Oshawa to Niagara, and is known as the Golden Horseshoe. Golden because it is rich; Horseshoe because it is lucky. It is also shaped something like a horseshoe.

This is the most highly-industrialized region of southern Ontario. It is also the most historical, the most densely populated, and the most polluted.

It is an area of paradoxes. Some of the most glorious and unspoiled natural beauty of southern Ontario is found here, along with some of the worst stretches of industrial ugliness: automobile graveyards, defiled beaches, rural slums, neglected orchards, putrid water, and spent gravel pits.

Two superhighways cross the area: the Queen Elizabeth Way running from Toronto to Niagara, and the newer Macdonald-Cartier Freeway (generally called the 401) cutting across the north side. Dozens of smaller highways and roads criss-cross the region, carrying farmers' trucks loaded with grapes or peaches, or happy tourists on their way to see the falls.

This part of the country is greatly influenced by a rather remarkable geological formation known as the Niagara Escarpment. It is actually a shelf of particularly durable limestone that extends in a jagged course from Niagara around the end of Lake Ontario (Hamiltonians call it The Mountain), and thence in a northerly direction across southern Ontario to Tobermory at the tip of the Bruce Peninsula.

It is the escarpment which accounts for Lake Erie's being 327 feet higher than Lake Ontario, and which accounts for the 167-foot drop of Niagara Falls. This abrupt height of land provides some great scenery in southern Ontario, including lesser waterfalls, spectacular valleys, beautiful gorges, and the Bruce Trail.

Because of its proximity to the United States, the Niagara Peninsula is rich in historical sites and monuments. Names like Lundy's Lane, Brown's Battery, Fort Mississauga, Butler's Burying Ground, and Beaver Dam are reminders of the days when Canada and the United States were enemies.

The Niagara River, which runs 35 miles from Lake Erie to Lake Ontario, forms the boundary between Ontario and New York State. Thus, in early days, the entire river front was known as the Niagara Frontier and was without doubt the liveliest stretch along the border between the United States and Canada.

During the American Revolution, anyone who wished to remain loyal to the British Crown needed only to cross the river to be in friendly territory. And when the Americans decided in 1812 that all they needed to do to conquer Canada was march into the country, they naturally thought of the trip across the Niagara as one good place to begin the march.

The first and deciding battle of the War of 1812 was fought at

Queenston Heights. Here Sir Isaac Brock, after galloping seven miles from Fort George, led a desperate charge up the escarpment and was shot dead before he reached the top. But the general's men rallied, fought their way to the top, and won the battle.

Twenty-five years later, the Niagara Frontier was again a hotbed of conflict. Rebels fleeing from the rebellion in Upper Canada set up a provisional government on Navy Island in the Niagara River. While militia patrolled the river banks at Chippawa in December 1837 and January 1838, William Lyon Mackenzie designed a flag, drew up a constitution, issued scrip, and acted as though his rebellion still had a chance of success.

Another place in the area that is loaded with history is Niagara-on-the-Lake, at the mouth of the Niagara River where it runs into Lake Ontario. It was first called Newark, and for a while was the capital of Upper Canada. It was also known as Butlersburg, in honour of Colonel John Butler, one of the most prominent of the United Empire Loyalists who left his home in the Mohawk Valley in 1775 and formed a hard fighting force known as Butler's Rangers. The burial ground of the Butler family, but not of the Rangers, is one of the tourist attractions of Niagara-on-the-Lake.

But today, most people go to the town to see the Shaw Festival which takes place every summer. Inspired by the success of the Stratford Festival, it was founded in 1962 by Brian Doherty, and is now well established. At first, plays were staged in the old Court House, but in 1973 a new festival theatre was built that seats 830 Shaw enthusiasts.

Niagara Falls, itself, was not always such a peaceful, well-regulated, well-ordered tourist spot. In fact, up until a hundred years ago, it was a wild, rowdy, raucous, rambunctious carnival where unscrupulous villains fleeced gullible farmers and sophisticated city dwellers alike. It was, according to newspaper accounts and reports of trials, a place where decent folk feared for their pocketbooks and their health. To be sure, it was a den of iniquity.

The whole of this nefarious action took place in the narrow "Front" between the escarpment and the river, stretching from the brink of the falls downstream to near the end of the gorge. This was supposed to be a military reserve of Upper Canada but since, after 1814, there seemed little danger from the Americans, the army tended to let it go to anyone with the gall to grab it.

The man with the most gall was a seedy old rascal named Sol

Davis who, along with his burly sons, blowsy daughters, and paid bullies, ran the Table Rock House, a combined hotel and curio shop. During a suit for slander that old Sol brought against the Hamilton *Evening Times* for calling his establishment the "cave of the forty thieves," it came to light that men had been threatened, beaten up, and thrown out, or even held for ransom by the Davis family for refusing to pay exorbitant prices for short trips and for pictures they did not want and other swindles.

But Davis was not the only one. Along the Front was a whole rat's nest of hotels, curio shops, and museums. On the walkway near the gorge, pitchmen in derby hats and carrying fancy canes accosted visitors with promises, flattery, and guile, and relieved them of their hard-earned cash. The noise of their hawking, it was said, drowned out the roar of the falls.

All manner of stunts were used to attract people to the falls. Sam Patch of Rochester, New York, a specialist in jumping off high places, drew a large crowd to see him leap from a 100-foot ladder into the river. Ingenious rascals picked up little white stones and sold them as "congealed spray from the falls," and when the local supply ran short, they imported boatloads from England.

Indian carvings and phony artifacts were always in demand, and one imaginative salesman boosted business by inventing a legend about a beautiful Indian maiden who was sacrificed by her tribe by being hurled into the falls to become the bride of the "mist god." This tale, combining as it did violence and sex, caught on with the people, and they bought thousands of little wooden, bare-bosomed carvings of this maiden. Honeymooners began coming to the falls. Local merchants, smelling profits, named the misty spot where the maiden was supposed to have landed The Bridal Veil. The first little boat to carry tourists that way was naturally named *Maid of the Mist.*

In the autumn of 1827 when business began to fall off, some of the promoters advertised that the old wooden pirate ship *Michigan* would carry a load of wild beasts over the falls. Although there was no sex connected with this stunt, there was plenty of violence, and thousands lined both sides of the gorge to watch the sport.

Sure enough, as the old ship came drifting downriver, the spectators could clearly see three bears, four foxes, along with raccoons, cats, dogs and geese frantically dashing around on deck. There was also a scruffy-hided old buffalo, but it was tied up. The bears jumped overboard and made it to shore, but the rest went over with the ship and, of course, perished on the rocks below. It was a great show.

But the greatest show of them all was the one put on by Blondin, the most daring, cool and audacious stunt man who ever put feet to a tightrope.

His real name was Jean François Gravelet, and he was a 140-pound Frenchman with amazing co-ordination and balance. Arriving at Niagara Falls with a troupe of acrobats, he announced that he was going to walk across the gorge on a tightrope, and if that went well he might just carry another man over on his back. This was in the summer of 1859, when Niagara Falls madness was at its height, and Blondin's wild boast attracted attention from the press of both the U.S. and Canada. Almost to a man they said he was crazy and could never do it.

Personally supervising every step of the work, Blondin had a three-inch hemp rope stretched across the gorge and made steady with some forty thousand feet of guy ropes. As he worked, the word spread and the crowds grew. Finally, when all was ready and the crowd large enough, Blondin took his balancing pole in hand and danced out onto the rope. He actually made it look easy, and after a couple of straight crossings began to do a series of stunts. He walked across blindfolded with his feet in buckets, took a table and chair to the centre and calmly sat down to a repast of cake and cocoa, took a small stove with him and fried an egg, turned somersaults, and swung hand over hand. He lowered a rope to the *Maid of the Mist*, pulled up a bottle of champagne, and calmly toasted the cheering crowd.

But all these were just warmups for his really big stunt, carrying a man across the gorge on his back.

Again the word went out and again the crowds began to gather. They came on foot, by oxcart, by coach, and by excursion trains from Buffalo, Rochester, and Milwaukee. Twelve hundred came by steamer from Toronto. There were bands and volunteer firemen and pickpockets and civic dignitaries and card sharks and even Sunday School outings.

It was a wonderful time, to be sure, and the assorted con men who controlled the Front were making thousands from the crowds. Being of a sporting nature, they also bet heavily that Blondin would never make it across with his human cargo and, to hedge their bets, tampered with the guy ropes that supported the main line.

On the late afternoon of the 19th of August, Blondin put on his show. The crowd was silent as Blondin stepped out onto the rope, accompanied by Harry Colcord. As the watchers held their breaths, the agile Colcord swung his 136 pounds up onto the shoulders of the only slightly heavier Blondin.

Slowly, carefully placing one foot ahead of the other, Blondin started down the incline of the sagging rope. It was painful work, and barely were they out over the roaring gorge when it was necessary for Colcord to get down off Blondin's back and stand on the rope to give the aerialist a rest. They had to repeat this performance seven times before they got across the gorge, and each halt took more out of the tiring men.

Nearing the middle of the rope where there were no guy ropes and the swaying was worst, Blondin actually lost his balance. In desperation he sprinted along the rope towards the nearest guy rope. He reached it, placed a trembling foot on it, and it broke. The gamblers had purposely weakened it. The main rope jerked sideways, pulled by the other guy rope. "Get down!" Blondin yelled, and Colcord did. Somehow they managed to keep from falling. After that, the trip up the 20 per cent incline to the other side was relatively easy.

The crowd went wild. They mobbed the two men. The band played jubilantly. People showered the men with gold coins and begged for their autographs. Surely it was the greatest day in the history of Niagara Falls.

Blondin and Colcord repeated their death-defying walk two more times, for the amusement of Edward, Prince of Wales, but the last walk was so hazardous that Colcord would never do it again.

For many years, other daredevils used Niagara Falls for their stunts. On October 24, 1901, a large crowd gathered to watch a huge round cylinder go over the falls, for inside it was the incredibly daring Anna Edson Taylor. When they fished the barrel out of the water and opened it, a shout went up from the watchers: Anna had survived the trip. Like swimmers of the English Channel, Anna was a one-day publicity wonder, and then nobody cared. She sat on the streets of Niagara Falls, N.Y., describing her feat to anyone who would listen and selling her autograph for pennies. Eventually she died destitute.

The most recent daredeveil was William (Red) Hill Junior who, in 1951, went over the falls in a flimsy rubber contraption which was smashed to pieces, causing the death of the famous river man.

People do not go to Niagara Falls to see daredevils today. Instead of the rowdy, raucous Front of a hundred years ago, there is the famous Queen Victoria Park whose lawns and flowerbeds are almost as famous as the falls themselves. Almost, but not quite. For Niagara Falls, like the Rocky Mountains or the Grand Canyon, is one of those truly great natural spectacles that must be seen and heard and felt to be appreciated.

Near Niagara Falls are the Welland Canal and the beautiful city of St. Catharines, described by its most ardent boosters as "the grape centre of the world."

The canal, certainly one of the wonders of Canada, cuts across the Niagara Peninsula for 27.6 miles, from Port Weller on Lake Ontario to Port Colborne on Lake Erie. An integral part of the St. Lawrence-Great Lakes Seaway System, the canal, by a system of eight huge locks, lifts ocean-going ships up to Lake Erie and gently sets them down again on their way back to the ocean. At almost any time during the shipping season, the traveller can park his car and watch the great ships easing their way through the locks.

It is a slow, painstaking process, but much speedier than the original method of transporting cargo between the lakes, which was to portage it on carts along a trail from Queenston to the mouth of Chippawa Creek above Niagara Falls. Then, in 1764, a system of hauling the bateaux and cargo up a six-mile incline by means of a capstan was devised, the charge for such service being £10 per bateau. Years later, between 1824 and 1829, the first ditch across the peninsula was dug, through the efforts of William Hamilton Merritt, a captain in the Canadian militia.

This first canal ran from Port Dalhousie (pronounced Portaloosie by locals) along Twelve Mile Creek to the summit level at Thorold, thence southerly to the Welland River at Port Robinson, to its mouth at Chippawa, and then up the Niagara River to Lake Erie. It had 40 wooden locks, each 110 feet long and 22 feet wide. By 1833 the route was extended south straight from Port Robinson to Port Colborne on Lake Erie.

After that, as the population increased and trade grew, the canal was enlarged and improved until in 1932 it was completed in its present form—8 concrete locks 859 feet long by 80 feet wide, with 30 feet of water over the sills.

Today the canal along Twelve Mile Creek, the site of the original canal, is used for the Royal Canadian Henley Regatta, one of the events that makes St. Catharines internationally known. The other is the annual week-long Grape Festival, held during the last week of September. There's a Grape Queen and a Grape King and even a Grape Prince. There's a gala parade and dances and banquets and sporting events and many other forms of frolic. St. Catharines is a good place to be during the Grape Festival.

The drive west along the Queen Elizabeth Way is over a narrow, flat, sand plain, with the cliffs of the escarpment on one side and Lake Ontario on the other. On both sides of the road are peach and cherry orchards and huge vineyards, along with other tender fruits. This is a part of Ontario different from any other. Protected by the wall of the escarpment and influenced by the slow temperature changes of the lake, the area is perfect for growing peaches. Because of the cooling properties of the lake, the blossoms come out two weeks later in the spring than they otherwise would, and so escape late frosts. During the summer the lake warms up, and in the fall this prevents early frosts that would ruin the peaches. Peaches can be grown elsewhere in Ontario, but nowehere as successfully as in the Niagara Peninsula, and tons of them are exported annually.

But this whole fruit-growing region is being threatened by people and "the needs of modern technocracy." More and more grape vines and fruit trees are being pushed out by bulldozers to make room for factories and the homes of the people who will work in them. For this is ideal industrial land, too, close to the great source of power at Niagara Falls and handy to all the markets of southern Ontario and the northeastern United States.

It is true that farmers whose families have been on this land are reluctant to sell. But fruit farming is a hard, grubbing, chancy life. Nobody works harder than the fruit farmer, and his returns are always subject to the whims of a fickle market. So the prospect of selling off the lands for fabulous amounts per acre, investing the proceeds and living a life of ease is very tempting. Anyone wishing to enjoy the Spring Blossom Festival when the peach trees are in bloom had better not delay his trip too long.

The city of Hamilton, at the extreme west end of Lake Ontario, is the most paradoxical city in Ontario. In some ways it is the province's ugliest and drabbest city; in others the most beautiful. Some people call it dull; local boosters maintain with conviction that

Hamilton is a glamorous city. Over the years it has had one of Canada's best football teams but until 1972 had never played host to the Grey Cup game. It is the centre of the steel industry, the focal point of half a dozen highways leading to Ontario's industrial heartland, and has one of the best natural harbours on the St. Lawrence Seaway. But its growth has been slow. Hamiltonians complain that they "live in the shadow of Toronto" which is a bare 35 miles away.

Hamilton is the city that tourists tend to by-pass, seeing only the steel mills and the smokey waterfront as they speed over the Burlington Skyway on the way to Niagara Falls. But anyone who stops and spends some time poking around Hamilton is well repaid, both in the beauty he sees and in the history he learns.

To begin with, at the northeastern entrance to the city, criss-crossed by concrete overpasses and underpasses, are 2,000 acres of natural park consisting of forests, marshlands, rock gardens, arboretums, one of the greatest displays of iris in the world, nature trails, winding creeks, and spectacular limestone cliffs.

This is the Royal Botanical Gardens, an unfortunate name, perhaps, as it suggests something formal and exclusive and a little forbidding. The Gardens are none of these things. They are for walking or driving, watching muskrats in the reeds, listening to the cur-a-lee of redwings, or observing the shy and elusive whistling swans pausing briefly in their March migration flight to the northwest. Visitors can help to make maple syrup or learn gardening from experts. And it is all absolutely free.

As is often true of parks, this splendid acreage is largely the result of the hard work and determination of one man. This was T.B. McQuesten, a formidable figure on the parks board of management some forty years ago.

Back in 1929-30 when much land was being sold for taxes, McQuesten persuaded the parks board to acquire some apparently worthless properties. Then he observed that the marshland and pond known as Coote's Paradise was Crown land. There was some more property that the Provincial Department of Highways had and did not need. The result of all this was that in 1941 the provincial government passed a Royal Botanical Gardens Act which provided for the perpetuation and maintenance of the Gardens.

Every summer, and to some extent in winter, too, hundreds of thousands of nature lovers and horticulturalists come to admire the floral displays, tramp the 19 different hiking trails that total more than 20 miles, admire the view from the brow of the Niagara Escarpment which runs through the Rock Capel Sanctuary of the Gardens, marvel at the geological exhibits, or watch the birds. Unfortunately hundreds of thousands more roar past, seeing only the small part of the Gardens visible from the highway and wondering vaguely what it is all about.

Hamilton's best historical site is Dundurn Castle, both for its connection with Sir Allan MacNab, who was surely one of Ontario's most colourful characters, and for the beauty and majesty of the house and the 60 acres of parkland that surround it.

Dundurn Castle is not really a castle in the sense of having turrets and battlements and moats and dungeons. It is simply a huge, gracious home built in the style of a Tuscan villa, and contains beautiful furniture of the early Victorian period. It was restored to its original state faithfully and painstakingly by Anthony Adamson for Canada's centennial in 1967, at a cost of $600,000.

The house is open to the public every day of the year, except Christmas Day. The pictures on the walls of the numerous high-ceilinged rooms reveal much of the social, economic, and political conditions of the day. One of the pictures is of Archibald MacNab, a cousin of Sir Allan, who attempted to set up a feudal system in the Ottawa Valley.

There are also pictures of the railways that Sir Allan built, and the bank that he founded. His old gout stool still sits in his study, as does the speaker's mace, a reminder that he was for a time speaker of the Upper Canada Legislative Assembly. And there are pictures of fighting cocks, for cockfighting, although illegal, was one of the laird's favourite diversions. From the study window you can see the cockpit where the contests were held. Sir Allan was constantly changing and adding to the house, so that he was nearly always in debt. Legend says his credit was cut off by the local tradesmen, and that he was reduced to rolling his supplies of flour up to the "castle" himself.

Gradually you put together a portrait of this fabulous character, by turns soldier, statesman, business tycoon, and patriot, who built this house in 1834 and lived there with his family until his death in 1862.

Born in 1798 in Newark (now Niagara-on-the-Lake) to Governor Simcoe's aide-de-camp, Allan MacNab was an adventurous rascally, energetic, capable lad who at the age of 14 fought with conspicuous bravery against the American invaders during the War of 1812. He was always lucky. At the defence of York he miraculously survived the explosion on April 27, 1813 of a gunpowder magazine that killed most of his companions.

After the war the young MacNab worked as a carpenter, actor, land agent, and finally as an articled clerk in a law firm. He studied law, was admitted to the bar, and cast about for a likely place to practise. The head of the lake was appealing for many reasons. There was a small but thriving village in Wentworth County on the south side of the bay which needed a lawyer. When MacNab moved there with his wife and infant son, he had but a few dollars in his pocket and no property.

But he did have something far more valuable: a tremendous fund of energy, a reputation as a soldier and patriot, and an entrée into the Family Compact. His father was already Sergeant-at-Arms in the Legislative Assembly (in which capacity, incidentally, he was more than once required to forcibly remove the battling, shouting, William Lyon Mackenzie from the chamber) and the young MacNab won the seat for Wentworth.

Always an ardent patriot and eager military man, MacNab endeared himself to the Compact by leading the "Men of Gore" against Mackenzie's rebels on December 7, 1837. As I walked through Dundurn Castle and was impressed by its splendour, I could not help but contrast it to the drab little house in Toronto where Mackenzie had spent his last disenchanted years.

MacNab continued to prosper in politics and business. He acquired great tracts of land, built railroads, was knighted by the Queen, became leader of the Tories, and from 1854 to 1856 was Prime Minister of the united Canadas. He lived opulently and boisterously. His motto was "Gun Eagal," which is Gaelic for "Without Fear," and he loved a fight of any kind. In many ways MacNab epitomizes the Ontario power elite: capable, shrewd, a mixture of pragmatism and idealism, stridently loyal to the British Crown, staunch believer in the individual's right to prosper by any means within the law.

McMaster University, which is not far from Dundurn Castle, is another of Hamilton's charms. Begun as a Baptist college in the 1830s, McMaster has developed into one of the finest science and engineering universities in the province. It has the first nuclear reactor to be found on any Canadian campus as well as a large research computer and a nuclear particle accelerator. McMaster has also instituted a new School of Medicine whose building and staff are the pride of Hamilton.

In 1968, William B. Ready, head librarian at McMaster, accomplished the literary coup of the half century by acquiring all of the papers of the late Bertrand Russell, so that Russell scholars must come to Hamilton for their source material. The library also acquired many of the papers and manuscripts of playwright Samuel Beckett.

Belying its situation in the midst of an asphalt jungle in the most heavily-industrialized area of Canada, McMaster has on its doorstep the sunken gardens and the nature trails of the Royal Botanical Gardens. "They're right there," one professor said. "When I feel the need to get back to nature I just take a walk. Within minutes I'm in the deep woods."

Also within walking distance for the faculty and their families are the ski slopes of the Chedoke Winter Sports Park. Although Hamilton is not in Ontario's snow belt, the slopes are kept serviceable all winter long by means of mechanical snow-making machines.

Wherever you are in Hamilton you are very much aware of the Mountain, for it cuts through the middle of the city with about one-third of the city's people living on the land above it. The Mountain is not really a mountain, of course. Not technically, anyway, but, as the mayor told me, "It gives the city glamour. We're the only split-level city in Ontario." He points out that all the land along the face of the Mountain is public land and will be used only for public purposes.

As I drove up the Mountain by way of the Jolley Cut, I had the feeling that little has changed here since the earliest settlers such as Robert Land or Richard Beasley came in about 1785 as Loyalist refugees after the American Revolution. At the top of the escarpment there are parks with flower gardens and lookout points from which you can see the flat land between the Mountain and the bay. The main business section is all down there: the civic square, the library, and the theatre auditorium. Beyond is the harbour, with huge ore-carrying vessels unloading at the docks, and the steel mills belching smoke into the sky and dumping their slag into the lake.

The paradox of Hamilton is that the visitor, although in the centre of Ontario's most heavily industrialized region, is never far from rural Ontario. The towns and villages of Wentworth County are rich in history and activity. Rockton, for instance, annually holds the Little World's Fair on Thanksgiving Day. It is a typical Ontario fall fair and a good place to be in the autumn sunshine to watch the parade of fat Aberdeen Angus and trim Holsteins, to bet on the harness races, to gnaw on hot dogs, and to see the biggest turnip grown in the county, the reddest roses, the tastiest jams, and the finest cakes. The horse show is the highlight. Here the horse, who once provided power, transportation, and recreation for people, is on display in all his glory. High-stepping hackneys and sleek coach horses, heads held high and tails over the dashboard, prance smartly in front of the grandstand. And the drivers, from eight to eighty, in their buggies all paint and silver, sit proud and straight on the leather seats. For good, warm-feeling, comfortable, gleam-in-the-eye nostalgia, you cannot beat an Ontario fall fair.

At Rockton, we went out among the lions. Not tame lions in cages; wild lions in fields. Great shaggy-maned male lions, sleek, sober lionesses, and frolicking cubs. They are used to cars, but not to people, so you are warned to keep your car windows shut and not to get out. There is a real spine-tingling, gut-tightening thrill about being that close to lions.

The lions are part of a 450-acre tract of scrub land called the African Lion Safari. Contrary to our preconceived notion, lions do not mind the cold at all. Like any other animal they simply grow more hair. There are monkeys in the Safari, too, and a great variety of other animals. It is a good place to take the kids.

Between Hamilton and Toronto along the shore of Lake Ontario is one huge industrial complex. Factories crowd in on either side of the Queen Elizabeth Way, and the towns and cities grow and prosper. Oakville, for instance, where the immense Ford plant is situated, was described by the Department of National Revenue as the richest community in Canada because the average income of its residents is higher than that of any other community.

A good chunk of this area, more than seventy thousand acres in fact, was incorporated on January 1, 1968, into the town of Mississauga. Its population of 160,000 persons and over a thousand industries surely make it the largest town in Ontario. Why a town instead of a city? Very simple. Towns receive a better deal in the matter of provincial grants and subsidies than do cities. Besides, being the largest town is probably better than being the twentieth largest city.

North of this area are the communities of Brampton, Streetsville, Milton, and Georgetown, all heavily industrialized. Brampton calls itself the Rose Centre of Ontario because of the hundreds of acres of greenhouses there that ship roses to many parts of the continent. Next door to Brampton is the planned satellite city of Bramalea, which was all laid out with residential, commercial, industrial, parks, and school areas before a single building was built.

The upwards of three million people who live in the Toronto–Hamilton stretch of the Golden Horseshoe are reasonably well provided with recreational facilities. There is Lake Ontario, of course, but outside of sunning and boating there is little recreation there. The water is just too cold. But north and west of Toronto, a few minutes by car from the industrial areas, are a series of lakes, hiking trails, fishing ponds, swamps where rare birds and flowers are to be found, ski slopes, and snowmobile runs. And much of it is a direct result of the worst calamity that has ever hit the Golden Horseshoe region.

During the early part of October 1954, Toronto weathermen were watching a hurricane that had developed in the south Atlantic. They called the hurricane Hazel, and expected it would probably hit Florida, as most hurricanes do, maybe wreak some havoc along the coast, and then go out to sea. Instead, this one swerved inland, and on the morning of October 15, warnings of possible high winds and unusual rainfall were issued.

Nobody paid much attention. After all, what harm can winds of sixty to seventy miles an hour do. Besides, this area with its ravines and creeks and hills was certainly not susceptible to floods. So people went out in their cars as usual and they took no precautions in their homes.

And then Hazel hit. She ripped across New York State and tore into the region around Toronto. The winds were not all that bad; they blew limbs off some trees to be sure, but no verandas, roofs, or barns were blown away. The rain, however, was something else. All day it poured, and all night, soaking into the ground and saturating it. And still it kept on raining and raining until 9¼ inches had fallen in just over 24 hours. And then it happened. The swollen creeks and streams and rivers could not hold the water any more, and it flooded over the banks, taking trees and debris with it. Bridges were carried away like toys, and with them many cars that should not have been on the road. Frightened people scrambled to the upper stories of their houses and, when the water kept rising, onto the roofs. But still the water came.

The Humber River and the Etobicoke Creek were the worst. In Woodbridge, where the river took a turn, houses on the low ground were washed away, and their people with them. Along the Etobicoke Creek a section of Raymore Crescent was completely carried away, leaving nothing but a muddy waste with no sign of life. Dozens of bodies were washed down into Lake Ontario.

When the rain stopped and a count could be made, 81 persons were known to have perished, and the damage was estimated at $25 million. Now the people knew that it could happen and might someday happen again.

There is nothing like a major catastrophe to produce funds, and after Hazel no one quibbled about money for flood control. The Metropolitan Toronto and Region Conservation Authority was formed, and raised during the next ten years no less than $39 million. It was obvious from the beginning that, while buying land for dams and other projects, some attention should be paid to the recreational possibilities. In fact the Authority has been accused by some of concentrating on recreation and being carried away by the need for it.

The results have been spectacular. Streams have been dammed to make lakes. Thousands of acres of land have been landscaped and supplied with picnic facilities. Fish ponds have been gouged out and stocked with fish from the Authority's own hatcheries. Nature trails have been established, and conservation schools set up. At Black Creek, which is just within the northwestern boundary of Metropolitan Toronto, a pioneer village has been created so that school children and others can experience life as it was in this area before Confederation. Everything is authentic—houses, tools, implements, furniture, butter churns that were run by dog power, threshing machines that were run by horses on a treadle, home-baked bread made from home-ground wheat, homespun clothes made from hand-woven wool, and so on.

Each year millions of harassed city dwellers leave the smog-filled air of the industrial sections to get up into the hills. At Heart Lake, just off Highway 10, the Etobicoke Creek has been dammed to make a beautiful little lake, where on a hot Sunday thousands of people swim and boat and fish. At Glen Haffey, just south of Mono Mills, the farthest out park, there is fishing, hiking, picknicking, and a view from the edge of the Niagara Escarpment of the beautiful hills of Albion. Each of the other dozen or so recreation areas has something special to offer.

Going eastward from Toronto along Highway 401 we pass through the industrial towns of Ajax and Whitby and come to the north tip of the Golden Horseshoe, the city of Oshawa, often referred to as "the town that Sam built."

For it was in Oshawa in the year 1907 that the McLaughlin Carriage Company made its first automobile. Sam McLaughlin, who died in 1973 at the age of 102, was a young man of 36 then, and a partner in the company. Later, the McLaughlin works became part of General Motors of Canada, which is still making automobiles in Oshawa.

The story of the McLaughlin family, as it has been told by Samuel McLaughlin himself, is in many ways the story of the development of this part of the country. In 1832, John McLaughlin, Sam's grandfather, emigrated from County Tyrone in Ireland, settled in the bush a few miles northeast of Oshawa, and founded a community which they called Tyrone.

He was no ordinary farmer, this John McLaughlin; he was in fact a genius at shaping wood, and an unusually astute man of business. He began to carve axe handles in his spare time after chopping trees, ploughing, butchering, making harness, and doing the hundreds of other jobs a farmer must do. These handles were made of the soundest true-grain hardwood, and they brought a good price in Tyrone.

Soon after this success, John McLaughlin decided to make a cutter from a design he had seen in a catalogue. Before it was finished, a neighbour asked him to make a similar cutter, and John McLaughlin was in business. He quit farming, built a shop for making cutters and wagons, and hired some men, including his son Robert. Tyrone proved to be too small a town, however, and soon he moved to a bigger shop in nearby Enniskillen and finally to a shop in Oshawa.

Robert McLaughlin then invented a special "gear" for carriages, which revolutionized their manufacture, and made the company the leading carriage makers in the province. By this time Robert's young Sam had quit school, apprenticed as an upholsterer, and joined the company as a partner. But soon the younger members of the firm became concerned about competition from the new "horseless carriages" that were appearing on the road. They persuaded Robert that they should make motor cars and, since the bodies would be made of wood, he reluctantly agreed. Thus the famous McLaughlin car was born. Later it became known as the McLaughlin Buick and, finally, just the Buick, still one of the mainstays of General Motors.

That is the Golden Horseshoe. An area containing more factories, more people, and more automobiles than any other area of Canada. It is by way of becoming one giant megalopolis of factories, shopping centres, and suburbs. Very soon all of the agricultural land will be snatched up for commercial, industrial, and residential purposes. All of the problems of great concentrations of people—pollution, overcrowding, noise, crime, slums, ghettos, and high taxation, to name a few—are already being felt and may ultimately overwhelm the area. For if there is a sure and permanent solution for urban blight and urban sprawl and urban pollution, nobody has yet come up with it.

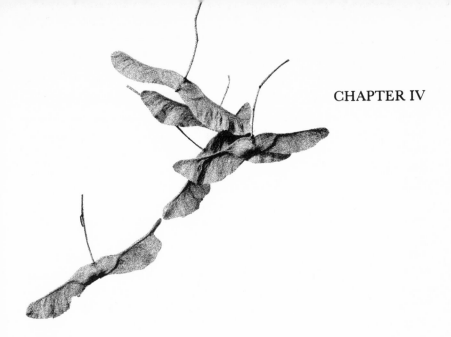

CHAPTER IV

Toronto

One evening shortly after arriving in Toronto in 1944, my wife and I went to a movie on Yonge Street. When we came out just after 11 o'clock, we were stunned to discover that there wasn't a single restaurant open where we could get a cup of coffee. Not one. Even in Saskatoon the Chocolate Shop stayed open later than that.

As we looked north and south on Yonge Street we could easily count the number of people on the sidewalk and the cars on the street. There were no bars or nightclubs, and few bookstores or record shops. Like the rest of Toronto, the city's oldest street was sedate, quiet, well behaved, and dull.

Not any more. When you walk down Yonge Street now, day or night, you can scarcely get through the throng of people. They are mostly young, many dressed in gaudy outfits, all in a buoyant holiday spirit. Record stores blare out the latest tunes, garish facades of bars and nightclubs beckon, bookstalls display their pornography, strip-tease joints entice the curious, and the road is jammed with cars. The street is alive.

An improvement? Many would say not. But certainly it is noisy evidence of what has happened to Toronto since the Forties. Toronto has drawn hundreds of thousands of people from Europe, Asia, Africa, the States, and from the other provinces of Canada.

Bus terminals, railway stations, and particularly Toronto's international airport, are jammed with people coming to the city. Many come by car, adding to the city's growing traffic problem. Others hitchhike. Sixty thousand newcomers a year swell Toronto's population, enough to fill a good-sized city.

A sportswriter in Edmonton develops a good style and some reputation; sooner or later he is invited to join the staff of one of Toronto's three large and thriving daily newspapers. A singer makes it big in Nova Scotia and soon finds herself getting "maximum media coverage" in Toronto. A Newfoundland artist opens a studio at the corner of College and Spadina. Radio announcers from Winnipeg, a doctor from Lac La Ronge, a magazine editor from Oxbow, a movie cameraman from Trail, a free-lance writer from Nokomis; all find their way to Toronto. Some prefer to stay home, of course, to make their reputations where they are, but to thousands of artists, professional people, and business people, too, Toronto is the ultimate goal.

People, of course, are flocking into almost every city in Canada, but because Toronto is the biggest and richest city in the richest province, it attracts the most. For Toronto has developed into a great metropolitan city with a world-wide reputation as an educational, cultural, entertainment, and industrial centre. It has grown up and has acquired big city status. You can feel it when you enter the city. You can see it on the faces of the people you meet. Toronto even smells like a big city—terrible.

Toronto's growth is as natural as that of a healthy child with all the advantages in life. For Toronto is a much-favoured city, geographically, historically, and politically.

In the first place, Toronto is close to the centre of southern Ontario. By the Macdonald-Cartier Freeway, which slices through the top half of the metropolitan area, the distance to the city of Cornwall near the eastern boundary of the province is 280 miles, while the distance to Windsor on the western border is 235 miles.

More important, Toronto is on the north shore of Lake Ontario, covering 25 miles of shoreline, and has an excellent sheltered harbour. Via the lake and the St. Lawrence Seaway, the city is connected by water with every port in the world, as well as with the Canadian and American ports on the Great Lakes. Lake vessels and ocean freighters call regularly at Toronto, making it one of the busiest ports in Canada.

The land around the city is flat and fertile, and has since the beginning of the province supported prosperous farms. The city has always been an important market-place from the day it was founded by Lieutenant-Governor John Graves Simcoe in 1793, and later became the seat of provincial government and an important military centre. People draw people, and despite the lack of coal or iron ore in the immediate vicinity, the city from the first developed factories that were later economically powered by electricity from Niagara Falls.

So there the city sits, Toronto proper and the five boroughs that make up the Municipality of Metropolitan Toronto, covering 241 square miles and containing more than two and a half million people, which means that about one out of every ten Canadians lives in Metropolitan Toronto.

Here are the things that have impressed me about Toronto, not necessarily in order of importance.

The entrance to the city from the west is, I believe, one of the most attractive of any city in Ontario. There is the Queen Elizabeth Way, the province's first four-lane expressway (opened in 1939), that comes from Niagara Falls by way of Hamilton. At the bridge over the Humber River it becomes the Gardiner Expressway, which was Metropolitan Toronto's first expressway; it is there largely because of the bulldozing vitality of Metro's first chairman, Frederick "Big Daddy" Gardiner.

South of the Gardiner, which sort of goes over the top of things, is Lakeshore Boulevard, a pleasant drive along the lake past green lawns and flocks of Canada geese and ducks and children's playgrounds. It also passes the old Argonaut Rowing Club, where in summer crews and singles do their training, and the grounds of the Canadian National Exhibition; and, across the road from the CNE and built out into the lake, Toronto's newest family playground, Ontario Place.

A pleasant drive today, and not too bad even in rush hour, but it used to be a horror. For years, before Big Daddy and his expressway, the only entrance from the west was along Lakeshore Boulevard, a two-lane road that ran right smack through the centre of the old Sunnyside Beach amusement park. Motorists who complain of tie-ups on the Gardiner today should have tried getting into or out of the city during the Forties and Fifties. I did a lot of commuting in those days, between our home in Streetsville and the offices of the principal magazines and the CBC, and I would sit for hours, hungry, tired and frustrated, part of a solid line of cars inching its way from Maple Leaf Stadium at the foot of Bathurst Street to the Humber Bridge. At Sunnyside Beach, where the amusement park drew customers by the thousands, I would wait while a Toronto cop held up his hand to let the mobs across.

As I sat there I would while away the time trying to figure out how I would solve the traffic problem if I were boss. I thought of tunnels, bridges out over the lake, and even crazier gimmicks, but I never came up with anything as good as that marvellous Gardiner Expressway. Even today, as I enter Toronto from the west and breeze along the Gardiner at 70 miles an hour, I think of those times and say a little prayer of thanks for the big, gruff, flamboyant character who made it all possible.

The waterfront was not always so neat and trim as it is today with breakwaters and retaining walls. For many years it was a muddy, weedy, pollution-ridden mess with rickety wooden wharves at the ends of the principal north-south streets.

In pioneer days it was the haven of smugglers specializing in the import of liquor, tea, spices, tobacco, jewels, and other valuable articles without the benefit of duty. One of the most colourful of these characters was a one-armed rascal named Michael Masterson who went by the nickname of "Fisty." In 1846 he lived in a cottage on the mudflats at the foot of Bay Street and carried on the trade of grinding razors. His real vocation, though, was illicit trade, and a certain King Street grocer, it is said, made a fortune selling tea that Fisty had fetched from clippers before they got to port. A customs man named Carfrae was watching Fisty closely and, when the time was right, went aboard his schooner to make the arrest. Fisty had other ideas. Seizing the customs man with his good arm, he dragged him overboard into the bay with the idea of drowning him. But both men were rescued, and Fisty had to pay heavy fines for his sins.

In 1911, by a special act, the present Toronto Harbour Commission was established with the powers needed to clean up the waterfront. They acquired the land at the lake's edge and began filling in the mudflats with earth dug from basements in the fast-growing city. Altogether more than two thousand acres of valuable real estate were created in this way.

The new Toronto Islands ferry wharf is an interesting part of the waterfront, and every weekend in summer thousands of Torontonians pile onto the ferries to spend a day on the island. For the Islands Park is one of the best in Toronto. No cars are allowed. Visitors can wander over acres of green grass, or rent canoes to paddle up and down the lagoons where, under the shade of immense willow trees, long-necked swans, dumpy ducks, and geese disport themselves in peace.

Not far from the ferry docks is old Pier 9 where, on the cold, dismal night of September 17, 1949, 119 pleasure seekers were burned to death when the cruise ship *Noronic* went up in flames.

The *Noronic*, one of the last of the Great Lakes pleasure cruise ships, was filled with passengers from Cleveland and Detroit. She had berthed for the night preparatory to setting sail for the Thousand Islands. A fire began in a linen closet and spread quickly through the gangways and cabins whose walls were thick with inflammable varnish. There was no alarm; passengers were caught completely unawares. Those who could, jumped over the side into the chill black water; some managed to get down the gangplank, but the rest were overcome with heat and smoke before they could escape.

Despite all efforts, 12 bodies never were identified or claimed; they were buried in Mount Pleasant Cemetery, where a plaque was erected in memory of all those who lost their lives.

The entire area of Toronto south of Front Street and between Yonge and Bathurst Streets is, in fact, undergoing a complete face-lift, and it needs it. When the railway first came to Toronto in the 1850s, the tracks were naturally built near the lake because that was the flattest and easiest place to put them. This led to a gradual and haphazard accumulation of vast railway yards, roundhouses, warehouses, and other industrial establishments, which do not make for an attractive waterfront.

All this is coming out, to be replaced by an exciting multi-use Metro Centre comprising 190 acres and costing an estimated one billion dollars. It will consist of housing, a convention centre, a transportation centre, a CBC English-language network headquarters, a new Massey Hall, and a park where people can actually see the lake and walk along it and enjoy it.

The most spectacular structure in Metro Centre is the already completed CN Tower, which reaches 1,805 feet above the ground, making it the highest free-standing structure in the world and, what is more important for communications, higher than any other point in southern Ontario. The upper observation tower at the 1,500-foot level gives visibility for 75 miles. On a clear day, they say, you can see Niagara Falls.

Yonge Street is the centre of Toronto. It is the city's oldest, longest, and most historial thoroughfare. It was built by John Graves Simcoe, Lieutenant-Governor of Upper Canada, shortly after the province was established by the Constitutional Act of 1791. Simcoe, an astute military man who had distinguished himself in the American Revolutionary War, knew that a fort was needed on the north shore of Lake Ontario, and he knew that fort must be connected with the interior by road. So he had his Queen's Rangers build Fort York and hack a trail north through the bush to Lake Simcoe.

There was nothing on the site of Toronto then. In the past there had been Indian villages and a French trading post. The last of these, Fort Rouillé, had been burned by the French in 1759 to prevent it from falling into the hands of the English.

On the east side of the Yonge Street Road, Simcoe built the town of York (as Toronto was first named), and a long trail, now Front Street, connected it with the fort.

On the corner of Front and Yonge Streets today is the city-run O'Keefe Centre, built to give Toronto a much-needed auditorium for operas, ballets, travelling extravaganzas, and other stage productions.

Yonge Street north from Front is a collection of buildings old and new. Many of the ornate old red-brick structures go back a hundred years to the time before Yonge Street was even paved. Some of these ancient buildings have had face-liftings, with fancy new facades and much bolstering of floors. But their basements betray their age, and building inspectors shudder when they go down the rickety steps.

Mixed in with these old-timers are the new concrete, steel and glass edifices of the banks and trust companies. The corner of King and Bay, for instance, probably Toronto's busiest corner, is surrounded by skyscrapers.

The names of the streets as you go north tell of Toronto's history. There is Temperance Street, which runs from Yonge one long block and one short one west to Sheppard Street. This was the site of Jesse Ketchum's tannery, an immense establishment filled with piles of hides and tanbark and vats and a putrid stench that filled all that part of old Muddy York.

Ketchum got off a boat at the Yonge Street wharf in 1799, just six years after the town had been established. A healthy, ambitious lad of 17 years, he had come from Spencertown, N.Y., to make his fame and fortune. He made both. Besides building the largest tannery in Upper Canada, he was prominent in real estate, education, and politics. A strongly religious man, he also endowed churches and other worthy establishments both in Ontario and Buffalo, N.Y., where he spent his last years. Why Temperance Street? Ketchum, like all good Methodists, was a determined foe of all alcoholic beverages, so naturally he named his street accordingly.

A couple of blocks north of Temperance Street is Queen Street, with the city's two largest department stores, Eaton's and Simpsons, facing each other. Despite the growth of modern shopping malls around Metropolitan Toronto, the corner of Queen and Yonge is still the place where most people come to shop, and the subway which runs beneath Yonge Street has a station connecting both stores.

The entire west side of Yonge Street, from Albert north to Dundas and stretching west to Bay, is being torn down to make way for the mammoth Eaton Centre which will fill this entire area with high-rise office buildings and retail stores. And with it goes a great deal of Yonge Street history.

One old building that is being saved is the Church of the Holy Trinity on Trinity Square, which was so completely surrounded by higher buildings that many Torontonians didn't even know it was there. But they found out all right when this tiny church was able to hold up the multi-million dollar project for many months.

The corner of Dundas and Yonge is one of the liveliest, being the centre of bars, nightclubs, and record stores. This is the part of the street strangers usually head for, because here they will see "the action"—mostly people just walking on the street, watching others, and being watched.

At College Street, Yonge becomes more sedate again largely because of yet another Eaton's store on the corner. But north of College until Wellesley, Yonge degenerates a bit.

The corner of Bloor and Yonge Streets fairly oozes history. This was the site of the Yonge Street toll-gate, where farmers from the north had to pay to use the street into town. So, to avoid paying two tolls, they usually spent the night at the Red Lion Inn on the northeast corner, which was conveniently close to Joseph Bloor's brewery.

Here the farmers gathered and drank and talked politics. And there was plenty to talk about. Roads that were axle deep in mud, bridges that would not hold up a cow, political heelers who were paid to maintain roads and never did. The nefarious Clergy Reserves that favoured the Anglicans and did not give the Presbyterians or Methodists a look-in. And that damned Family Compact, friends of that nincompoop Lieutenant-Governor Bond Head, who refused to make any reforms. It was enough to make a man think of fighting for his rights.

Across the street was the sombre, desolate Potter's Field, or strangers' burial grounds, where the lost and the neglected and the destitute were buried at night with no one to mourn their passing. When the street was developed their bones were moved, but nobody cared very much where.

North of Eglinton Avenue on the west side of Yonge Street stands a post office building bearing a plaque which states that it was the site of Montgomery's Tavern, where a small band of rebels and their leader, William Lyon Mackenzie, met on a cold December day in 1837 to march on Toronto and capture it.

Mackenzie figured that since the element of surprise was in their favour, and since most of the regular troops were away from the garrison fighting rebels in Lower Canada, he could march on the town, seize a quantity of arms in the town hall, and carry out a bloodless coup.

Other leaders had other ideas. Long, wearisome discussions went on far into the night, envoys were met and argued with, and before the coup could be accomplished, news of the secret meeting in the tavern reached the garrison and a group of between fifteen and thirty loyal militia men were marching up Yonge Street.

The first skirmish went something like this:

Mackenzie, on a horse, was leading his men who were under the direct command of Colonel Samuel Lount. A few dozen rebels in front had muskets, but those in the rear had nothing more formidable than pieces of sharp iron on the ends of long poles, or axes and cudgels. When they got within range, the militia fired a volley of shots and the men in the front rank of the rebels returned the fire. Then the militia men turned and retreated back down Yonge Street. The front-line rebels fell on their faces so that the men behind could fire a volley over them. But the men behind thought their companions had been shot, so they took to their heels, too.

"We shall all be killed," their pikemen cried in panic as they threw down their weapons and ran.

Mackenzie tried desperately to rally his forces. He galloped about explaining the reason for the misunderstanding, but nobody was in a mood to listen. He believed, and he was probably right, that there was still time to take the town.

That opportunity, however, did not last. Reinforcements arrived, and soon a well-disciplined force with artillery led by Sir Francis Bond Head himself was marching up the street. The rebels met them near Montgomery's Tavern and, for a while, fought bravely. But the cannons were too much for them. Shells ripped through the tavern itself, and Mackenzie ordered a retreat.

Sir Francis immediately issued a proclamation offering a reward of £1,000 for Mackenzie's capture, dead or alive. But Mackenzie's friends and supporters hid him in barns and caves, fed and clothed him, and provided him with horses. He finally managed to escape to Navy Island in the Niagara River and from there he carried on an abortive struggle for a number of years. He was finally included in the general amnesty of 1849 and returned to Toronto to live out his life, a broken and disillusioned man.

The house that Mackenzie's friends gave him and in which he and his daughters lived still stands on Toronto's Bond Street. It is furnished as it was in the year 1861, with the old pianoforte and the actual bed in which Mackenzie died. His high top hat is there, too, and his steel-rimmed spectacles, and in the basement is part of the printing press on which he printed the *Colonial Advocate*. It had been pitched into the lake in 1826 by a band of irate young Tories when Mackenzie was the establishment's sternest critic, and was hauled up by workmen digging in the harbour fill many years later.

There is something else there, too: the ghost of the fiery rebel himself.

When my wife and I were in the house for the first time in 1960, we were the only visitors. The caretaker, who had already resigned and was soon moving out, showed us some things that he did not usually show visitors, including erasures in the family Bible that had possibly been made to protect somebody's good name.

Just as we were about to leave, I jestingly asked the caretaker, "Do you ever see any evidence of the ghost of the old boy about?"

He immediately became dead serious and told us of a couple of very strange incidents. Once in the middle of the night his wife was awakened by being severely slapped on the face by someone standing beside the bed. When she turned on the lights no one was there, the door downstairs was still locked, and there was no stranger in the house. But there on her face were the welts left by a hand that had slapped very hard.

Another night they were awakened by a noise from the front bedroom that sounded as though someone was watering the plants on the window sill. Again no one was there, and the doors were locked tight, but the room was a frightful mess; water all over the window sills and floors and walls. The caretaker showed us the stains to prove it.

There was absolutely no doubt in his mind that the ghost of William Lyon Mackenzie walked the house. Why, he had been seen leaving the front door one night with hat, glasses, and walking stick, and carrying the same old carpetbag he always took on his travels.

That same day I told Rex Lambert what the caretaker had said. Rex was at the time Toronto's unofficial resident expert on ghosts, and he subsequently spent a night in the house in Mackenzie's own room, watched over only by television cameras, but no ghost appeared. Mackenzie always was a contrary man.

Yonge Street, which is also Highway 11, continues north through the borough of North York, the towns of Thornhill, Richmond Hill, Aurora, Newmarket, Bradford and on to the city of Barrie.

Just as Yonge Street grew out of the old Yonge Street Road, many other Toronto streets had similar origins. Kingston Road was the road to Kingston. Dundas Street grew from the old trail that led from the town of York west into good farming country. Other streets had been private laneways into the estates of early residents, a fact which accounts for the numerous short, curved streets, roads, and crescents that seem to lead nowhere.

Unlike western cities, Edmonton for instance, where the streets mostly run one way, and the avenues are at right angles to them and are numbered, Toronto's streets are a hopeless hodgepodge. Very few streets are numbered and the house numbering system on one street bears no relation to the system on the next. A street may be called a place, a road, a drive, an avenue, a crescent, or may along its length have two or more of those designations. Thus the long street that cuts through the centre of the city from west to east is variously called Bloor Street, Danforth Avenue, and Kingston Road. And the same name is used many times. "Indian" is one favourite. There is Indian Grove, Indian Line, Indian Mound, Indian Road, Indian Road Crescent, Indian Trail, Indian Valley Crescent and Indianola Drive. The Metropolitan Street Index reads like a telephone book with over eight thousands names from Abbeville Road (followed by Abbey Lane, Abbotsfield Gate, Abbotsford Road, Abbott Avenue and Abbotswood) to Zoo Road and Zorra Street.

Spadina Avenue, one of the city's old and interesting streets, was originally the long lane running north two miles from the lake to the country house of Dr. W. W. Baldwin, (father of reformer Robert Baldwin), which stood on the brow of the hill where Casa Loma now stands. This was back in 1840, before the western outskirts of the city reached to Spadina, and Baldwin donated his lane in the hopes that it would some day become the main street. This possibly accounts for the fact that it is one of the widest streets in the city.

Spadina is to some extent Toronto in miniature, embodying as it does some of the poorest and some of the most gracious aspects of the city.

The lower part of Spadina, originally named Brock Street, was part of Toronto harbour. An early picture shows great lumber rafts being prepared at the wharf for the hazardous trip along Lake Ontario and down the St. Lawrence to Quebec.

North of the tracks is the garment district. Old brick buildings bear signs stating that dresses, fur coats, girdles, socks, and other articles of clothing are manufactured here. And during their noon hour break on a hot summer day, the women who work the thousands of sewing machines in crowded "sweat shops" are out on the street getting a breath of fresh air.

North of Queen Street is the part of the avenue that is the domain of race track touts, pimps, prostitutes, pushers, gamblers, tiny restaurants, and churches. The centre of this domain is Dundas Street. Here, on the corner across from a Catholic church, is the Victory Burlesk theatre, one of the few old-time burlesque houses on the continent. The lurid marquee and posters announce that the show features such internationally-renowned strippers as Lolita Love, Helen Bed, Vera Shapely, Rose Mary Baby, and other artists.

Near the Victory is one of my favourite Toronto establishments, the hat store of Sammy Taft. While fitting me perfectly with just the hat or cap I want, Sammy fills me in on what is happening. He was born on Spadina above his father's barber shop over sixty years ago, and he considers Spadina to be the "most foreign street" in Canada. On the walls of his shop are pictures of some of the world's great hat wearers, like Bing Crosby and Gordon Sinclair.

Just a block west of Spadina is Kensington Street, which runs north into the area called Kensington Market. The market is packed with shoppers from the area who speak mostly Chinese, Italian, Greek, Portuguese, Yugoslavian, and other languages. The stores are small, for the most part the fronts of ancient houses built up with plywood and packed with merchandise. There are dozens of poultry and egg markets, fruit and vegetable stands, cheese stores, and fish markets. A customer chooses a live chicken from a crate sitting on the sidewalk and has it killed and prepared to his specifications.

A few blocks farther north is the corner of Spadina and College, the northern boundary of the strip. This corner has special interest because in the late 1900s it was one end of the famous Belt Line of the Toronto Railway Company. The streetcars could be converted to fresh air vehicles by removing the sides, and were pulled by horses until 1892, when electricity began to take over. They were available in the evenings to private parties of people who wished to travel the tree-lined streets of the Belt Line down Spadina, east on King to Sherbourne Street, and north to Bloor. This ride, as the company advertised, encircled "the major part of the city" and passed through "the splendid retail stores of King Street, as well as the handsome residences of the merchant princes in the surburbs."

A wrought-iron drinking fountain stood at the southeast corner of the Spadina-College intersection, so that horses and passengers alike could refresh themselves.

North of College, Spadina Avenue splits to go around an ancient brick Gothic-style building surrounded by an iron fence. Built in 1875 as Knox College, this is one of the first buildings erected on the avenue. Since then it has been used as an extension of the University of Toronto's Connaught Laboratories. Penicillin was manufactured there and more recently polio vaccine was manufactured from viruses grown in the culture from Rhesus monkey kidneys.

This building serves notice that, north of College, Spadina is about to become respectable. For here it forms the western boundary of the University of Toronto property, and the great brick and stone houses that have been there for a hundred years or more are gradually being torn down to make room for new university buildings.

At Bloor Street Spadina Avenue becomes Spadina Road. Before it gets to St. Clair Avenue, Spadina takes another jog at Davenport Road to skirt Casa Loma. The grounds are surrounded by a high stone wall costing some $250,000, built in 1912 by Scottish stone masons imported especially for the job.

The castle was built by an imaginative millionaire named Sir Henry Pellatt who, besides being a financial tycoon, was a soldier, world traveller, and lover of big houses. He lived in it for a while, but the cost of servants and general upkeep—he once housed 1,000 men of his regiment, the Queen's Own Rifles, in the basement—became too great, and he finally turned it over to the municipality for taxes. After a couple of tries at getting rid of it, the city leased Casa Loma to the West Toronto Kiwanis Club, who rent it out for receptions, parties, proms, and other affairs; they also conduct tours.

Each year some two hundred thousand visitors tramp through its 90 rooms marvelling at the beautiful teak and mahogany woodwork, the turrets from which they can get a fine view of Toronto, the 30 bathrooms, 25 fireplaces, and the quarter-mile-long tunnel that leads under the streets to the stables.

North of St. Clair, Spadina Road runs through Forest Hill Village. The very name suggests stylish homes, wide curving streets, spacious lawns and piles of wealth. So the old Spadina of the garment and market areas has gone high class indeed.

In this respect Spadina is typical of most of the north-south main arteries in central Toronto, Dufferin, Bathurst, Sherbourne, etc., but whereas the southern portions of some of these are becoming respectable with new apartment buildings replacing the old, dirty brick structures, Spadina still has its strip. There is little doubt, however, that the strip and the crowded, lively shops of Kensington Market will be replaced by efficient, sterile high-rise apartments.

At Eglinton Avenue, Spadina Road just ends, and the motorist finds himself faced with a host of curving streets that lead he knows not whither. And this brings up a word of warning for motorists coming into the city from the west by way of the 16-lane Macdonald-Cartier Freeway. Shortly after you pass the modest off-ramps at Dufferin Street, you will come to one of the grandest and most elaborate clover-leafs to be found in North America. There are over-ramps and under-ramps and a sign that proclaims that here you can enter the Allen Expressway south.

Don't do it. For this is the entrance to the unfinished Spadina expressway, which represents the strength of "people power" in the city. The planners planned a four-lane freeway to take cars into the city's core. The people said, "No. There are too many cars downtown now." The provincial government stepped in and stopped construction. Result, an increase in construction of public transportation facilities.

The principal cross-town streets of the downtown area are Front, King, Queen, Dundas, College, and Bloor. Front Street, as its name implies, once fronted on a row of wharves which stretched far out into the shallow, reed-filled, muddy lake. After the lakeshore was filled with good solid earth, and the railway came to the city in the 1850s, Front Street fronted on the tracks. Thus the most imposing building on the street, and the one many people see first when they arrive in Toronto, is Union Station. It was opened in 1927, following a series of other structures on or near the same site, the first of which was a little wooden shack erected in 1858.

Front is a relatively short street, stretching from Bathurst on the west to the Don River at the eastern end. Many of the old buildings are gone, of course, but there are enough left to tell much of Toronto's history.

Old Fort York is just west of Bathurst Street in the midst of the railway yards. One of the original buildings of the fort is still there. The others are slightly younger, having been built to replace those burned by the Americans in 1813. It is a good place to see how military men lived (to a large extent self-sufficiently), and to witness a re-enactment of the changing of the guard and the explosion of a tiny cannon, pointed at a large brewery which stands today between the fort and the lake.

East of Bay Street, Front slants off a bit to the north, following the original line of the shore, and in the area of Jarvis and Front is the St. Lawrence Market, where every Saturday thousands of city shoppers come to buy produce "straight from the farms." Many of the buildings on Front have been rebuilt and modernized, but some of them are the old originals. In the front of the market on the south side of the street are traces of what Torontonians call the old-old city hall. It was built in 1844 and used until 1899, when the mayor and council grandly moved to the *new* old city hall at the corner of Queen and Bay.

Near the market is the magnificent St. Lawrence Hall, completed in 1851 and for ten years the centre of an exciting and brilliant

Toronto social life. World famous actors and singers performed on its stage. Then, as bigger buildings went up, it gradually fell into disuse, finally became a warehouse, and was slated for demolition. It was saved by a group of citizens dedicated to the cause of preserving Toronto's grand old buildings, and was renovated in 1969.

King Street, a short distance north of Front, was once Toronto's most fashionable residential street. An old drawing showing the street in 1836 includes a church, a school, a public building, an oxcart, and a row of two-storey houses. Ladies in sunbonnets and hoop skirts escorted by men in top hats stroll along the board sidewalk, while a man on horseback canters down the muddy road.

Today, King, between Yonge and York, is the street of skyscrapers. When we first came to Toronto there were two skyscrapers on the street, one owned by a newspaper and the other by a bank. The bank building, completed in 1930, was the tallest (34 storeys, 476 feet) and was proudly described as "the highest building in the British Empire."

For a long time this description held true, and it looked as though King Street, along with the rest of downtown Toronto, might stagnate. Then the subway was built below Yonge Street, to the howls of downtown merchants who complained about the disruption to their business, and the core of the city was saved. Bank buildings sprang up along King Street like mushrooms after a rain, each new one higher or grander than the last. Then one bank built a "complex" including an underground shopping mall and two black glass and steel towers, the tallest of which was 56 storeys, 740 feet, making it a little higher than Place Ville Marie in Montreal. Then, not to be outdone, another bank built just across Bay Street a skyscraper which is one storey and 44 feet higher, and whose observation tower will look right over the top of the previously "highest building."

Just south of King on Bay Street is the Toronto Stock Exchange, the second largest in North America. This is the real heart of Ontario from which flow the financial decisions that direct the lives of farmers, labourers, businessmen, and industrialists alike. A serious fluctuation of prices on the Toronto Stock Exchange will bring forth more concern and comment than anything said or done in the legislative buildings. And so the market has an air of excitement and vitality about it. From a special gallery, visitors can watch as the representatives of dozens of Toronto brokerage houses shout and gesticulate and dash about the floor like kids at a party, while on an immense board incredibly agile young men scribble the changing prices.

Queen Street, originally called Lot Street, has become, since the completion of the new city hall in 1965, the core of the city which for years lacked a real core.

Everything happens in Nathan Phillips Square in front of the city hall. Rock groups hold their festivals, public "days" are held for venerable elder citizens, sculptors put on open-air shows of their work, young people skate in winter and picnic in summer, old men sit and meditate, and tourists snap pictures of each other with the twin curved towers in the background. Born of debate and wrangling, the new city hall, most Toronto citizens now agree, is the greatest thing that ever happened to the city.

Across Bay Street from the new city hall, broods the old city hall. It is big and stolid. If the new city hall represents the spirit of the new and changed Toronto, surely the old hall is a reminder of the city's conservative, establishment-centred, Orange-dominated past. There it sits, silently warning against the folly of too quick and violent change.

For this reason, and because it is sitting on valuable real estate coveted by enterprising developers, many people feel that the old building should be knocked down, its big clock silenced for good, and its immense sandstone blocks put to better use. Others say no, it would be a crime to destroy such a fine old building which represents a distinctive style of architecture. This controversy is the essence of Toronto's ambivalence. Like many another city it cannot quite make up its mind whether or not to plunge whole-heartedly into the modern world.

Just west of the city hall stands a constant reminder of Toronto's beginnings. This is the iron fence surrounding Osgoode Hall, Ontario's principal law school and court for many years. The fence has a cow gate, especially constructed to permit persons to pass through but not cows, a device much needed in the early nineteenth century when Lot Street was the northern limit of the town of York.

Like many other streets in Toronto, College Street has two names. East of Yonge it is Carlton Street, and the most notable structure on Carlton is Maple Leaf Gardens.

On Saturday nights and often on Wednesdays during the winter months, the Gardens is the most popular building in Toronto. For on those nights the Maple Leafs are playing at home and, whether the team is first or last in its league, ten times as many people as the Gardens will hold are crazy to get in to see them play. So, on hockey night, as you approach one of the main doors, you are aware of a small scattering of men; some old, some young. They keep in the shadows and, without really looking at you, mutter "Got any hockey tickets?" These are the scalpers who buy season tickets from their owners who can't go to the game and sell them again at greatly inflated prices to others who will pay just about anything to get in.

A short block east of Bay Street on the south side of College stands one of my favourite buildings. It is a huge, ugly, red sandstone building which for 60 years housed an establishment that tells a lot about Toronto's past wealth and poverty, The Hospital for Sick Children.

Sick Kids, as it is known to most Torontonians and a surprising number of people throughout the world, is one of the world's largest hospitals devoted entirely to the care of children. Wonderful things were done in this old building, and continue to be done in the "New Sick Kids" a block south and a block west at 555 University Avenue.

Here those two great pioneer surgeons, Doctors Clarence Starr and Edward Gallie, performed their miracles of healing. And Dr. A.B. LeMesurier rebuilt tiny faces deformed with hare lips and cleft palates. Dr. Alan Brown ruled like a little czar for 43 years as surgeon-in-chief and bullied many a mother into giving her children proper care. In a laboratory on the third floor, a team of nutritionists led by Doctors Theodore Drake and Frederick Tisdall developed the mushy but nutritious baby food, Pablum.

The Hospital for Sick Children had its beginning in the spring of 1875 in a tiny, dilapidated house on Avenue Street, which used to run through the area now taken up by the Toronto General Hospital. It was begun by a young, energetic matron named Mrs. Samuel F. McMaster and a group of ladies who believed that it was their Christian duty to help the poor and relieve suffering.

So great was their faith that they had no doubt that if they prayed to Him sincerely, God would provide money and food and furnishings for their hospital. And, through the agency of generous souls, He did provide. The hospital grew in size and influence until houses could no longer contain the work. Then that truly great Torontonian, John Ross Robertson, planned and built the College Street hospital.

Robertson is perhaps my favourite Torontonian of the past. A tough, irascible, energetic Scot, he founded the Toronto *Telegram* and, with the money he made from that, supported numerous charitable institutions. But the cause dearest to his heart was that of sick children. After he built them a home on Toronto Islands, he took over the complete running of The Hospital for Sick Children, booting out the Ladies' Committee in 1899. In addition to all this, he wrote and published many books about Toronto and preserved thousands of pictures of the city's early days.

Across College Street from the Toronto General Hospital is the Banting Institute, which is part of the University of Toronto. In fact the whole area here north of College to Bloor Street and west to Spadina Avenue is taken up by the University and various provincial government buildings, including the stately Queen's Park building where the Legislature of Ontario has met since 1886.

It is difficult for an outsider such as I to write much about the University of Toronto. Before coming to Toronto I'd heard something about the U of T. There was the famous Hart House String Quartet on the radio, and every kid taking music lessons strove for an ATCM (Associate of the Toronto Conservatory of Music). The Varsity Blues football team won the Grey Cup three years in a row (1909, 1910, and 1911), and the Varsity Grads won the Olympic hockey championship for Canada.

Later, when I became head schoolmaster at HMCS York in Toronto, there were several Varsity graduates on the staff. They beguiled me with stories of professors such as John Satterly, famous for his annual liquid air demonstration, a three-ring circus featuring song, poetry, sleight-of-hand, and quick-frozen goldfish that shattered like glass. And Professor Coventry, who sometimes welcomed students to his attic room in Hart House attired only in tobacco smoke. And the story of the University College ghost that was sometimes seen on campus. To a man, these alumni took it for granted that Varsity was the biggest and best university in Canada, if not in the world.

For a long time I was never quite sure just where the university was. Unlike most Canadian universities that are set apart from the city, Varsity is right in the middle of Toronto and is comprised of a conglomerate of different architectural styles. Several Toronto streets, Harbord, St. George, and University Avenue, to name three, run through the university and carry a goodly amount of Toronto's downtown traffic.

The University of Toronto is Ontario's oldest university. It was founded in 1827 by that determined Anglican, Archdeacon John Strachan. He called it King's College in honour of William IV, who granted the charter, and it was to be a Church of England institution endowed by the state. This meant, of course, that for a while all but Anglicans were excluded from higher education, but it was 1843 before King's College was opened in a small building on Front Street.

These were troubled times, as we have seen, and there was much agitation from the Methodists and other denominations to open the school to all. The reform government of Robert Baldwin did this in 1850, at the same time naming it the University of Toronto. Strachan was furious. He called the new setup a "Godless imitation of Babel" and founded Trinity College.

Ultimately Trinity (Anglican), Victoria (Methodist), St. Michael's (Roman Catholic), and others all joined together to make the University of Toronto. There is still considerable rivalry among the different colleges, but most graduates are proud enough to say that they made it at the University of Toronto. They are proud, too, of the university's tradition of liberalism, as for example, when John McCaul, the second president, admitted the first black student over a hundred years ago. And when the Hepburn government wanted history professor F.J. Underhill fired because he was campaigning for the CCF party, Canon H.J. Cody flatly refused to do it. Similarly, president Sid Smith (as he encouraged students to call him) would not fire the brilliant Polish physicist Leopold Infeld just because he was a communist.

They are proud, too, of their fellow alumni who include hundreds of famous Canadians in all fields, among them Stephen Leacock, Mackenzie King, Vincent Massey, Doctor Frederick Banting, operatic tenor Jon Vickers, and comedians John Wayne and Frank Schuster. Most of the doctors who staff Toronto hospitals are Varsity graduates, as are most of the province's highschool teachers. So Varsity has left its mark on the province, if not quite in the way John Strachan wanted.

Today the University of Toronto is bursting out all over. New buildings, massive structures of brick and stone, open every year. There are more students in the university now than there were people in the entire town of York at the time of its founding. And they represent all classes and creeds, a blend of conservatives, radicals, and free thinkers. Black students from the Caribbean play soccer on the field in front of University College. There are so many brilliant medical students from other countries that some sons of doctors of "old established Ontario medical families" cannot find a place.

In short what has happened to the U of T reflects what has happened to Toronto since the war. It has become a huge, multi-cultured, multi-racial establishment with a strong international flavour.

North of the Parliament Buildings is Queen's Park, the favourite of the university students and many others. The park is not very big and is completely surrounded by roaring traffic, but it has immense maple and oak trees, many friendly squirrels, numerous tables and benches for picnics, and in the centre a huge equestrian statue of a bronze King Edward VII, haughtily astride a magnificent bronze stallion.

A stroll through the park on a summer Sunday afternoon is a joy. Young people sit on the grass and discuss the problems of the world. Others chase each other among the trees, sit on the benches and study, or join King Edward on his horse. Young parents take their kids to the park to play tag through dried leaves and to feed the squirrels. Old folks bask in the dappled sunlight watching the young. There are art shows, and in winter a small skating rink. Among all the rush and roar around it, Queen's Park is an oasis of peace and tranquillity, yes, and gentleness in the very heart of the city.

I guess the street I like best in all Toronto is Bloor. For four years we lived a short block north of Bloor, practically across the street from Varsity Stadium, and if we have to live in a big city, that is the place to live.

Step out the door and we were at the St. George Street entrance to the subway where we could get on trains going east or west, or south and ultimately north. The subway is, I believe, the city's greatest creation—fast, efficient, clean, and relatively quiet. That is, unless it is necessary to ride it during the rush hour crush, and then it is hot, packed, and unbearably noisy.

Bloor, which almost rivals King Street for skyscrapers, has been called the Mink Mile by a Toronto newspaper because of its high-class shops, and is the hangout of many of the city's "beautiful people," as well as being the northern limit of the university. Within the half-dozen blocks of its central section it changes character many times.

Everyone who visits Toronto should walk along Bloor Street and take some excursions north and south from it.

Starting at Yonge Street and walking west to Avenue Road, you are in the centre of fancy shops, elegant shopping plazas, and movie theatres. A block north is Cumberland Street with excellent night clubs and restaurants, and north of that is Yorkville Avenue.

Yorkville, once part of a village outside of Toronto, is now an area of ancient houses, mostly with rebuilt fronts, fixed up as tiny discotheques, specialty shops, nightclubs, and art galleries. All the teenagers in Ontario and many from much farther away have heard of Yorkville. It used to be the place to come to, baby, the place where the "real" people were, and for some time this part of Toronto had a bad reputation for drugs. However, it has become well ordered and quiet and, some people say, dull.

On the southwest corner of Bloor and Queen's Park Crescent (north of Bloor this street is called Avenue Road) sits the Royal Ontario Museum, a huge, venerable pile of stone, modelled after the Royal Museum in London, England. An Ontario institution, this museum draws kids from all over the province. "Dad, let's go to Toronto and visit the museum," they plead. When they get there they dash through the great high-ceilinged rooms, their eyes big with wonder at the thousands of displays. The dinosaurs are the favourites; huge skeletons of creatures that lived millions of years before any man appeared on the earth. The kids stand and stare, while teachers or parents try to give them some idea of the immensity of time.

There is nearly always a bus loading or unloading kids in front of the museum, while popcorn vendors try to catch them on the way past. This corner of Bloor is probably better known than any other to Ontario citizens from outside the city.

Covering an area of six acres, the museum has 22 different curatorial departments and a staff of 280. Research teams go to many parts of the world in search of material. The mineralogy and geology departments in particular attract crowds, and the Chinese collection has a world-wide reputation.

Immediately west of the museum on Bloor Street are two huge stone gateposts, and a flight of steps leading down to a pathway going south through the university grounds. It has been called Philosopher's Walk by the thousands who have used it in the past, including Stephen Leacock, Morley Callaghan, and Lester Pearson, but I prefer to call it lover's lane. It is a great place to walk. One step and you are off busy, noisy, sweaty Bloor Street and among green lawns and in the deep shade of oak and maple. Young people sit on the grass beside the asphalt walk, holding hands and watching the squirrels that beg for handouts, or walk with arms about each other talking, making endless plans as young people have always done. The great red, brown and grey buildings of the university are all about them, closing them in, protecting them, providing them with a place for youth.

Farther west of the museum, past a couple of university buildings, is Varsity Stadium. It fronts Bloor Street with a long high red brick wall, from behind which on an autumn Saturday afternoon come the wild cheers of students and alumni as the Varsity Blues clash with the Golden Gaels from Queen's, the Mustangs from the University of Western Ontario, or some other rival. Other sounds come from behind the great brick wall, too; the clarion call of bugles, or the raucous howl of rock bands, for Varsity Stadium is the site of international bugle band competitions and many a pop concert.

On the northeast corner of Bloor and St. George Streets, and surrounded by another impregnable wall, is the venerable York Club, once the home of the Gooderham family. It is a beautiful Victorian mansion with solid copper drain pipes on the outside, and highly polished mahogany and oak panelling in the spacious rooms inside. It is ultra-exclusive, the York Club. Presidents and senior officers of powerful financial and industrial firms meet for lunch here to discuss matters that the secretaries, students, and old ladies passing along St. George Street to the subway entrance next door do not even know exist.

Across St. George Street from the York Club is the Medical Arts Building, which is synonymous with success for doctors and dentists. Here the busiest specialists have their offices, and in the huge parking lot behind are automobiles from every part of the province.

Across the street from the Medical Arts and a little farther west is a 20-storey building which for years housed what was certainly the most controversial establishment in Toronto, Rochdale College. According to who was talking, Rochdale was a "profoundly impor-tant educational idea" in higher education or a "dope-infested stable of free love and a hangout for bums." Either way, while it was in existence it certainly did liven up the neighbourhood. All manner of people lived there: students, transients, professors, artists, retired ministers, and others who liked the atmosphere of freedom. Unfortunately it gained a reputation as a drug centre, and the viewers-with-alarm blasted it in all the media and demanded its extinction. The police had a hard time there, too. When they conducted raids, heavy objects sometimes fell from high up and smashed the roofs of their cars. Residents jammed the elevators and locked their doors. Despite determined efforts by its management to counteract Rochdale's bad reputation, the complaints persisted. Finally the place was far behind in its mortgage payments and a judge decreed that it should be taken over by a "receiver."

From Spadina west, Bloor Street is a robust, vital, thriving neighbourhood where immigrants from a dozen countries live and play and work together. They live in rented rooms, two and three families to a dwelling, in ancient two- and three-storey, patched-up brick houses on the streets that run north and south of Bloor. The people work hard for the day when they will have a better place to live.

There is more non-English than English spoken on these streets: Markham, Brunswick, Palmerston, Euclid, and in the shops along Bloor. We noticed one sign in a store window, "English spoken here," and the movies are in Greek, Italian, Spanish, Portuguese, and other European languages.

The unofficial centre of this district is the corner of Markham and Bloor. Many people in the district refer to Edwin Mirvish, a small, dapper man, with a mixture of envy and admiration as "Fat Ed," and vow he should be mayor of Toronto. Mirvish's store, called "Honest Ed's," is a low, sprawling establishment whose windows are covered with humourous signs, such as: "Honest Ed should be jailed for cutting prices the way he does." In fair weather and foul, before opening time the customers stand for hours, grim-faced and determined, because inside are the big bargains: nylon hose for 11¢, a pair of boy's jeans for $1.29. As the people file past the big armed security guards, they are dedicated to one purpose, making their paychecks go as far as possible.

Like sheep they go down a long, narrow hall and must keep on going to the end of the line in order to get out. The merchandise, of every kind and description, is piled around in careless profusion, and each customer picks up a shopping bag with the legend "It's Fun To Shop At Honest Ed's" painted on the side, in many cases the first sentence of English that the newcomer to Toronto learns.

And the shopping bags are free! At other stores they cost money, but not at Honest Ed's. They are tucked into every corner of that vast emporium, and the security guards, who look as though they would shoot you for heisting a hankie, beam benevolently as you scoop up as many bags as you want and walk off to fill them with bargains. Thus, with one stroke of genius, Ed Mirvish has ensured that his advertising will walk the streets for days.

Markham Street south of Bloor is a two-block-long art centre with dealers in exotic antiques as well as theatres, boutiques, art schools, and art galleries. The most prominent gallery, a 17,500-square-foot ultra-modern establishment owned and operated by David Mirvish, son of Edwin, has been described as "the most beautiful private gallery on the continent" and is one of the many galleries that have made Toronto an important centre of painting and sculpture.

When we lived in an apartment in Toronto, as millions do, the city parks saved our sanity. A quick ride east on the Queen streetcar and we were in Kew Beach Park, walking the dog along the mile-long boardwalk at the water's edge. Hundreds of others were there doing the same thing. Some were playing tennis, or badminton, or swimming in the olympic-size pool; farther north in Kew Gardens, others were watching an open-air play. In many ways park and gardens are as much a community centre as they are an outdoor playground.

Altogether there are more than two hundred parks within the boundaries of Metropolitan Toronto, operated by the city, the five boroughs and Metro. Many are in the ravines of the numerous small rivers that flow through the area into Lake Ontario. Others, like Kew Beach and Exhibition Park and the Toronto Islands Park, are along the shore of the lake. Within the parks are facilities for hiking, biking, horseback riding, fishing, canoeing, sailing, baseball, tennis, soccer or, in fact, for engaging in nearly every sport known to man. Kids can swim, skate, ski, toboggan, fish, watch plays, listen to rock groups, pat cows, ride ponies, chase each other among the giant oaks and maple trees, and stuff their faces with hotdogs and pop.

The best-known park man in Metro is Thomas W. Thompson, better known as "Tommy Thompson," who puts up signs that read "Please walk on the grass." As head of the Metropolitan Toronto Parks Commission, Tommy and his staff keep an eye on some twenty parks, including Exhibition Park and the new Metro Toronto Zoo, which covers 1,250 acres in the Rouge River Valley in the northeast corner of Metro. Tommy, a friendly, loquacious, energetic, roly-poly man who likes to tell how his father was chief gardener for Casa Loma, frequently leads as many as four hundred hikers at a time on long walks through his parks, expounding on the flora and fauna, geography and history, to those who can keep up with him.

Another park we rather fell in love with is at the corner of Bloor and Christie Streets, and goes locally by the plebeian name of Christie Pits. It actually is the site of an old gravel pit whose innards helped to make buildings and sidewalks in early Toronto. Here old men sit in the shade and play checkers for fun, while younger men gather around tables and play cards for money. There are a couple of soccer fields, numerous softball diamonds, a noisy swimming pool, and a first-class baseball field where the Toronto Maple Leafs play their home games. Since the Triple A team and Maple Leaf Stadium both left town a few years ago, this is Toronto's only ball club. People sit on the grassy slopes and watch the Leafs play Kitchener or Hamilton and pay for it by dropping whatever they feel like into a coffee pot that is passed among them. A great way to spend a summer evening.

In the early Seventies, three of our kids lived close enough to the pits to go there for pick-up softball games. I really liked those games. None of your cut-throat competition here. Not infrequently one team would complain that the pitcher on the other side was too good and suggest, "Why don't you let that girl in centre field pitch?" The request would be granted, to the benefit of everybody's batting average. Our son Colin, who has a knack for such things, dubbed his team the Christie Pit Beasts and got sweatshirts with the words emblazoned on the chest. I think the Beasts were probably my all-time favourite ball team.

Another park at the corner of Eglinton Avenue and Don Mills Road contains the Ontario Science Centre, which houses a remarkable show of modern technology. Hordes of school kids visit the centre where they are encouraged to handle various scientific gadgets and become involved in "participational exhibits."

But of all the parks, the one we have enjoyed most is High Park in the west end, which stretches from Bloor Street to the Lakeshore and covers over four hundred acres. High Park has beautiful trees, a zoo, ponds with swans, acres of green grass, playgrounds, stunning flower gardens, rugged ravines, an outdoor school, some outstanding sculpture, and Grenadier Pond which people say has no bottom. It also has Colborne Lodge, the former home of John G. Howard, Toronto's first City Engineer, who in 1873 donated his farm to the city in return for certain concessions. Now a museum, his house still sits on a hill overlooking the lake.

Just as it has all kinds of parks, Toronto has all kinds of people. Some idea of their diversity can be derived from those who speak to and, supposedly, for them. For instance, the most popular and richest radio news reader and commentator is a 74-year-old pundit who almost daily ridicules the Bible, scoffs at a vengeful god who would drown "every man, woman and child" in the world at the time of the flood, and is an avowed and jubilant atheist. All this in a city that has a reputation for church-going.

Or take one of the most widely-read columnists on a morning newspaper. This gentleman regularly rails against anybody with hair longer than his own, derides modern music, prattles on about high society parties he has attended, advocates compulsory military service for teenagers, and stoutly states that his allegiances are to God, the Queen, his country, and his family . . . in that order.

On the only remaining evening paper, another popular columnist says all the opposite things. He keeps wondering in print when people will give up all this royalty nonsense and avers that the only reason Canadians joined the armed forces during the last war was because anything was better than being unemployed, or because they could not get out of it.

There are many more churches and more cocktail lounges in Toronto than in any other city in English-speaking Canada, more rich people and more poor people, more preachers and more winos. Almost every religion on the earth has its adherents in Toronto, including a fair number of Druids, and the Hare Krishna with their saffron robes and rhythmic chanting.

There are nightclubs where middle-aged and young men can paint pictures on the bare breasts of nubile young ladies, for a price, and numerous topless massage parlours. The citizens support one of the finest symphony orchestras in the country and fill Maple Leaf Gardens to hear a group of rock singers. It is known as "a good sports town" and "a good show town." All the top-rated entertainment personalities from England, the States, France, Germany, Russia, and other countries, sooner or later come to Toronto, and almost without exception say they would sooner perform there than anywhere else.

Many visitors to Toronto find their way to the Canadian Broadcasting Corporation's headquarters on Jarvis Street. Here and at other locations around the city it is possible to take guided tours and see dramas in production and other behind-the-scenes activities. Panel shows are always looking for guests who will applaud and laugh on cue.

Actually the CBC has done a great deal for Toronto's growth. Because of it, actors, singers, musicians, dancers, directors, writers, artists, puppeteers, and other entertainers and artists have been able to make a living and remain in Canada. From the CBC they have branched out into live theatre, nightclub acts, and revues. The CBC has done more than anything else, perhaps, to make Toronto an important cultural centre.

What of the future? There is much talk of more and higher skyscrapers, a go-transit system that will top anything in the world, and a domed stadium for sporting events and conventions. As fast as is humanly possible, old buildings are being ripped down and new and bigger ones put up in their place.

As the dapper ex-mayor of New York, Jimmy Walker, once remarked about his city, "It will be a great town, if they ever get it finished."

But regardless of what the planners and developers and politicians think and do, Toronto has a vitality of its own. A vitality that comes from the great variety of people who live and work there, expressed in its fine historic buildings, its new discotheques, its theatres, its skyscrapers, its parks, its Casa Loma, its restaurants and bars, its newspapers, the "beautiful people" on Bloor Street, the shrewd people on Bay Street, its bankers, its colourful politicians, its writers, its artists, its labour movement, its concerned people, its nuts, its university students, its harassed commuters, its mothers, and its kids. All this and much more make Toronto a good place to visit and, despite the choking smog that periodically envelops the city, a good place to live, too.

This drawing, "Indians Catching Game" from Champlain's "Voyages et Descouvertues" probably is the beginning of our misconception of the American Indians. The park-like countryside bears as much resemblance to Ontario primitive forest as the dancing figures do to hunting Hurons.

Top Right: Winter travel was actually easier with sturdy sled dogs doing all the work. The fort on the river bank indicates the ever-present danger of attack from rival traders.

Left: For a hundred years or more the main means of summer transportation was the voyageur canoe. *Coureurs de bois* and explorers needed all the protection that the church could give.

Top Left: Education in the bush. Pupils came when work was slack at home. Grade eight was high achievement.

Bottom: Loyalists at Johnstown on the St. Lawrence, 1784, with all that remained of their homes and property.

Top Right: Early loyalist farm in the bush. A man's home and farm depended largely on his skill with the axe.

March of Intellect

School in Adelaide
erected Dec 1845
Teacher Mr St Leger
Sketched at the time
W. L.

Top Right: Surrender of General William Hull to General Isaac Brock after the defeat of the American forces at Detroit on August 15, 1812. For his great work Brock was made a Knight Commander of the Bath.

Bottom: The Battle of Queenston Heights, October 13, 1812, ended in a British victory. The Americans suffered 300 casualties, had 958 taken prisoner and were discouraged in their attempt to conquer Canada. General Brock was killed in the charge up the heights. Other British casualties numbered 150.

Top Left: Death of General Pike during the siege of York by the Americans, April 27, 1813.

Laura Secord warns Lieut. James FitzGibbon that the Americans plan to attack Beaver Dam.

Bottom: American fleet in Toronto Harbour shelling Fort York. They burned the Parliament Buildings and stole the mace.
Top Right: Death of Tecumseh at the Battle of Moraviantown, October 5, 1813.

Top: Political meeting in 1837. Each candidate stood or fell on the strength of his voice.

Below: Mackenzie's men marching down Yonge Street in December, 1837. Determined, angry, confused and defeated. But they brought about change.

C. W. JEFFERYS

Cartoon of the attack on Mackenzie's people on Navy Island in the Niagara River. Mackenzie returned to Canada during the amnesty of 1849.

Below: The steamship *Caroline* was attacked on the American side of the river by Captain Drew R.N., burned and sent over the falls.

Below: On the lawn of a house on Beverly Street, Toronto, 1875.

Top Right: Lord and Lady Dufferin throw a fancy dress ball at Rideau Hall, 1870.

Bottom Right: Sunday was a day of worship, bible reading and boredom. Children were forbidden to whistle or play.

Top Left: Oil well drilled by
Mr. J.M. Lick in Kent County, 1863.

Bottom Left: Noon meal on an
Ottawa River timber raft.

Top Right: Adam Beck (second from
right) and his travelling electric circus.

Bottom Right: McLaughlin carriage
works at Enniskillen, 1877. The little
boy is Sam.

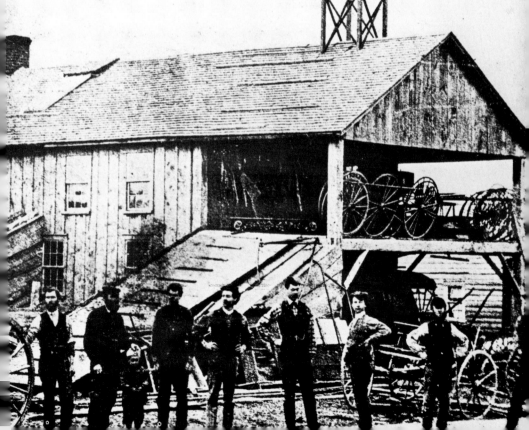

He did call! Life changed in Ontario after the invention of the telephone in 1875. Alexander Graham Bell lived in Brantford, Ontario.

CHAPTER V

Shakespeare and Oil

In the summer of 1952 I went on assignment for a magazine into a part of Ontario where thousands of tourists go today but which, then, had not much to offer. I discovered a part of the province where some years earlier there occurred one of the most important developments in modern times. And I met a man who typifies the good, solid, hard-working people of Ontario towns.

We were headed for the city of Stratford, and when we got to the twin cities of Kitchener-Waterloo (which will be dealt with in a later chapter), we got off the highway and travelled along lesser roads so that we could see and meet some of the farmers who live in this fertile region. We passed through towns that have not changed much since they were established 150 years ago. We drove by farms with big yellow houses built of bricks that were manufactured right on the farm, and bank barns and old orchards, and fat cattle feeding on the hillsides. Then we were on a flat plain with straight roads. And we crossed the river Avon to enter the city of Stratford.

The Avon is not much of a river really, hardly bigger than its namesake in England, but it is beautiful. Immense willow trees lean over its banks, and in the water ducks and swans amused us by gobbling up soggy bread and bits of popcorn. Rustic bridges cross here and there, and the lawns are wide and smooth and

71

inviting to the hundreds of thousands who come each year to the Stratford Shakespearean Festival.

The Shakespearean Festival was the brain child of a Stratford man, Tom Patterson, who believed that Shakespeare's plays could be brought to life on the banks of the Avon. There was not much enthusiasm for the project at first, but Patterson kept talking it up and finally managed to get an exploratory committee organized. Then the possibility of doing Shakespeare's plays on the type of stage on which they were originally performed—with the audience almost completely encircling it and sometimes sitting on it—caught the imagination of theatrical people, and Tyrone Guthrie was invited to come from London, England, to direct the first production.

Guthrie was enthusiastic. The Stratford Shakespearean Festival Committee was organized, a stage was designed, and a huge tent built to hold hundreds of people. The first production in 1953, *Richard III* starring Sir Alec Guinness, with many Canadians in the cast, was a smashing success. So was *All's Well That Ends Well*, and audiences looked forward to the next year's production. It was also a success, and in 1957 a permanent theatre was built in the Shakespeare Park on the banks of the Avon. Since then the festival has branched out to include a great variety of entertainment and has gained world-wide recognition.

But none of this would have been possible if it had not been for the efforts of one man who is never mentioned in the festival brochures, or in any of the many books that have been written about the Festival.

His name was Tom Orr, and when I talked to him in the spring of 1952 he was a spry, neat, twinkling, grey-haired, slim man of 81 years. He never held an official office in Stratford more august than that of Chairman of the Parks Board. He was variously described by officials I talked to as "the stubbornest cuss I've ever seen" and "Stratford's leading citizen."

In 1904 Tom Orr was a young, handsome man-about-town of 33. His job was selling insurance, but his great interest was in improving his town and, as he put it, "Believe me it needed improving."

When the town got its first Parks Board under the Ontario Parks Act, Tom Orr had his chance. He was appointed secretary of the board.

Stratford then had one small park on the river at its eastern limits and another, Queen Victoria Park, at its western limits. In between ran a muddy, marshy stream whose banks resembled a park as much as an ash heap resembles a flowerbed. An old wooden dam held back just enough water to form a weedy, stump-filled marsh called Victoria Lake.

Tom Orr said: "There is just one thing to do—join the two parks at each end of the city and make the entire river front, on both sides, one big park."

Others on the Parks Board said: "You're crazy." The battle was on.

The Parks Board finally did accept the plan, but had no notion where to get enough money to buy all this land. Orr persuaded the City Council to issue debentures for the $10,000 asked, by pointing out that the sale of ice and water-power rights would take care of the payments.

The Parks Board then built a dam in the centre of the town and began to clean out and dredge the lake for boating.

In 1912, after some lively skirmishes with local industrialists who wanted to build factories on his parkland, which Orr won handily, he faced his biggest fight. His adversary was no less a power than the Canadian Pacific Railway.

The company was determined to run a line through the heart of the park, along the Avon River from one end of town to the other. Stratford was already served by the Grand Trunk, but most citizens as well as the mayor and 12 of the 14 aldermen were convinced that the town needed another railway.

Stratford is still without the blessings of a second railway, but the battle was not easily won. It came to a head in a public vote; the citizens of the town were faced with the choice of another railway, or a pretty piece of land to walk and play games on. The final result was a majority of 100 in favour of the park, and against the railway.

Subsequent fights over the park were by comparison mere skirmishes, though each one stirred up its quota of dirt and recriminations. Most of them were over money, but Orr usually won.

In his insurance business Tom Orr had built a reputation for sound, solid dealing. In his park dealings he used every cunning manoeuvre and horse-trading ruse in the book. "If you want a park, you've got to be firm," Orr told me.

There is no monument in Stratford to Tom Orr, but there is little doubt that without his stubbornness, vigour, and hard work, there would have been no park and no Stratford Festival. They are his monument.

About thirty-five miles southwest of Stratford is the city of London, fourth largest city in Ontario, proud of its cultural achievements and history, and certainly one of the most attractive cities in the province.

London is, naturally enough, on the river Thames, and the two main branches of this river come together to form a perfect "T" in the downtown section near the courthouse. This spot was planned as the site for the capital of Ontario when John Graves Simcoe visited the region in February of 1793. It was far enough removed, he considered, from the Americans threatening Fort Niagara, and had in addition many natural advantages. The river, called by the Indians Aspenessippi, was beautiful and capable of limited navigation. Somehow it reminded Simcoe of his favourite river in England and so he renamed it accordingly. The forests were thick with good timber and had an abundance of game. In fact London's coat of arms shows a deer and a bear holding up a shield inscribed with wheat sheaves, and a beaver hard at work. Across the top is an old-time railway locomotive, to indicate that the city is a shipping and distribution centre, and at the bottom are the inspiring words, *Labore et perseverantia.*

But London had no easy access to the Great Lakes, and when Lord Dorchester came to make his final decision for the capital, he gave the nod to Toronto. Nothing more happened in the London area until 1826, when a Scotsman named McGregor, assisted by Patrick Smith and another man named McManus, built the first residence there. It was, of course, a crude log house, and it stood on the corner of today's King and Ridout Streets. A tablet marks the spot.

Soon after this, the judicial centre for the area was moved from Vittoria near Lake Erie to the Thames region, and the town of London began to grow. The first courthouse there was a two-storey log structure. The one that replaced it on the same site was a copy of the castle of Malahide near Dublin where Colonel Thomas Talbot, founder of the town of St. Thomas, was born. It is one of the city's most popular tourist attractions.

By 1830, according to one writer, there were between forty and fifty houses scattered about in the bush of the area. Most of the inhabitants were British, Welsh Baptists, Irish and English Methodists, and Scottish Presbyterians. And many of them were violent enemies of the Anglican Family Compact centred in York.

During and after the Rebellion of 1837, many of these people had an exceedingly bad time of it. Although there was no actual uprising in the area, feelings ran high and many a man took the opportunity to get back at his neighbour for some previous grievance. Anyone who had made a derogatory remark about the government was likely to be picked up and thrown into jail.

In 1838, 43 men of the district were found guilty of treason and sentenced to death. Six were hanged, and most of the others were "transported" from the colony. Altogether 160 persons of the district were arrested for their part in the rebellion, although it was never proved that any of them had fired a shot.

London grew and prospered as a distributing centre for the thriving farming communities that developed in the Thames region. After the discovery of oil in the Oil Springs–Petrolia area to the west, the city became involved in that industry, and a good deal of its prosperity was due to the oil refining carried on there. For one short, exhilarating, cap-waving day London had an oil well right in the city limits.

In the year 1865, during the great oil boom in the town of Petrolia, the people of London went oil crazy. And where there is ungoverned enthusiasm, there are always shysters to oblige by relieving the greedy of their cash. London's sharpy was a character named Hicks. According to an account in an old book titled *Illustrated London*, Hicks persuaded some of the local business geniuses to invest in an oil well which he proposed to sink on a farm located where Woodland Cemetery now stands. There was great excitement that day as the derrick was erected and drillers went to work. And sure enough they struck oil. It spouted out of the hole and ran down into the creek. The boom was on. Speculators offered fabulous prices for surrounding farmlands, and the farmers turned it down. They soon wished they had not, though, when it was discovered that the enterprising rascal, Hicks, had buried a cask of crude oil in the hillside, and that was all the oil there was down there.

The University of Western Ontario, situated on the river in the northwest corner of the city, has many claims to fame. Ever since Sir Frederick Banting did his preliminary work on insulin there, the university has concentrated on medical research.

"London-in-the-bush," as it was called by the early settlers to distinguish it from "London-in-the-smoke," is a well-treed, rather quiet city with wide streets and fine homes. It is probably the most British city in Ontario and has borrowed many of its place names from London, England: Blackfriars Bridge, Oxford Street, Piccadilly, Pall Mall, Covent Garden Market, Cheapside, and Chelsea Green, to name but a few.

Another writing assignment took us about forty-five miles west of London to three small towns where, in the middle of the nineteenth century, industrial history was made.

These are the towns of Petrolia, Oil City, and Oil Springs. As we drove into Petrolia through a gate, on either side of which is mounted a miniature oil derrick, we noticed a peculiar saltwater-sulphury smell. We also heard a peculiar clanking sound and, as we looked about, we discovered that we were surrounded by oil well pumps moving slowly up and down, operated by a jerker-rod system that joined them all together. Beside each was a dirty round tub, and trickling into it from a spout on the oil pump was a thin stream of black liquid. This mixture of petroleum and saltwater was separated by specific gravity in the tub, and the oil drained off through a system of collector pipes, ultimately to become gasoline.

These ancient oil wells within the town limits of Petrolia and in the surrounding country are all that remain of Canada's, and indeed North America's, first great oil boom that began in the early 1850s and lasted almost half a century.

Most encyclopaedias say that the oil industry in North America began when Colonel Edwin L. Drake drilled the first oil well near Titusville, Pennsylvania, on August 27, 1859. But anyone in Petrolia will tell you that "it began right here in Enniskillen Township on the banks of Black Creek nine miles south of here a good four years before that." And they have plenty of evidence to prove it. The facts about the discovery of oil and the boom days have been very carefully collected and documented by R.B. Harkness.

The first petroleum in Canada was found about thirty miles southeast of Petrolia on the Thames River, around where the town of Bothwell now stands, by Lieutenant-Governor John Graves Simcoe in the spring of 1793. Simcoe was on one of his inspection trips through the bush when he came upon "a spring of an oily nature which upon examination proved to be petroleum." The Indians and whites with him gathered the stuff by tossing a blanket on the surface of the spring, wringing it out, and then skimming off the oil. They used it as a liniment and a medicine.

Fifty-three years later, Dr. Abraham Gesner, an enterprising physician of Hillsboro, Nova Scotia, who was also something of a geologist and chemist, demonstrated a method for making kerosene out of petroleum. Since whale oil was becoming scarce and "burning fluid," a mixture of refined turpentine and alcohol, was dangerous, petroleum was much sought after as a means of lighting the darkness.

In 1849, Sterry Hunt, chemist to provincial geologist Sir William Logan, reported gum beds in Enniskillen Township which were suitable for "the construction of pavements, paying [coating] the bottoms of ships, and for the manufacture of illuminating oils."

Around this time, Enniskillen Township had only 400 of its 86,800 acres under cultivation, and supported 37 settlers, 34 cows, and 16 dogs. The rest was hardwood bush with two creeks running through it—Bear Creek, which runs through the present town of Petrolia, and Black Creek nine miles south, where the town of Oil Springs now stands.

Logan sent his assistant geologist, Alexander Murray, into this area, and Murray made a *Report of Progress* in 1852 in which he described the bituminous springs of Enniskillen and stated that he had heard of a well being dug there to a depth of 30 feet. This well was probably on Black Creek. It is believed to have been dug by Henry Tripp of Woodstock, which would make him the first oil-well digger in North America.

At any rate, the oil rush to Enniskillen was on. Men began arriving through the bush by whatever means they could, bringing whatever equipment they could. Charles Nelson Tripp, a foundry-man from Bath and a brother to Henry, organized the International Mining and Manufacturing Company and applied for a provincial government charter to refine petroleum in 1852. He got it in 1854.

However, Tripp ran out of cash and sold his interests—some say that he gave them away in payment for a wagon—to James M. Williams, a carriage maker from Hamilton. Sterry Hunt, who knew Williams personally, reported that Williams built an oil refinery at Oil Springs and began refining oil in 1857. He says also that "by sinking wells in the clay it was possible to obtain great quantities of the material in liquid state."

There is little doubt that first Tripp and then Williams dug oil wells along the Black Creek around the year 1857, and possibly as early as 1855. This would be four years before the Pennsylvania drillings.

January 1862, is a big date in the Canadian oil industry. On that day a Cooksville merchant named Hugh Nixon Shaw struck the first oil gusher at Oil Springs. He had dug into the clay to a depth of 50 feet, cribbed in the well, and then with a primitive drill that operated with two men on a "kick board" begun drilling a small hole through the rock. He ran out of money but managed to persuade his men to work on for "one more day." When it finally came, the oil pitched his rig high into the air and shot out of the well at the rate of an estimated 500 barrels a day. His find was reported all over the world, and speculators flocked into the area.

A plank road was built from Oil Springs and Petrolia to Sarnia by laying squared timbers side by side in the marshy ground. Over this road went a constant stream of rigs, loaded with barrels of petroleum and hauled by oxen or horses, to the port at Sarnia from which the oil was shipped to refineries in Hamilton or the U.S.A. Later, refineries were built in Sarnia, leading to its development as Canada's oil refining centre.

Old-timers say that the 35-mile round trip over the plank road could take the better part of a week, and the hard-drinking teamsters often spent more than they earned on booze and lodgings along the way. The toll on the road was 15¢ a load, and the fact that the owners got rich on this gives some idea of the traffic it carried.

November 23, 1866, is a day they still talk about in Petrolia. Up until that time all the drilling had been done on the Bear Creek flats on the theory that the lower you are, the closer you are to oil. Then one November day a well-heeled driller from St. Catharines named B. King hitched a team of horses to his drilling rig, hauled it up the hill west of the creek, and started to put down a well in the bush near where Eureka Street is now. Everybody else laughed at his stupidity, until on the 23rd he struck a gusher that threw his rig 30 feet and poured out rich black petroleum at the rate of hundreds of barrels a day.

Whereupon nearly everybody else hauled their rigs up the steep hill, later known as Quality Hill, and began digging wells side by side. Oil was worth $10 a barrel then, as compared with 75¢ in 1863. Every man, woman, and child in the area had oil fever.

The oil poured out of the new wells faster than it could be hauled away. It was stored in hastily built tanks above ground, but much of it lay on the surface, a black gooey mess. Then, one Saturday night in August 1867, the inevitable happened. A derrick caught fire, and it spread to one of the tanks. Before anyone could stop it, the whole works went up in flames that shot 100 feet into the air. For two weeks the fire burned uncontrolled over ten acres, consuming the oil as fast as it came out of the ground. One report states that the very soil itself was charred to a depth of two feet. The total loss in oil and equipment was estimated at $100,000.

After that costly disaster, the big oil men looked around for a better way to store their product. They hit on the idea of digging into the clay and building cylindrical, board-lined tanks 30 feet in diameter and 60 feet deep. Some of these huge tanks remain on the northern outskirts of the town, with signs warning that there is still some danger of explosion of gas fumes.

After the fire, the King well came back stronger than ever. Hundreds more were drilled close to it. The field extended to the northwest to the present village of Marthaville, where 400-barrel-a-day gushers were brought in. The Petrolia field was well on the way to becoming one of the biggest in the world, with a peak production in the 1890s of a million barrels a day.

Getting the gushing oil from the crowded wells to the railway was the problem. When it rained, the town was a mudhole. In the 1870s an estimated 800 teams of workhorses sloshed about in the mire among the derricks and pumps and shouting men and staring children, hauling in equipment, pulling up pipe, and drawing out the heavy tanks of oil. Those were the days, old-timers say, when Petrolia men were men.

Then, in 1872, the over-production in the Petrolia field, and in the Pennsylvania field about 150 miles to the southeast, dropped the price of oil to $1 a barrel, where it remained for 25 years. Ingenious men thought of ways to cut expenses. Two men named Vanalstyne and Smith invented the first oil pipelines—small "gathering lines" connecting the wells and carrying the oil to the gravel roads.

About the same time the jerker-rod system of pumping up to thirty wells from one steam engine was invented by J.H. Fairbank. It was subsequently used in many other oil fields, and most of the present wells in Petrolia are still pumped in this way.

The total number of oil wells in Petrolia in the 1890s is unknown, but estimates run between five hundred to a thousand. Scotty Miller, a scar-faced, rotund native of Glasgow, Scotland, who started in the oil business in Petrolia before he was in long pants, once stated, "Why, they'd even haul the kitchen off a house to make room for an oil well. There were oil wells in every second yard, and two or three in some."

As the oil industry grew in different parts of the world, the men who had learned their trade in Petrolia were in great demand. They travelled to Europe, Borneo, Mexico, Venezuela, Columbia, Equador, and the Middle East. In Petrolia today they still talk fondly of those "foreign field drillers" who came home with strange stories, and street names in the town with unpronounceable names like Oozloffsky and Ignatiefna bear witness to their influence.

Today the oil wells of Petrolia still produce a trickle of oil, amounting to about enough in one year to keep a modern refinery going for 12 hours. The pumps rattle away, worked by the same jerker-rod system introduced a hundred years ago. They do not interfere with the business of life in this pleasant, busy town and they serve as a constant reminder that the whole marvellous, rambunctious oil business began right here.

There is no direct highway replacing the old plank road that once connected Petrolia to the city of Sarnia on the St. Clair River, just where it leaves Lake Michigan. But, because of the oil fields, Sarnia became, besides the gasoline refining centre of Canada, the centre of the whole chemical manufacturing industry.

One of the salient characteristics of the "chemical valley" is the smell. It is not really a bad smell, the inhabitants of Sarnia will tell you, when you get used to it. And it is relatively easy to tolerate a smell that comes from industries that produce your job. Besides, to make up for the smell they raise, the chemical companies spend a considerable amount of money in beautifying the city.

Sarnia's problem is not a unique one. Every community in southern Ontario wants industry and will go to any lengths to acquire factories, refineries, fertilizer plants, smelters, meat-packing plants, or whatever. But with the industries come the problems. The air begins to stink, and a sign goes up on the old swimming hole that the water is not safe for swimming. This means more municipal expenses and requires the acquisition of more industry to provide the tax base for expenditures. In the meantime, new schools must be built to accommodate the children of the workers, and that requires a great deal more money, as does better street lighting, sidewalks, sewage disposal plants, improved water mains, and so on.

As one harassed mayor put it, "I sometimes wish we'd never got a factory and could go back to the nice pleasant days of the Thirties when I knew the first name of every man in town."

CHAPTER VI

Along Erie's Shore

The toe of southern Ontario, tiny Essex County bounded by Lake St. Clair, the Detroit River and Lake Erie, has been called the "sun parlour of Ontario." It is also the region where the first white men established farms in what is now Ontario, and the place where the province was almost lost to the Americans in 1812.

It was in 1749, when all of what is now southern Ontario was still forest, that the Governor of New France decided that the region along the Detroit River should be settled by farmers. Accordingly, he proclaimed that "Every man who will go to settle at Detroit will receive gratuitously one spade, one axe, one ploughshare, one large and one small auger." He would also get a cow and seed which could be paid for later, and the women and children would be supported for one year. All this, of course, was contingent on the new settler sticking with farming and not going into the more lucrative fur trade.

A number of adventurous Frenchmen took up the offer and, after long and difficult canoe trips, established themselves on farms along the Detroit River. And they prospered. Not only was the land flat and fertile, but the climate, since this area is almost three hundred miles farther south than Quebec City and surrounded by water, proved to be much milder and gentler than they were accustomed to. They found that they could grow grapes, peaches, apples and other fruits. We are told that many of these settlers had the advantage of black and Indian slaves to do the really hard work.

When this area became British in 1763, the French settlers stayed. The town they had called L'Assomption became Sandwich. Their other important settlement, Fort Amherstburg, was 16 miles farther south on the Detroit River.

During and after the American Revolutionary War, a number of United Empire Loyalists crossed the Detroit River and settled with the French. Thus this area is the only region in Ontario that can claim a continuous white settlement antedating the British Conquest.

Being so close to the Americans on the other side of the river, the towns of Sandwich and Amherstburg were the first to experience American hostility in the War of 1812. The first man killed in the war was a soldier named Hancock who was guarding a bridge near Amherstburg. The short skirmish amounted to little more than that.

Then two extremely important men entered the picture. One was the Lieutenant-Governor of Upper Canada, General Isaac Brock, and the other was the Shawnee Indian chief, Tecumseh, who had fought the Americans before, during the Revolutionary War.

It is a happy accident of fate that both these military geniuses happened to be at the right place at the right time. The two men met at Amherstburg and appreciated each other at once. Tecumseh said of Brock: "This is a man." Brock's assessment of Tecumseh: "A more sagacious or more gallant warrior does not exist." A good argument can be made that without the help of Tecumseh and his large force of well-trained warriors, Brock could not have pulled off the coup that broke the spirit of the Americans before their invasion had begun.

Brock decided to advance across the river and capture the powerful fortress of Detroit. In preparation he used some astute psychology on the American general, William Hull, by sending him a letter which for sheer audacity has rarely been topped:

> The force at my disposal authorizes me to require of you the immediate surrender of Fort Detroit. It is far from my inclination to join in a war of extermination, but you must be aware that the numerous body of Indians who have attached themselves to my troops will be beyond my control the moment the contest commences.

Hull did not surrender, of course, but he certainly began to worry. There were many women and children in the fort, including his own family, and the idea of an Indian attack on them was pretty horrible.

Brock and Tecumseh crossed the river with their men under the protection of shore batteries, and the guns of the sloop *Queen Charlotte* and the brig *Hunter* anchored in the river. It made quite a sight, the Indian war canoes filled with painted warriors, and the boats carrying the troops in their bright uniforms, with General Brock standing in the lead boat.

It was no battle really. After some desultory firing, General Hull sent out a man with a white flag and the fight was over. Thus with one stroke Brock captured the fort, 2,500 troops, great quantities of guns and ammunition, and control of all of southern Michigan. Not only was this a terrible blow to American morale, but it put a lot of mettle into the Ontario settlers who, up until that time, had been unsure about their chances in standing up to so powerful an enemy.

This was not the last brush with the Americans along the Detroit River border. In December of 1837, following William Lyon Mackenzie's abortive rebellion, over one hundred adventurous and carefree Americans, members of one of the notorious Hunters' Lodges, crossed the river to the village of Windsor, which had been established near Sandwich a few years before. They burned some buildings and the steamer *Thames*, which was anchored in the river, and committed other acts of violence. Much more serious, they shot four men whom they happened to meet, one of whom was an army surgeon named Hume.

Colonel John Prince who was in charge at Sandwich at the time heard of the attack, got together 170 militiamen, and marched out to meet the invaders. The fight took place in an orchard whose location is now within the boundaries of the city of Windsor. Twenty-one of the Americans were killed, and a number were taken prisoner. Prince selected four of these and had them shot in reprisal for the Canadians who had been shot. In his report he stated that the prisoners were "shot accordingly." After that he went by the nickname of "Shot Accordingly Prince."

Another invasion by an American some years later was more peaceful and friendly. This was Hiram Walker of Massachusetts. He built a distillery and began manufacturing liquor for the local trade. As most distillers did, he prospered mightily, and in 1858 the town that had grown up around his establishment was named Walkerville.

In the meantime the town of Windsor continued to grow, and in 1892 was incorporated as a city. Then, with the advent of the motor car and the establishment of Detroit as the American headquarters of the industry, the region grew and expanded. In 1904 the Ford Motor Company established a plant employing 17 men and producing 117 cars the first year. The settlement around their plants became known as Ford City. Later it was named East Windsor.

In 1935 all the border towns of East Windsor, Walkerville, Windsor, and Sandwich were amalgamated into the City of Windsor, which became the centre of Canada's automotive industry. Today, although some of the companies have moved part of their operations elsewhere, Windsor continues to be a leading manufacturing centre.

From Windsor, Highway 3 traverses a flat plain southeast to the town of Leamington. A short side trip west will bring you to Kingsville, which is principally noted as the location of the Jack Miner Migratory Bird Foundation.

Visitors are welcome here, and during the spring and fall migrations, thousands of geese, ducks, and song birds can be seen feeding in or around the artificial ponds. There is nothing to compare with the sight of an immense flock of Canada geese circling the ponds, making sure this is the place where they are safe. For a moment the sky is black with their wings and the air is full of their cries; then they land with the noise of kids at a picnic. They stay as long as they wish, and then take off for the migratory flight north or south, depending on the season.

It was here that in 1904, Jack Miner, who had once been a commercial hunter of quail, first managed to attract and gain the confidence of the wild birds. He began the practice of attaching bands to their legs, bearing his name and address along with a short verse of scripture. When the bands were returned to him by hunters, he knew where the birds had gone on their migration flight. Most of what we know about bird migration began with the work of Jack Miner, which today is carried on by thousands of bird banders around the world.

The whole of Lake Erie's north shore is, in fact, the delight of birdwatchers. For this is the centre of one of North America's great flyways, and before or after they cross Lake Erie the birds stop to rest.

Each spring and fall, hundreds of eager birdwatchers gather at

Point Pelee to observe and count the birds. If they are lucky, they will see whistling swans resting in Pigeon Bay in the lea of the long sand point. Often the birdwatchers camp in the campgrounds of the Point Pelee National Park and bathe off the long sand beaches.

All of Point Pelee is a naturalist's delight. More than six hundred plants flourish in the sandy soil, including many found nowhere else except on Erie's shore. There are hackberry trees, red cedar, black walnut, red mulberry, and sassafras, along with a variety of flowering shrubs.

In the large ponds and marshes, water plants grow in profusion, including the rare swamp mallow, while spatterdock form floating islands of green.

Oppossums live on the point, and the rare (in Canada) eastern fox-squirrel. Birdwatchers extend their lists of sightings with cassin's sparrows and yellow-billed cuckoos.

South of Point Pelee and, incidentally, the southernmost point in Canada, is Pelee Island, which can be reached by steamer from Kingsville or Leamington, or by aircraft. The island is flat and bare (in French *pelé* means bald or uncovered), and was once a grape and tobacco growing centre. A well-remembered vendor's cry at the fall fairs throughout southwestern Ontario was "Pelee Island Grapes!" Now the island is more noted for soybeans and pheasant shooting.

Highway 3 east of Leamington runs close to Lake Erie but to the north of the highway, on flat, fertile land, farmers grow beans and peas and tomatoes to be put into cans and shipped all over Canada, and great white cobs of corn used in the manufacture of corn flakes. The centre of this industry is the city of Chatham on the Thames.

Chatham was one of the terminals of the "underground railway," an ingenious system used before emancipation for smuggling slaves out of the U.S.A. into Canada. Settlements of freed slaves were established in different localities in southwestern Ontario, one of the most famous of which was the Dawn Institute near Dresden. It was here that Josiah Henson lived and preached and became the model for Uncle Tom in Harriet Beecher Stowe's novel *Uncle Tom's Cabin*.

The towns on and near Lake Erie are small except for St. Thomas, a marketing and manufacturing centre where, in 1885, the largest elephant that ever lived in captivity was killed in a railway accident.

His name was Jumbo, and that name became synonymous with everything large from hotdogs to sweaters. The famous circus man, P.T. Barnum, bought him from the London Zoo, where he used to carry gleeful children about on his back, and made him the star of his great Barnum and Bailey Circus. Jumbo and the circus travelled all over North America, and wherever they went great crowds came to marvel at the size and gentleness of the massive pachyderm who stood 11 feet tall at the shoulder and weighed six and half tons.

On September 15, 1885, the show reached St. Thomas on its way west through Canada. The roustabouts quickly put up the immense tents, and a colourful parade went through the main streets, with horses and lions and tigers and beautiful women. Of course, the parade was led by the biggest monster of them all, Jumbo.

There was an afternoon show and an evening show, and right after Jumbo's final performance he was led by his trainer, Matthew Scott, out the back of the tent towards his special car on the circus train. To get there, however, they had to cross the main line of the Grand Trunk Railway. And here is where tragedy struck. As Jumbo and a tiny elephant named Tom Thumb were being led towards their car, Special Freight No. 151 came roaring down the track, its coal-oil lamp throwing an eerie light before it.

Jumbo saw it coming, trumpeted with terror, and took off down the track as fast as he his big legs could carry him. Afraid to get off the track because of a six-foot embankment on one side and the circus train on the other, the big elephant just kept on going. The engineer plied his brakes but to no avail. The iron locomotive hit the big elephant and banged him into the side of the circus train, fracturing his skull and mutilating him horribly. He died in a matter of minutes.

Thus the greatest attraction of the Greatest Show on Earth met his fate, and most citizens of St. Thomas can point out exactly where it happened.

To get back to Erie's shore, the most spectacular characteristics of it are the long sand spits that extend out into the lake, built by the swirling currents of shallow water. The three main ones are at Point Pelee National Park, Rondeau Provincial Park, and Long Point Provincial Park. On Long Point, which extends like a great crescent 20 miles into the lake, can be seen every spring and fall one of the greatest collection of song birds to be found anywhere. And it is here that the Ontario Bird Banders Association have their station.

Long Point is a perfect place for the bird banders. Since it is privately owned by a group of American sportsmen who come there only to hunt, it is, except for a lighthouse keeper and his family, devoid of humans.

I was lucky enough to be invited to spend a weekend at the Long Point bird banding station with an official of the association, Donald Baldwin. If you are going birdwatching, it's a great advantage to go with an expert, and Baldwin is an expert.

It was early in April when the song birds were returning from across the lake. Baldwin instructed me to meet him at 9 pm at the Harbor Lunch at the base of the spit. There we loaded our gear into a land rover and set out for the point. It was a cold, windy night and the only trail was on the sandy shore about two feet from the pounding waves. Also on the shore were enormous chunks of ice around which Baldwin dodged without reducing speed. One of them he couldn't dodge, however, and we went into the water, got stuck, and had to walk, carrying gear, about four miles along that cold, windy, wet beach. Birdwatching isn't for softies.

We spent the night at the Number Two Station about half way along the point, sleeping on the floor as close to the oil-burning heater as possible.

In the morning I got up and looked out a picture window onto an immense marsh filled with bulrushes, reeds, and water plants. There were also ducks, hundreds of them; and a great whistling swan lifted from the water and flew to another part of the marsh.

We went outside and I saw that the cottage was surrounded by big trees: oak, poplar, cottonwood, and elm. The walnut trees were stunted because deer ate the tops off them each winter. "There are plenty of animals on the point," Baldwin said. "Deer, brush wolves, rabbits, small rodents, raccoons, skunks, and so on. Funny thing, the garter snakes here are black. A mutation. They'll be coming out by the hundreds any day now, and then the hawks gather and have a rare old feast."

But we weren't spending any time at the Number Two Station. Number One Station right out on the tip of the point was our goal. So after Don had carefully made notes on all the birds he had seen, we got back in the land rover, which had been pulled from the lake by the lighthouse keeper, and drove the remaining 13 miles to the station.

It consisted of a bungalow set about two hundred yards back from the shore and surrounded by sand dunes. Farther back, on the other side of the point, was the lighthouse and the buildings of the lighthouse keeper. There was also a pier and a boathouse there. Between the station and the tip of the point were the birdcatching traps, about a dozen of them, ranging in size from 60 feet long to tiny cages attached to trees.

"Come on," Don said. "Let's go out and find the birds." Flitting in among the scrub cottonwoods and sparse grass were dozens of small brown birds. "Song sparrows. This is going to be a song sparrow weekend. Come on, we'll catch some in the Heligoland trap."

The Heligoland trap was a huge wire structure about sixty feet long and twenty feet high, made of chicken wire strung on poles. One end was open, and the trap narrowed down gradually to the other end where there was a wooden ramp leading up to small box that was backed with window glass. "The birds see through the glass, think it's a way out, and get caught in the box. Come on, let's chase some in."

He spread his arms and began to shout as we walked through the brush towards the open end of the trap, and I did the same. The frightened little birds flew on ahead of us and, of course, without realizing flew into the large open end of the trap. By the time they realized they were in some sort of enclosure, they were too far in and so they went forward. Just as Baldwin said, they saw the window glass in the box, bumped into it, and fell down into the box. He fished them out through a little trap door, placed them carefully into a carrying box, and reset the trap. We carried the birds back to the bungalow for banding, weighing, measuring, and checking for fat.

It is all very carefully done, recorded on proper forms, and submitted to the International Bird Banders Association. Banders, Baldwin explained, must be trained and licensed before they can legally do this work. He said also that trained banders are scarce: "What we need is bird banders with broad backs and money in their pockets."

After the first batch was completed and released through the little trap door in the banding room, we went out to inspect other traps. Besides the three large Heligoland traps, there were house traps baited with millet or bread crumbs for catching ground-feeding birds; creeper traps consisting of little wire cages on the trunks of trees, with wire wings to direct the creepers up into the trap; and ground or Mason traps which are like tree traps only sitting on the ground. Mist nets, made of fine, tough, almost invisible thread, are spread from tree branch to tree branch to catch flickers, redwings, robins, and other birds as they fly through.

The most spectacular device of all, used for catching ducks and geese, is called a boom net. It consists of three small cannon arranged in a row; fired together electrically, they carry out a net which settles down over the birds that have been enticed to the beach by grain. All of the birds caught in these nets and cages are carefully handled and released. It is all regulated by the International Migratory Birds Convention Act.

Why so many birds on Long Point?

Don Baldwin explained that sticking out 20 miles into the lake as it does, Long Point is the first land the birds encounter during their long flight across the lake on the way north. Being tired and hungry, they naturally stop for food and a rest. Thus, during the migration seasons, there is a great concentration of birds on the point. They stay for a day or two, and then resume their migration.

Sometimes there is real tragedy on Long Point. Since migrating song birds always fly at night, they are guided by stars. But when there is a sudden overcast, they may be attracted by the bright beam from the lighthouse and fly to it. Then, completely confused, they just fly around and around the light until they drop dead from exhaustion. It does not happen often, but on one occasion the banders counted close to a thousand dead song birds at the base of the lighthouse.

The waters of Erie, the shallowest of the Great Lakes with a maximum depth of not more than 210 feet, can be extremely cantankerous in a blow. Many ships have foundered on the sand banks of Long Point in the past, and it is a rare fall that there is not a report of duck hunters lost in a high wind or snowstorm. And great deeds of heroism have been performed by rescuers.

No modern deeds, however, can compare with that of Abigail Becker who, in 1854, lived with her trapper husband on Long Point. One terrible night in November, the schooner *Conductor*, loaded with timber and hides, ran aground on a sandbar. The captain and crew, not knowing the shallowness of the water, climbed into the rigging to escape the icy waves that were breaking over the hull, and there they stayed the long night through.

In the morning Abigail saw them and realized that without help they would all perish. Her husband was away, so she undertook the task alone. First, she kindled a big fire of driftwood on the beach, and then waded through the icy water to the side of the ship. She shouted to the men to jump into the water so that she could help them to shore. The first to venture was the captain, who was picked up by a great wave and deposited at Abigail's feet. Somehow she managed to get hold of him and drag him ashore. Then she went back for the others. One by one, she fetched seven men from the freezing water to the warmth of the roaring fire.

North of Long Point, in Norfolk County, is the heart of Ontario's flue-cured tobacco industry. This is sandy land, flat, with never a stone nor boulder to break the surface. It was originally covered with great stands of white and red pine, but when the settlers came they cut down the trees so they could farm the land. They grew crops of grain and vegetables and fruit, and prospered. But then, lacking the binding of tree roots, the light soil began to blow away in the wind and wash away with the rain, and gradually the fertile land was transformed into weed-infested drifts of sand. The once-flourishing farms were useless. Many were abandoned.

Then, in 1923, two farmers named H.A. Freeman and W.L. Pelton became interested in tobacco. Flue-cured tobacco, the kind used in cigarettes, requires a sandy, well-drained soil, plenty of fertilizer, and abundant water. The ground must be relatively flat so that it can be irrigated. Since all of these conditions exist on the sand plains of Norfolk, the tobacco thrived. Soon farms that were worth nothing became among the most valuable in the province.

When you drive through Norfolk, you are struck by the fine homes, big barns, greenhouses, and green or red tobacco-curing sheds. In the spring you will see the tobacco being planted by men sitting on the low platforms of tractor-pulled planting machines, sticking the small tobacco plants that have been grown in greenhouses into the ground. Later you will see whole families—men, women, children—in the fields plucking the flowers off the tops of tall tobacco plants, or removing the suckers from the base of the leaves.

And then, about the middle of August, you will see the tobacco primers out there doing the hardest job of all. Bent double, they go along the rows removing the bottom leaves (sand lugs) first, and putting them into a box pulled by a single horse. Gradually, they work up the stalks of the plants, straightening up, until they have reached the top leaves, and the crop is all picked.

During tobacco harvest time, the towns of Delhi, Aylmer, Tillsonburg and Simcoe are besieged in the evening by itinerant pickers from far and near: university students earning their fees; travelling workers who follow harvests of fruit, vegetables and tobacco; imported pickers from Holland and other European countries brought over at government expense. Sometimes there is not enough work for all, and then there can be trouble in the streets.

As soon as the tobacco leaves are picked, they are tied in bundles, and hung in the drying sheds where oil burners keep the temperature just right. Usually, experienced tobacco experts from Georgia or Virginia supervise this vital process. After being properly dried, the leaves are bundled and stored in huge barns, later to be graded and taken to market.

The entire tobacco-growing industry is as heavily regulated as any in Canada. A board made up of growers determines exactly how many acres of tobacco shall be grown.

"Go to Normandale. You'll find something interesting there," an old-timer at Delhi told me. And so I went to Normandale.

There isn't much of a road leading to Normandale, and there isn't much of a town when you get there. A few scattered buildings at the mouth of a tiny creek, named Potter's Creek, that runs into Lake Erie halfway between Port Rowan and Port Dover. It is a town that history has completely passed by, and yet in its heyday, during the first half of the nineteenth century, it looked as though it might become the industrial centre of Upper Canada. As many as three schooners a day loaded up with Normandale products for export across the lake to the U.S.A., and just about every farmer and householder in the province depended upon the workers of Normandale.

A bronze plaque on the wall of a fish hatchery gives some indication of the story. It states that the town was founded in 1818 by Samuel Mason, and that Joseph Van Norman built and worked Ontario's first blast furnace here, producing fine iron stoves (that can still be seen in museums), ploughshares, shovels, kettles, pots, frying pans, and other iron goods needed in the new province.

Iron works on Lake Erie? I had thought that iron ore was a product of the Canadian Shield, that it was taken from immense open-pit mines and shipped to Hamilton for manufacture. Subsequent investigation, however, told me that iron is also found in swamps, that it is called bog ore, and that it can run up to 50 per cent pure.

The first man to dig up the Erie bog ore and smelt it down in a blast furnace was the enterprising, irascible Englishman Samuel Mason. He worked hard and he worked alone. He built a crude version of a blast furnace, charged it with bog ore and charcoal, inspired it with a blast of air from a bellows, and extracted a thin trickle of molten iron. But he worked too hard, it seems, and he could have done with some help. His makeshift furnace fell down, and Mason died a discouraged and worn-out man.

Then along came three enterprising Yankees, Joseph Van Norman, George Tillson, and Hiram Capron. They knew a good thing when they saw it, rebuilt Mason's furnace, and went into business. Tillson left and founded the town of Tillsonburg; Capron went farther afield and founded the town of Paris, named after plaster of paris, the making of which was Capron's trade.

That left Van Norman, who built a blast furnace of brick on the side of the hill. Charcoal was made from the hardwood that grew in abundance in the area and was dumped, along with the big, rust-coloured chunks of bog ore, into the top of the furnace. Potter's Creek turned a water wheel that worked a huge bellows to provide the "blast" necessary to produce enough heat to melt the ore. The iron and slag were drained off at the bottom, just as they are in blast furnaces today, and the molten iron was poured into sand casks to make kettles and other iron products.

Van Norman worked a sort of you-help-me-I'll-help-you system with the settlers of the area. They needed his iron goods, and he needed their muscle, so they paid for their purchases by digging and hauling ore and doing other necessary jobs around the furnace.

So great was the need for iron wares, and so good were Van Norman's products, that his business flourished. He designed kitchen ware, and even built a stove which needed no bolts, but which could easily be taken apart and stored for the summer. Not only did settlers make the long trip from other parts of the province to buy his iron goods, but an excellent export trade was developed. A pier was built where schooners could load up with iron goods to be delivered across the lake to the States and, after the first Welland Canal was dug, down the waterways to Toronto, Hamilton, and as far as Montreal. Goods were shipped the other way as far west as Chicago.

Bad luck finally caught up with Van Norman, however. His supply of bog ore ran out, and the nearest he could find any ore was hundreds of miles away at Marmora, which is north of Belleville near the eastern end of Lake Ontario. At great expense he moved his works to this site, built a new furnace, and went into business. But nothing was the same. Iron products had to be hauled 30 miles through the bush to the lake, cheap iron was coming in from the States, and Marmora ore was of poor quality. Van Norman lost just about everything.

So the action moved elsewhere. Railways were coming in, and they needed a harder iron than Van Norman could produce. Hamilton became the iron and steel centre. The iron workers moved away, and the town of Normandale, like so many other once-bustling towns, slowly dwindled away. There is nothing now to remind the visitor of Normandale's former glory, except the plaque on the fish hatchery and the odd hunk of green slag half buried among the weeds and brush along the bank of Potter's Creek.

Besides ironmongering, Joseph Van Norman was involved in construction and shipping. During most of the nineteenth century, the harbour enclosed by Long Point was important in shipping lumber and other products to the U.S.A. and through the Great Lakes–St. Lawrence River system to Britain. Ships were built in the the ports here, and manned by the men of the lakeshore.

The shore was also vulnerable to attack from across the lake by the Americans. In the summer of 1814, a small detachment of the enemy landed at Port Dover and burned the town, established only 13 years earlier, to the ground. Port Dover quickly recovered and, over the years, developed as the largest fresh-water fishing centre in Ontario. Hundreds of turtle-back boats put out into the lake every day to fish for the delicious blue pickerel and herring. But those fish have gone now, some say because of pollution in the lake caused by fertilizers and sewage, others say from too much fishing. Today, the few remaining fishermen use trawl lines instead of gill nets, and their quarry is the lowly perch.

Not far from Port Dover, near the little town of Vittoria, stands an old colonial house that few ever give a second glance. The house was built by Colonel Joseph Ryerson, a United Empire Loyalist, who was in command of the First Regiment of Norfolk Militia during the War of 1812. Joseph was an ardent churchman and when he and his wife, Mahetabel, had six sons, he trained five of them to be Methodist ministers. And in those days a Methodist minister spent much of his time on horseback, riding the circuit and bringing the Word to isolated homes and communities in the bush.

All of the five became eminent churchmen, but none was more eminent than Egerton, a heavy-framed man with a fiery nature and enough energy for ten. All his life he fought the good fight for the Methodist religion in Ontario (and equal rights for all denominations), taking on such formidable foes as Archdeacon John Strachan, the equally fiery and energetic churchman who fought the good fight for the Anglican Church.

A writer, editor, and founder of Upper Canada Academy, which later became Victoria College, Ryerson is most noted for the fact that as Chief Superintendent of Education for the province of Canada West, he established the free educational system of Ontario.

North of Port Dover, but connected to the lake by a canal that was once the community's lifeline, is the city of Brantford. The early settlement derived its name from a shallow section of the Grand River where Joseph Brant once crossed with his braves. Hence Brant's ford.

Joseph Brant, a full-blooded Mohawk Indian, became the darling of London's high society during the time of the American Revolutionary War for his fighting ability against the American rebels. So to us in Canada he has always been a "good Indian," while in American history books he is a "bad Indian."

Certainly Brant was a courageous man. But whether he was any more savage than the white men he fought against is doubtful. He once stated, when asked why he preferred the Indian way of life to the white man's:

> Among the Indians you will find no prisons, no pompous parade of courts. We have no written laws and yet our judges are highly revered among us. And for what are many of your people imprisoned? Debt. You put a man in prison perhaps for life, for circumstances beyond his control. I would rather die by the most severe torture than languish in one of your prisons for a single year.

Besides being proficient with the tomahawk, Brant knew Latin and Greek; as well, he translated the "Gospel of St. Mark," and the psalm book and the liturgy of the Anglican Church into the Mohawk language. For his services on behalf of the Crown, Brant was granted by Lieutenant Governor Sir Frederick Haldimand six miles of land on either side of the Grand River.

There is a statue of Brant in Victoria Park in Brantford, a fine museum of Indian lore and relics, and a Mohawk church called His Majesty's Chapel of the Mohawks, where Brant was buried after his death at the age of 65.

Also in Brantford is the Bell homestead where in 1874 Alexander Graham Bell conceived the telephone. In Bell Gardens in the centre of the city there is a monument to the inventor created by Walter S. Allward, and in front of the Bell Telephone Company offices a great bronze statue, the work of Toronto sculptor Cleeve Horne, broods over the traffic.

Port Colborne at the south end of the Welland Canal is a heavily-industrialized town, but in recent years it has become internationally famous for something far removed from the refining of nickel or the milling of flour. This is the annual meeting of writers, teachers, media people, and others interested in the arts called Canada Day. It was Jim Foley, the energetic head of the English Department at the Port Colborne Highschool, who in 1971 determined that highschool students should become better acquainted with current Canadian writing.

There was at that time no Canadian literature course on either the highschool or university curriculum in Ontario. Jim set about to remedy this. He invited writers such as novelist Hugh Garner, poet John Newlove, myself, and many others to come to his school to meet the kids. The affair was given good local publicity and turned out to be a big success. The writers and the students liked each other on sight.

The next year's Canada Day was even bigger, with Farley Mowat and Pierre Berton as the headliners, and this time it attracted attention from the American and British press as well as from the Canadian media. Each year the affair has become bigger and better, with the result that the Canadian Studies Foundation has been established with Jim Foley at its head. Now, highschool literature courses actually include works by Canadian writers.

Fort Erie is the last town of any size along the north shore of the lake. Actually it is on the Niagara River at the Canadian end of the Peace Bridge, but Fort Erie's history has not been a peaceful one. Proximity to the States has meant trouble both at the time of the Fenian raids and during the War of 1812. The fort, about a mile south of the present town, was built in 1764. It was taken by a strong American force in July of 1814, and held by the invaders until November 5 when they blew it up and withdrew across the river. The fort has been restored and is a fine place to study early military history.

The town of Fort Erie is chiefly known in Ontario now as the setting for race meets of the Ontario Jockey Club.

CHAPTER VII

The Highlands
of Southwestern Ontario

The highlands of southwestern Ontario is that land west of the Niagara Escarpment and north of the Erie plain, in whose swamps and bogs dozens of small rivers rise. Rivers with beautiful names like the Nottawasaga and the Humber and Saugeen, and tributaries with saucy names like the Mad and the Pretty and the Noisy. The land of hills, long ridges, moraines, drumlins, long winding eskers, and pointed kames. A rough land to be sure, but we believe it to be the most beautiful of all southern Ontario.

Highway 10 from Toronto leads most directly into this country, but we followed the side roads that keep pretty close to the Credit River, which makes up for the plainness of its name by the beauty of its surroundings.

We turned off the Queen Elizabeth Way just a little west of Highway 10 onto the Spring Bank Road, which follows a trail the Indians travelled to get down to Lake Ontario. It got its name from a spring that still gushes out of a bank just as it did a thousand years ago when the Indians stopped there to drink. Today commuters short of good drinking water in their wells stop to fill large containers and load them into car trunks.

North of Highway 5 the Spring Bank Road becomes the Streets-ville Road. There is a small stone church perched high on a hill at this crossroads, the church Mazo de la Roche wrote about in her Jalna books. The Streetsville Road more or less follows the river through orchards, and past lovely homes and the entrance to Erindale College, a part of the University of Toronto. You can see the river soon at Minzenti Park, where the rapids burble and boil, and where each spring adventurous paddlers don rubber suits and climb into kayaks and canoes to race through the freezing, dashing water.

The town of Streetsville (now part of the town of Mississauga) is next, and just north of Streetsville is the "small holding" where I went after the war to begin the precarious trade of free-lance writ-ing. And it was here I met one of Ontario's most important and most shamefully neglected citizens.

It was one and seven-tenths acres we had near the bank of Mullet Creek, and when we moved there in the spring of 1946 I knew that I was going to do all right. I would raise fruit trees (apples, peaches, pears) as well as grapes and raspberries. And I would grow a whopper of a garden, enough to feed my family and all my friends. Back to the land, that's the stuff. The man who sold me the property said that he had been permitting a retired gentleman to grow Chinese elms from seed in the garden but that, of course, if I wanted all the land, he could go. I said he would have to go.

So we moved in and, as soon as the land was able to be worked, the old gentleman showed up and began mucking about in the mud of my garden. He came to the house and introduced himself. "Hello. I'm old John Mitchell."

The name didn't mean anything to me but his appearance certainly did. A finer looking man I've never seen. Not because of the classic lines of his face, but because of the character, under-standing, suffering, and compassion that were written there. He had a fine head of white hair and his skin was tanned brown.

I invited him in and we had a drink and talked. "I'll get my stuff out of here as soon as I can," he said. "I know you'll want the land."

"There's no hurry," I muttered.

The sharp blue eyes twinkled. "Oh, I know how it is. You can't wait to start farming the land, eh? You want to be an agriculturist."

"A what?"

"Agriculturist. A farmer makes his money in the country and

spends it in the city, while an agriculturist makes his money in the city and spends it in the country."

How right he was. All around me were commuters driving frantically into the city every morning to office, factory, school or what have you, and frantically driving back to the country every evening to breathe the fresh air. And on weekends spending their earnings and savings on new roofs, septic tanks, ponds, garden tractors, lawnmowers, trees, plants, horses, and all the other things that brought them to the country in the first place.

From neighbours I learned John Mitchell's story. He had been a lawyer by profession but not by temperament, was careless with clients' monies, and finally found himself in court charged with a misappropriation of funds. His friends rallied to his defence and, it is said, even the judge wanted to see him acquitted, but there was something about John Mitchell that made him insist on paying the penalty. So he went to jail, which of course ended his law career. Before his downfall, he had written a book about an Irish orphan boy's experiences in the town of York and the hills of Mono Mills. He called it *The Yellow Briar*, and signed it with the penname of Patrick Slater.

The Yellow Briar is a fine, sensitive story about Ontario around the 1860s; in fact there has never been a finer one written. It has been reprinted many times and has given much pleasure to many people. It is a sad book, too, not just in its story but in the fact that, although it was a success, it never earned its author enough money to support him. So he grubbed in the mud of my garden growing Chinese elms for commercial tree sellers, and he died in poverty.

North on the Streetsville Road, the farms present an interesting study in the old and the new. Original brick houses that have been reroofed many times, decorated with "gingerbread" carvings; old bank barns still standing and housing the great herds of Holsteins that this region is famous for. And rail fences. The same cedar rails that were split and put there by the settlers a hundred and more years ago. There are even a few stump fences, made by piling the immense maple and oak stumps in a row. It takes a long time for a hardwood stump to rot away. And amidst all this, shiny new barns and sheds for raising chickens or turkeys, with aluminum roofs gleaming in the sun.

And then the hill country where there are more trees. Wood lots, as they are called, consisting mostly of maple and preserved as a conservation measure. They stand out on the hillsides, green in summer and in the autumn, patches of brilliance that you can hardly believe. Red and yellow and bronze, bright against the blue sky. There is no scenery anywhere like it.

Farther north a road winds down by the river bank to the little village of Terra Cotta. Not much there but old houses and a mill, and a restaurant that is famous throughout southern Ontario. It is great to sit on the veranda, eat fine foods, sip fine wines, and listen to the singing of the Credit River nearby as it comes running down out of the hills.

There are other villages to drive through and savour. Cheltenham, Inglewood, and Belfountain, all river bank towns. And near Belfountain is The Forks, a place where two branches of the Credit come together with a great rushing and bouncing over the stones of their limestone beds. Nearby is a bold, heavily-treed cliff, one of the many of the escarpment, known as Rattlesnake Point, though there are no rattlesnakes this far south.

The Bruce Trail runs through this area. Hikers can get on it at Brimstone, a beautiful little village just north of The Forks, and walk along the river either north or south. Paths have been cut through dense cedar bush on the river bank, with steps here and there where the climb is steep. All were put there by the sweat of Bruce Trail members on Saturdays and Sundays (I know because I helped with some of them) and carefully marked with little white blazes on trees, rocks, and fence posts.

You can walk as far as your legs will carry you here: 5, 10, 50, or 100 miles, for the trail has been built from Niagara to Tobermory, a distance of more than four hundred miles. It is a nature trail and a natural trail. Only enough steps and stiles have been provided to enable hikers to manage steep inclines and climb fences. The rest is a simple path through the forest or across meadows, with only the debris of fallen branches cleared away. In the autumn the path is ankle deep with fallen leaves.

The trail crosses the Hockley Valley road near the hamlet of Glen Cross and goes north through some of the most attractive forest country of its entire length. Hikers walk through shady dampness beneath huge oak, maple, and beech trees, climb over snake rail fences, tramp across meadows, investigate fox dens, pick hard apples from wild trees, cross bubbly streams on fallen logs, climb hills as steep as stairs, and flop exhausted in the long grass on the top of a hill with a view for miles.

I was living in Orangeville when the Bruce Trail was new and its promoters were desperately seeking supporters and workers. As I was one of the few walkers in Orangeville (an activity that made me slightly suspect by some of the townspeople who owned two cars), I naturally enough became involved. The chief trail organizer and hiking advocate in our area at that time was Phil Gosling of Guelph. Phil was the kind of man who would phone you up on a Sunday morning just after you had gotten out of bed, still in your pyjamas, and say, "It's a great day for trailing. A gang of us are meeting in the cataract area. We'd like you to join us. Oh, and bring a shovel and a sharp axe . . . and a pick if you've got one. Better bring a lunch, too."

At that, the pick and shovel work was better than calling on farmers and asking their permission to cross their property. The Bruce Trail Association owns no lands and has no contracts with land owners. It uses the land by permission, and the owner can withdraw that permission at any time. Naturally some farmers who have been plagued with dude hunters from the city shooting everything in sight (including cows) and careless smokers and litterers do hesitate a little in granting this permission. But most can be persuaded, and Phil Gosling was a powerful persuader.

It is due largely to men like Phil, and Ray Lowes of the Federation of Ontario Naturalists (who actually first had the idea for the trail and is considered to be its founder), and Tom East, and dozens of others just like them that there is a hiking trail there at all.

From The Forks, the road goes north through the village of Alton, also on the river, and ultimately to the town of Orangeville, county seat of the county of Dufferin.

Orangeville in many ways is typical of towns within a 50-mile radius of Toronto. It is a town in transition with the old houses, streets, mills, and retired farmers mixed with new office buildings, apartments, suburban homes and bright young executives. For Orangeville has been greatly affected by the diversification trend in Ontario industry. Get away from the big cities, is the cry of many companies, to the towns where living is cheaper and more pleasant, labour is plentiful and reasonable, and community involvement immediate and real.

This is the part of the province to which the Irish and Scottish immigrants of the mid-nineteenth century trekked from Toronto, partly because the flat lands of the plain had already been taken, and partly because the hills and streams and rugged bush of the country reminded them of the highlands of Scotland and the hills of northern Ireland.

Protestants they were to a man, those who came up the hill to this part of the highlands. One man, who grew up at Laurel just outside of Orangeville, told how as a boy he hid in the hayloft to peek down on his first Catholic. "He'd come to buy some grain from my father, and from the terrible things we'd heard about Catholics we didn't really know what kind of creature to expect. But he turned out to be an ordinary man, just like our father." There was still a faint note of surprise in his voice as he said it.

Two of the townships of Dufferin County are named Luther and Melancthon, and the story of how they got their names, although probably apocryphal, tells something of the attitude of those times. It seems that the first surveyor to chart this mess of bogs and swamps that make up much of the townships was a devout Roman Catholic. And so, since this was the worst country he had ever seen, he decided to name it after the worst men he could think of, the two leaders of the Reformation, Martin Luther and Philip Melanchthon. The Protestant settlers who later came, of course, looked upon this as a great honour.

It is considered by most that Orangeville was naturally named after the Orange Lodge, which was strong there from the beginning. The truth is, however, that it was named after its founder, a Scotsman named Lawrence who had the unlikely first name of Orange. Like almost every other town in southern Ontario, Orangeville began with a mill, built on a small creek which is one of the headwaters of the Credit River. Lawrence came up into the bush from Halton County in 1843 and bought the saw and grist mills that had been built by James Greggs 11 years earlier. A hard-working, flamboyant man, Lawrence provided a store and a blacksmith shop besides the mills for the convenience of the settlers, and soon a town grew up around him. Like all towns, it was destined to be, according to its boosters, the great metropolis of Ontario. At least that was the opinion of the editor of the Orangeville *Sun* in the fall of 1896:

Aye the visions . . . visions of the distant day when Orangeville shall be a city wondrous and sublime . . . with roaring mills and factories . . . with street-cars thundering down the ways . . . with great buildings rearing their glittering domes to the upper vaults . . . when the name of Orangeville shall be sounded on the boulevards of Paris . . . and its glory shall rival the glory of London

. . . and its wealth shall have transcended the wealth of New York. . . .

Well, Orangeville never made it, but neither did any of the other towns nearby, Caledon or Caledon East or Mono Mills. Mono Mills particularly. Situated six miles east of Orangeville, it was once the biggest town in the district, with stores and mills and hotels and taverns and churches that were the envy of the countryside. And then the railway came, and it went through the tiny village of Orangeville instead of through Mono Mills. Today Mono Mills is nothing. The crumbled remains of some of the buildings can be seen amid the weeds. There are a half-dozen houses and an antique shop and nothing else. A deserted village.

Two streams of the east branch of the Credit River meet in Orangeville, and one of these has been dammed to make a 400-acre lake on the edge of town which has great possibilities. It has been designated as a wildlife sanctuary and already is crowded in spring with nesting ducks and bitterns and other water and shore birds. In winter snowmobiles criss-cross its snow-covered surface and some hardier chaps from town even go there for walks.

The Credit River flows south to Lake Ontario, and not more than a hundred yards from a stream that feeds it is a stream running into the Nottawasaga River which runs north to Georgian Bay at Wasaga Beach. The Nottawasaga has cut a deep valley called the Hockley (locally pronounced Huckley) to provide some the fine scenery.

The hills on either side of the river, once farmland, are in great demand by Toronto commuters and the developers of ski resorts. The Hockley is on the edge of the snow belt and often receives enough snow for skiing. Its resorts are most popular with the beginning and casual skiers who drive up from Toronto in the morning and back in the evening. On a busy weekend the doctors on duty at the Orangeville hospital will set a dozen broken bones. Serious skiers tend to go father north to Beaver Valley or Collingwood.

Highway 10, which is variously called Hurontario Street, Centre Road or the Prince of Wales Road, goes north again through relatively flat country with good farms on each side. It cuts Highway 89 running east to the town of Alliston, where potatoes and tobacco are the principal crops, and where there is a school named Sir Frederick Banting, because that is the town where the co-discoverer of insulin was born.

Straight north are the hills of Mulmur, wild rugged country, mostly hills and cedar bush and swamps and streams, where more and more city folk are finding their way to build retreats and dig ponds to stock with trout.

West is the town of Shelburne. It's not a big town, but it's a lively one that somehow has managed to get and hold one of the major international festivals. This is the Old Time Fiddlers Contest held in the town arena every summer. The people go all out for this event with old-time costumes, street dances, and parades. Thousands of people pour into the town, along with the best fiddlers from North America and even from Europe. The CBC gives it full coverage, and each year a new champion is proclaimed.

Just north of Shelburne are the headwaters of the Boyne River, which runs eastward through Alliston and then north into the Nottawasaga. North of the Boyne is the Pine, and on the Pine is the small village of Horning's Mills, which is chiefly noted for the story of the kidnapped children. It is an old story and probably has gained something over the years, but the facts are that the Horning family and some others had driven oxcarts from Hamilton, more than seventy miles through the bush, and established the town of Horning's Mills. Some time after, four children of the settlement, Jane, Susan and Oliver Vanmear, and Lewis Horning, went into the bush searching for a new-born calf and were never seen again. Since the girls were in their teens (the boys were only nine), it seemed unlikely that they would get lost. The settlers searched and searched for days, but no sign of the children could they find. Some said they were eaten by wolves, but others firmly believed that the Indians had kidnapped them.

North of the Pine is the Noisy River, which runs into the Mad, a branch of the Nottawasaga. The Mad River got its name from the experience of a woman who, it is said, walked 30 miles through the bush from her home north of the river to Horning's Mills, carrying a sack of wheat on her back. She had the wheat ground into flour and was returning through the woods, when she came to the river which she had previously crossed on a log. But a heavy rain had swollen the river, and the madly rushing waters had taken away her bridge. When she attempted another crossing, she fell into the water and, of course, ruined her bag of flour. Ever after that when relating the story, the woman would say: "And then I came to that mad, mad river. . . . " Hence the name.

From Shelburne, Highway 10 goes towards the Bruce Peninsula across Dufferin and Grey Counties, where fat beef cattle can be seen feeding in the fields on either side of the road. At Flesherton is the beautiful Beaver Valley, created over the centuries by the Beaver River cutting its way through the limestone of the escarpment. The sides of the valley provide the best ski hills in the area.

Farther on is the city of Owen Sound, at the end of a long, funnel-shaped sound that goes inland from Georgian Bay. Before highways were built, Owen Sound was an important shipping centre for this entire area. Today it depends for its prosperity mostly on manufacturing.

The Bruce Peninsula is long and narrow, with a jagged shoreline. It is an extension of the Niagara Escarpment which juts between Georgian Bay and the rest of Lake Huron. In many places the limestone is on the surface, and fissures wide enough for a pig to fall into are common. It is not much good as farmland, but as rugged scenery it is superb.

The Bruce Trail runs along the top of the steep limestone cliffs of the east shore of the peninsula, and this is the part of the trail that separates the family-outing type walkers from the real hikers. You need proper boots, plenty of agility, and a good strong constitution to walk this section of the trail from Hope Bay to Tobermory, but it is worth it.

From the edges of the cliffs you can look out over the blue waters of Georgian Bay and listen to them breaking on the rocky shore. If you are lucky, you might surprise a short, fat massassauga rattler sunning itself on a rock. These are the only rattlers left in Ontario, and Georgian Bay's shore and the islands in the bay are the only places they are found. It is best to walk around them because their bite is poisonous, but massassaugas are not aggressive and do not look for trouble.

In some places the trail leads right down onto the beach where the water is good for swimming or fishing. And along the rocky cliffs in various places are deep caves for the more adventurous to explore. Some are small, others as big as cathedrals. They have been cut there over millions of years by the action of water wearing away the softer limestone and leaving hard dolomite walls.

There is a good chance that you will find, particularly along the north shore from Cabot Head to Driftwood Cove, caves that no one else has ever seen. Inside there are deep pools of water and stalactites over a foot long. It is good to carry a coil of sturdy rope along this portion of the trail for lowering yourself down to the mouths of otherwise inaccessible caves. And it goes without saying that you should not try this section of the trail alone.

You can camp on Flower Pot Island off the tip of the peninsula and marvel at the weird pot-shaped pinnacles of rock formed in the same manner as the caves, by the water washing away the softer limestone and leaving the hard rock.

If you do not feel up to hiking, there is a good road leading through the centre of the peninsula from Owen Sound to Tobermory. And you can drive your car onto a ferry that will carry you across to Manitoulin Island, reputed to be the largest fresh-water island in the world.

Like the Bruce Peninsula, Manitoulin is limestone thinly covered with soil, a farther extension of the Niagara Escarpment. There are rugged cliffs and flat limestone plains and beautiful beaches. Before the white man came, Manitoulin was the home of the Ottawa Indians, who had a legend (very similar to our Adam and Eve story) which relates how the Great Spirit created life there and gave the island to the Ottawas to hold and enjoy forever.

Unfortunately it did not work out that way. Some of the Hurons who had not been killed by the Iroquois in 1649 sought sanctuary on Manitoulin, but the Iroquois found them. Today there is a large Indian reserve on the island and, during harvest time, groups of Indians are brought into the fruit and vegetable growing areas of southern Ontario as cheap pickers.

The west side of the Bruce Peninsula is flat and swampy and here, if you know where to look, you will find rare flowers that grow only in this region. There is the calypso orchid, for instance, and the prairie white-fringed orchid, the rare Alaska rein, and the dainty ram's head lady slipper. The best place to see them is in the Dorcas Bay Nature Reserve, established in 1962 by Malcolm Kirk with the help of the Federation of Ontario Naturalists, who somehow found the money to save this natural beauty spot from the bulldozers.

At the base of the Bruce Peninsula on the Lake Huron side is Sauble Beach, a great stretch of sand where many thousands of Ontario citizens find relief from the heat each summer.

At Southampton is Highway 21, usually referred to as "the Blue Water Highway," although very little of the blue waters of Lake Huron can be seen from the road, which runs down the east shore of Lake Huron through such beautiful little towns as Port Elgin and Kincardine, with their fine brick and stone homes and shady streets.

We turned south off the Blue Water Highway at Amberley for a special reason. Highway 86 took us through the town of Lucknow, and south of Lucknow on a farm stands a big stone house that was the birthplace of a man I want to talk about. I knew and admired him because he represented a generation of Ontario youth who, around the turn of the century, went West to help found new provinces and contributed greatly to their development.

His name was Bob Treleaven, and you will not find it in the *Encyclopaedia Canadiana*. But you will find it in the hearts of his six children and their children and their children's children and the hundreds of friends he made from one side of this country to the other.

He was born in a narrow room in the big stone house where he lived as a boy with his six brothers and sisters. And when we visited that farm with him he remembered, at the age of 73, every corner, every closet, every mark on walls and floors, from the musty basement where russet apples were stored in winter to the attic where the boys slept.

Bob was a lively, wiry boy who did all the things on the farm that farm boys did then, which means he worked just about all the time. But there was time off for county fairs and dances and taking girls out in the buggy. And sometimes he would visit and tease a pretty, pert neighbour girl named Amy Reid, whom he never could get out of his mind. He passed his "entrance" (Grade 8), which represented considerable education for farm boys in those days, and he was ready to lick the world.

The talk then was all of the West, of the great fields of grain and the threshing outfits and the barrel of fun a fellow could have on the harvest excursion. So when he reached the age of 17, Bob took the harvest excursion to Saskatchewan (return trip $12) and pitched bundles on a threshing outfit in the Hanley area, where an older brother and an uncle were already established.

The next year he set out from Hanley with a load of door and window frames and household goods on a wagon pulled by oxen. Along with his brother, he filed on a homestead in the Rosetown area, and built a sod house on the property. He stayed in the West for the next three years, proving up the homestead, which he later sold, and working with his brothers in a store in Hanley.

Then he returned to Toronto and found Amy Reid, prettier than ever, working there as a stenographer. He married her and took her west to Saskatoon, and then to a homestead in the sandhills west of Hanley. But the soil was miserably light and Bob broke his back, but never his heart, trying to make a living on it. Finally he moved to Hanley and opened up a butcher shop. But even there luck never smiled on him.

All this time he and Amy were having their family about as fast as children can be born. Two boys and four girls, all healthy and strong and bright. I know, because I married one of the girls.

Through all their troubles and work, Amy and Bob Treleaven never lost their optimism or their humour. They both came from the old-type Ontario WASP family and they raised that type of family and their children are doing much the same. They are the kind of family that built Ontario. There are still many such to be found, but each year there are fewer. Changing times and mores are gradually phasing them out.

Following the same highway and branching off on Highway 85, we came to the twin cities of Waterloo and Kitchener. They are close enough together to be one city, but they remain separate municipalities. For the sake of brevity and ease, I will call the community Kitchener-Waterloo.

Kitchener-Waterloo is a German community. The first settlers were the Pennsylvania "Dutch" who, finding their religious views incompatible with those of the newly-formed United States, travelled upwards of 500 miles by boat, on foot, and by Conestoga wagon to their new home. They spoke German and, after that, German immigrants seeking a new home naturally tended to go where they could be understood. It is a community built on German efficiency, hard work, zeal, and discipline, and it displays those virtues to this day.

This fertile land along the Grand River was so densely covered with oak, maple, black walnut, and other hardwoods that the Huron Indians, who needed cleared land for agriculture, could make no permanent settlements there. The early British settlers, too, passed it by and settled where there was not so much back-breaking chopping and stump pulling to be done. But it was the land of promise for the Pennsylvania Mennonites who previously had emigrated from Holland, Germany, Switzerland and Denmark, and they came by the hundreds.

The first to arrive, in 1800, were Joseph Sherk and Samuel Betzner and their families. They were soon followed by other settlers who camped under trees, made crude shelters, and began swinging their axes. But immediately they ran into a situation that threatened to end their project. The tract of land they thought was to be theirs turned out to have a $20,000 mortgage against it. So Joseph Sherk and Samuel Betzner made the long trek back to Pennsylvania to get help from their fellow Mennonites there. After much argument, the brethren were persuaded that helping the Ontario group was a Christian duty, and Betzner and friends made the trip back to the Grand River location carrying 20,000 silver dollars in a wooden box.

The settlement developed in the usual way and as time went on immigrant artisans from Germany, particularly furniture makers, began working at their craft in small sheds that grew into factories. Thus the new community gradually became the centre of an extensive furniture manufacturing industry that spread to the neighbouring towns. Textile and food processing industries soon followed.

The town that grew up where Kitchener now stands was, naturally enough, named Berlin after the capital of the Fatherland; and the language of the street, the home, and indeed of business, was predominantly German. So proud were they of their German heritage that a bust of Kaiser Wilhelm, spiked helmet and all, was erected in the park. And so proud were they of their industry and success that they nicknamed their town "Busy Berlin," and the trademark "Made in Berlin" became famous throughout the land.

Then, in 1914, when Canada found herself at war with Germany, trouble began. Loyalties were divided. There were fistfights in the streets, and friends of long standing became bitter enemies. People of German background, no matter how upstanding they had been before, suddenly were considered villains. An agitation began to discard the opprobrious name of Berlin for a more patriotic one. Besides, who would buy anything with "Made in Berlin" stamped on it?

The bitter fight was finally settled by democratic means, and the vote went 1,569 to 1,488 in favour of a change. Kitchener was finally chosen as the new name, and during World War I you could not get much more patriotic than that.

But despite its good British name, Kitchener-Waterloo continues to have a distinctive German flavour. The influx of immigrants following the Second World War saw many of German origin going to Kitchener, and there are many German clubs, German choirs, and German associations in the community. The area is famous for its German food, with schmierkase, schwadamagha sausage, sauerkraut, and other such delicacies.

At the market there are many Mennonite men and women dressed in their black suits and dresses. In fact, throughout the countryside, as you roar along the highway at 60 or 70 miles an hour, you will pass Mennonites in black buggies pulled by black horses on their way to the market or the meeting house or to visit neighbours.

There is still a large Mennonite community in the area. Their farms are neat and prosperous, and many of the young men and women are perfectly content to remain on the farms and follow the old customs. They pay their taxes, send their children to the schools for as long as the law requires, and live their own lives in peace and tranquillity.

Each spring in Elmira, a few miles north of Kitchener-Waterloo, there is a Maple Syrup Festival. Thousands of people from all parts of Ontario crowd into the little town to get a breath of country air. On the streets there are soap makers, quilt makers, and other artisans plying their trades. You can buy pancakes smothered in maple syrup, and eat them at tables set up in the street; you can buy maple syrup in quart sealers or gallon jars; and you can even take a ride on a horse-drawn sleigh through the sugar maple bush. There is usually a fairly high ranking representative of the government on hand to make a speech from a platform on the main corner, and when he is finished the folk singers, square dancers, and magicians take over.

The city of Guelph, twelve miles northeast from Kitchener-Waterloo on Highway 7, is as British in its origin as Kitchener-Waterloo is German. It is one of Ontario's first planned communities. While others grew up more or less haphazardly around a mill, Guelph's location, name, nature, and even some of its buildings were deliberately planned by John Galt.

Galt, an enterprising young Scotsman, had become head of the Canada Company, charged with the task of bringing settlers to the western portion of Ontario. (The town of Galt, now part of Cambridge, was named after him although he did not found it.) With a flare for publicity, he chose St. George's Day (April 23, 1827) for the founding of Guelph because, as he wrote in his autobiography, "I was well aware of the boding effect of a little solemnity on the minds of most men, especially of the unlettered . . . ." He had chosen the name of Guelph in honour of George IV, whose family name it was. At a spot on a hilltop near where the Speed and Eramosa rivers join, he even took a whack at the first tree to be cut down in the clearing.

Situated on good agricultural land, which originally sold for the equivalent of 25¢ per acre, Guelph grew and prospered. The land around is rolling and pastoral, making the drive from Guelph to Georgetown on Highway 7 one of the most attractive in the province. Guelph has been called the Royal City and the Agriculture City and several other names, but I prefer "the greystone city." For Guelph more than any other city in the region has a predominance of buildings made of the grey limestone of the area. Almost every building on the main street, in fact, is made of squared limestone.

But the most striking of all the limestone buildings is the Roman Catholic Church of Our Lady of the Immaculate Conception. The site for it, along with that of other churches, was set aside by John Galt himself.

The name of Guelph is best known internationally because of the hundreds of graduates from its veterinary college. Until recently the veterinary college in Guelph was the only English-speaking veterinarian school in Canada, and so drew students from across the country. Because of the high calibre of teaching and research, students also came from the United States and as many as twenty other countries. In 1964 the Ontario Veterinary College, the Ontario Agricultural College and MacDonald Institute, famous for its home economics graduates, were incorporated as the University of Guelph, which now offers a full arts program as well.

There is much more to see in the highlands of southwestern Ontario; more towns to visit, each with its own story, and many with historic museums; more hills to climb and more swamps to explore. During the many years that we have lived in Ontario, my wife and I would often take off on an afternoon for a drive through the countryside, following back roads, sometimes finding ourselves at a dead end in the bottom of a ravine and having to be hauled out by a farmer's tractor, exploring old buildings, and visiting towns. And in those many years we didn't come close to seeing all there is in the highlands of southwestern Ontario.

CHAPTER VIII

The Mighty Saint Lawrence

A trip along the north shore of Lake Ontario and down the St. Lawrence River, from the Golden Horseshoe to the Quebec border, is a great experience, especially for a prairie boy. For not only is this one of the great lakes of the world, and one of the world's truly great rivers, but along their shores is the evidence of the lives, the work, the play, and the battles of the first white men who came there.

Many of the narrow, stone-lined canals are still there, built to carry the bateaux and Durham boats and small steamers around the wicked rapids of the river. Bateaux were open, flat-bottom boats often driven by poles or sweeps, and Durham boats were larger than bateaux, and usually had sails. Only pleasure boats and fishermen use them now, while big freighters from the world's ports climb upriver through the great canals and locks of the St. Lawrence Seaway.

Old river trails are there still, disappearing in places where the waters of new-formed lakes have drowned them. Forts that fell into ruin when the threat of hostile American invasion disappeared have been restored in recent times for the edification of a horde of invading tourists. For a small fee you can see and hear the re-enactment of a great battle of the War of 1812.

But mostly there is the St. Lawrence itself: the great powerful river with mist hanging over it at dawn, and its great, tree-covered

115

islands where herons nest and geese congregate. The water is not as clean as it once was when settlers drank it, but is still clean enough for swimming in by the thousands of campers who dwell along the banks in summer. A great man-made lake obliterates the fierce Long Sault Rapids which, along with the International Rapids, were such a discouragement to fur traders and early settlers. Immense power dams feed generating stations which supply electric power to the industrialized towns along the shores.

Enough is left of the old towns to show you how it was: sturdy limestone buildings with foot-thick walls and narrow windows; old churches, reverently kept in repair, and functioning now as they did in pioneer times to give the people strength of spirit to face the terrors of their times; old taverns where rivermen stopped to rest and swap yarns and get the news of events along the river.

Many of the farms are still there, looking much as they did when the lake or the river was their lifeline to neighbours and markets. The farms have big houses, big barns, apple orchards now decaying away, old smoke houses, and rail fences. Many have been bought by city people and made into weekend homes, but others still function as farms with herds of Holsteins grazing on the slopes of the river bank.

It is best to keep off the super, zip-along Macdonald-Cartier Freeway which by-passes all the towns, and from which you only rarely catch glimpses of the river. Stay with Highway 2, which runs right along the shore and crawls through the main streets of the towns.

The towns along the north shore of Lake Ontario after you leave the Golden Horseshoe—Bowmanville, Port Hope, Cobourg, and Colborne—are still picturesque. Each has a harbour, once crowded with sailing ships and rafts of squared timbers, but now mostly used by pleasure boats. Each is at the mouth of a small river or creek that comes tumbling down from the hills to the north, and that in early times provided power for grist mills and sawmills.

These towns are a blend of the old and the new. Ancient limestone and brick buildings still in use are gradually being torn down to make room for more functional structures of concrete and glass. Great, beautiful old houses, surrounded by great, beautiful old trees, go back to the first half of the nineteenth century when these towns were founded, mostly by Loyalists. By contrast, there are modern shopping centres. Each town has a museum where the curious can discover the names of the first settlers and the kind of lives they lived.

It is interesting just to drive through these towns and observe them; it is even more fascinating to park your car and stay for a day or two. It is risky though, for these towns have a way of causing visitors to begin looking at old houses and calculating what it would cost to restore the roof or the old balcony. After all, it is not much more than an hour's drive to Toronto. The air is much easier to breathe. The pace of life is slower, and the chance for community involvement much greater. There are good schools, too. Port Hope has famous old Trinity College School where proper discipline and thorough scholarship are still emphasized. A fellow could get a little sailing boat and join the yacht club. And then there is the beach for summer swimming. Property prices are a lot more reasonable, too. Yeah . . . it would not be a bad place to live at all.

The town of Trenton, which sits at the mouth of the Trent River where it empties into the Bay of Quinte and thus is the beginning of the Trent Waterway, is another of the old Loyalist towns. It is a town of bridges, rivers, canals, commercial fishermen, and factories.

The 240-mile long Trent-Severn Waterway begins here with the first lock just off Highway 401. Here some 1,300 pleasure boats a year, about 10 per cent of which are American, are lifted 18 feet from the level of Lake Ontario to the Trent River. Thence they follow the old Champlain Route northwest through rivers, canals, the Kawartha Lakes, Lakes Simcoe and Couchiching, and finally by the Severn River to Port Severn on Georgian Bay.

Houseboats 50 feet long and costing up to $500 a week to rent, cruisers, small boats with outboards, canoes, and even rowboats begin their long summer voyage at this first lock. The lockmaster provides them with charts, a copy of the Waterways regulations, and a small booklet called *Safety Afloat*. Each year more boats make the trip, which takes them through 43 locks to a high point near Kirkfield, 598 feet above Lake Ontario and 262 feet above Georgian Bay.

I followed Highway 2 from Trenton to the city of Belleville and drove along Belleville's Moira River, whose banks are layered shelves of limestone. I was on the lookout for two things, a tourist information centre and a museum. (Since the Centennial celebrations of 1967, most towns have both.) Belleville had done a fine job of hiding theirs from the casual eye of the tourist. I drove down Church Street where the museum was located but saw no signs designating its presence. After three enquiries, I located the information centre on a one-way street. When I asked for a history of the town, they produced typed sheets which they were sorry they could not let me have because there was only one copy. I suggested that maybe they could photocopy the pages. The lady in charge said, "I'll see; wait here," disappeared into a back room, and finally came out with the photocopied sheets.

They were worth waiting for. From them I learned that the first inhabitants of the area were Mohawks who lived in a village called Kente, from which the word Quinte has evolved. There was a mission at Kente run by the Sulpician Order as early as 1666.

When the United Empire Loyalists came in 1789, John W. Meyers built a sawmill and a grist mill on the river, which he called Meyers Creek. The town supplied timber for Britain and served as a centre for the farmers who settled on the drumlin-pocked clay plains to the north.

In 1866 gold was discovered in the rock country 30 miles north of the town in the area of the present village of Eldorado, and this increased the growth of Belleville, which called itself the "Gateway to the Golden North." So prosperous and uppity did the town become, in fact, that the citizens actually petitioned Queen Victoria to make Belleville the capital of Canada. Dunbar Moodie, husband of Susanna Moodie, who wrote the classic *Roughing It In The Bush,* was one of the early officials of the town. The Moodie stone house still stands at the corner of West Bridge and Sinclair Streets.

I crossed the narrows of the Bay of Quinte by bridge and headed south across the Quinte Isles on Highway 14. The Bay of Quinte is a lovely place: heavily-treed islands all over the place, long, winding channels with little farmhouses and cottages along them, and swinging bridges. It really is the beauty spot of Ontario.

Farther south, Quinte Island is a great limestone plain with the layered stone cropping out among the trees and grass. Trees become scarcer because of this, and many fields are dotted with red cedars ten feet tall or less.

Quinte Island offers, as the tourist posters say, a paradise for the sightseer, the historian, the fisherman, and the sailor. The island is rich in historic plaques, famous old stone houses built by Loyalist settlers, and no less than five museums.

I could visit only one of these, the United Empire Loyalist Museum at Adolphustown on Highway 33, just after crossing Adolphus Reach on the Glenora free ferry.

There I met Mrs. Speers, who had plenty of time to talk to me, because I was the only visitor to the museum. She told me that this is where the bulk of the first contingents of Loyalists to this part of Ontario landed in 1784. They came upriver by bateau, canoe, rowboat, or raft, through the furious International Rapids section, from Sorel near Montreal where they had spent the winter. They claimed the land granted to them by a grateful British government and settled in the area. Many are buried in the historic burying ground at the site.

There are original documents on the walls, including Lord Dorchester's decree, and Mrs. Speers pointed out that there is a difference between a "Loyalist" and a "United Empire Loyalist." "You had to join the Royal Standard in America," she said, "before the Treaty of Separation in the year 1783. That's the key to the whole thing. You can be a Loyalist without being a United Empire Loyalist." You cannot get into the organization unless your ancestors were United Empire Loyalists.

Highway 33 from Adolphustown to Kingston is never very far from the St. Lawrence. Old farms are on either side of the road, many of them with their yards facing on the river. At the gap between Amherst Island and the eastern tip of Prince Edward County is the place where on November 9, 1812, the British corvette *Royal George*, chased by an American fleet of seven ships, escaped into the Bay of Quinte's north channel. She was later pursued into Kingston harbour but, with the aid of the batteries that lined the shore, fought off the Yankees.

The remains of those shore batteries still sit on Kingston's waterfront, rescued and converted into shore parks from the railway and old warehouses that for years hid the lake. In fact a trip along Kingston's waterfront tells a lot of history for anyone looking for it.

First of all there is the old town hall, which was designed in 1843 by architect George Browne "in keeping with Kingston's status as a provincial capital" (1841-44). A plaque describes it as "one of the most ambitious examples of 19th century municipal architecture." The big solid building made of blocks of local limestone originally housed—besides the municipal offices—various shops, the Kingston market, and a saloon. The saloon is no longer there, but the market is, and each morning in the summer farmers fetch in truckloads of garden-fresh fruits and vegetables to sell in the market square behind the municipal building. The structure, including the graceful front portico, was restored in 1967 as a Centennial project, and there it stands facing the lake and new Confederation Park and the modern marina.

The time to see a city is early on a summer morning. It is cooler then, and the tourists are not yet abroad. The people you see are those who work in the city or, like yourself, prefer to walk when the streets are not crowded. On this warm August morning I walked up King Street past fine old limestone buildings with their red- or green- or yellow-trimmed windows. (A local historian claimed that Kingston has retained so many old buildings because it could not afford to tear them down for new ones.) At the entrance to Macdonald Park, flanked by two ancient cannons (cannons are everywhere in Kingston), stands a statue of the city's most famous citizen, Sir John A. himself, looking wise and cunning as usual.

There is a plaque in the park telling how the Sieur de la Salle in July of 1673 assembled the Iroquois to hold council here with Governor Frontenac, following the contruction of Fort Frontenac, as Kingston was then called. La Salle was placed in command and granted the seigneury of Cataraqui. He set out from there for his voyage to the mouth of the Mississippi and never returned.

Sitting on a bench in the park was a small, thin elderly gentleman in a neat cardigan sweater and grey tweed cap. He had a little black Manchester terrier named Tiny who was ten years old and who sat up on the bench beside him and listened to our conversation. The old man said that his grandfather had come from Ireland during the potato famine. "He was six months coming over . . . they were blown off their course and went everywhere." He had been born at Kingston Mills, a few miles north of the city where the Cataraqui River joins the Rideau Canal. His father, he said, had worked at the locks for many years. There were mostly freight barges and coal boats on the Rideau Canal then, but some passenger boats. "The *Rideau King* and the *Rideau Queen*. One coming and one going, you see. They left here in the morning and they'd be in Ottawa next morning."

I left the old man and the park and walked farther along King Street to another park, this one on the lake. In the park is Murney Tower, a round structure made of limestone blocks with a deep

moat around it, but the moat is now empty of water. A plaque said
that it was a martello tower, one of four erected in 1846-7 at the
time of the Oregon crisis to defend the city dockyard and the
entrance to the Rideau Canal.

From the number of old cannons, battlements, and towers along
the waterfront, it is obvious that the people of Kingston stood on
constant guard against the United States just across the water. On
a point of land east of the city stands the great limestone fortress
of Fort Henry, built in 1813 "as a bulwark against American
aggression."

Fort Henry must have acted as a great deterrent to the Americans
ever ready to spring on their smaller neighbour, for the guns of the
fort never fired a shot in anger. A brochure contends that all the
guns faced the wrong way, as a matter of fact, and the designer of
the fort committed suicide on his way back to the mother country;
but local historians say that this is a lot of rubbish.

Brochures also tell of famous regiments of the line that were
stationed there between 1813 and 1870; of gay dances in the officers'
quarters, and white muslin gowns of ladies fluttering on tennis
courts; of rebels hanged there; of Royal Visits; and of the impris-
onment in the fort of German sympathizers during the Second
World War.

The fort was restored in 1936 as a tourist attraction, and since
then hundreds of thousands of curious visitors have filed through
the place, gazing at the splendour of the officers' quarters and the
stocks where prisoners sat and the old dungeons and storage rooms
and cannons that stand guard on the walls. A guard of university
students dressed in red coats and funny hats and carrying muskets
regularly stages gun drills of marching and shouting and shooting
as a reminder of those early days.

Kingston is still the most military of all Ontario cities. Across
Navy Bay from old Fort Henry is the Royal Military College, where
young men can obtain their university degrees while learning to be
officers in the Canadian Armed Forces. Also, the Royal Canadian
School of Signals and the Royal Canadian School of Electrical and
Mechanical Engineers, the Naval Defence College, and the Canadian Army Staff College, are all in or near Kingston.

Being really more interested in the pursuits of peace than of war,
I walked farther along King Street to Queen's University. Here the
great grey limestone buildings, set among fine green lawns with

immense maples and oaks, look out over Kingston harbour. This is a university that feels like a university. It makes you think of the great institutions of learning in Europe. I decided to find out something about it.

Queen's is patterned after the University of Edinburgh, and was established through Royal Charter in the year 1841 by the Presbyterian Church, largely because their young people would rather not attend the Anglican colleges already established. And the early football teams were called, of all things, the Presbyterians. ("Come on, you Presbyterians! Kill them!")

Since then, of course, Queen's, like other universities, has become largely non-denominational and is supported by government funds.

Queen's is the only university in Canada to have a rector, who is a sort of students' representative chosen by the students, on the Board of Trustees. The most famous of all their rectors and one of the most appreciated was the late Leonard Brockington.

A couple of stories reveal something of the spirit of the student body. In 1956 for instance, a group of them invaded Watertown, New York, in the dead of night and took down all the American flags from public buildings and replaced them with Union Jacks. The Watertown students retaliated by storming old Fort Henry.

On another occasion a group of students became incensed at the American foreign secretary, John Foster Dulles, who owned an island off Kingston on the Canadian side of the international boundary. According to the legend, he used to shoot deer and ducks there out of season. The students sent him a strong letter telling him that if he was going to live on Canadian soil, he had better obey Canadian game laws. They received no reply, of course, and so once again in the dead of night they stormed his stronghold and painted his boathouse a garish colour. Thus do the students of Queen's keep alive the spirit of 1812.

After leaving the university, I walked down to Centre Street where there is a house that Sir John A. Macdonald rented for a year and which has been made into a museum.

It is a big, three-storey, white stucco house sitting in an immense yard full of trees. Macdonald was a successful young lawyer when he lived there. At the age of 33, he had already been a minister of the Crown and was the leading light of the Conservative Party, then in a bad way. His wife, Isabella, was an invalid, and the room in which she spent most of her time is there, fitted out as a bed-sitting room with a note that tells that the young lawyer occasionally took his meals in there with her. And it was while he lived there that his infant son, John Alexander, died.

A house of sorrow; but also the house of an energetic, indomitable young man who would let nothing stand in the way of his ambitions and his strong devotion to the British way.

From Macdonald's house I went on to visit the bastion of British justice, the Kingston Penitentiary. In this great ugly heap of stone, Ontario people have been shutting up their lawbreakers since June 1, 1835. In 1850 a prison commission made a thorough investigation and reported that the warden, one Henry Smith, charged Kingston people admission to watch prisoners being tortured by the lash, the chain, the Oregon boot, the water hose, and the sweat box.

Not only that, but this worthy warden permitted his sons, one of whom later became a member of the provincial legislature, to chase prisoners about the prison yard shooting at them with a bow and arrow. At the same time, Smith swindled everybody he dealt with, and made a fortune out of short-rationing his prisoners. When finally brought to task by the prison physician, James Sampson (who later became the first Dean of Medicine at Queen's and still later Mayor of Kingston), and the redoubtable George Brown of the Toronto *Globe,* Henry Smith was defended by no less a figure than John A. Macdonald.

The St. Lawrence River begins at Kingston, where it is 245 feet above sea level, and about ten miles wide. For the first 40 miles of its north-easterly course it is a wide, tranquil stream with scarcely any current and containing no less than 1,768 islands.

The "Thousand Islands," as they are called, are part of the Frontenac Axis, a ridge of precambrian rock that stretches down into New York State. Some of the islands are pink granite with the usual pine, birch, and poplar growing on them; others are of lime-stone covered with a greater depth of soil. Some are big enough to contain farms, others so small that one tiny building covers them. Altogether they form eastern Ontario's oldest playground for the rich, and a major tourist attraction. Since the Thousand Islands first became popular around the turn of the century, they have lost little of their grandeur and beauty.

The shore downstream from Kingston is covered with marinas, motels, and tourist homes, while young men stand by the side of the road near Gananoque, selling tickets for Thousand Island cruises.

And cruising the river is, of course, the best way to see the islands.

The boats go along narrow channels between the rocky shores, while the guide gives details about the most interesting of the islands. Here is Heart Island, with the great, square limestone Bolt Castle standing on it. Begun in 1898, it was never completed; the builder's wife died in 1902, and in his grief and despair millionaire George Bolt decided that it never would be finished. You can even walk through some of the forlorn, debris-filled rooms and tunnels if you have a mind. Bolt's personal chef, Oscar of the Waldorf-Astoria, concocted the Thousand Island salad dressing in honour of this area.

And there is the Island of St. Helena, with a structure resembling Napoleon's tomb on it, and a house built in the shape of the emperor's hat. And there, the shortest international bridge in Canada; it stretches over the Canada-U.S.A. boundary between the two Zavikon Islands. And the houses of Kate Smith, Irving Berlin, Arthur Godfrey—the Thousand Islands are almost as good as Beverly Hills for gawking at the splendour of the great.

Near the American shore of the river you can see great ocean freighters from Greece or Britain, France or Germany, or a score of other countries, ploughing quietly along upriver through the St. Lawrence Seaway channel, their pilots taking it easy after passing the last of the locks at the town of Iroquois.

There are camp grounds on the islands and, since many a tourist has a boat along behind him, they are well used. Unfortunately, there is no car ferry, so that an ordinary traveller cannot cover this stretch of his trip downriver.

I came to the town of Prescott, which is not big, but it is lively. That Prescott wants you to stay for a while is obvious. They have an immense sign across the street to welcome you, and at the tourist booth they give you a map of the town with a history tour marked on it. The tour took me through restored old Fort Wellington with its guns pointing straight at Ogdensburg across the river, past the house on Dibble Street where writer Bruce Hutchison was born, and past a lot of other stone and brick houses of the earliest settlers. For a small town, Prescott knows well how to put its best foot forward. The river towns, after a long slump, are staging a comeback.

Prescott is where the rough water of the St. Lawrence begins, a prelude to the fierce International Rapids section that made navigation on the river a horror until the Seaway was built. Thus Prescott became a "forwarding centre," where lake steamers were unloaded of passengers or freight, and the loads were carried through the rapids by Durham boat or other smaller vessels, while bateaux were pulled by plodding horses through the narrow canals built along the bank. Even grain was trans-shipped from Prescott.

Just east of Prescott, on a lonely limestone cliff overlooking the turbulent river and Ogdensburg on the further bank, is a tall, whitewashed stone tower about 60 feet high with square red windows. It was originally a windmill and then a lighthouse and now is an historical monument. Here, on November 13-15, 1838, an heroic battle was fought.

A young hothead named Nils Shojtewsk Von Schoultz, who posed as a Polish revolutionary (later research has thrown doubt on this claim), organized a group of adventuresome Americans, Canadian leftovers from the recent rebellion, and Poles, for an attack on Canada.

A huge plaque on the site says:

After the rebellion of 1837 in Upper Canada, some rebels sought refuge in the United States where their tales of oppression by the Family Compact and the monarchial system found a sympathetic audience. Firmly convinced of the virtues of republican democracy, many Americans banded together in the Hunters' Lodges whose purpose was to help the Canadian 'patriots' liberate their homeland. In November 1838 a band of 'patriots' and American sympathizers ... mostly the latter ... crossed from Sackett's Harbour to attack Prescott.

On Monday, November 12, the 150 invaders landed at Windmill Point and without any trouble took possession of the windmill and the surrounding stone buildings.

But the next night a force of British regulars from Fort Wellington, together with Canadian militia from the surrounding counties, was collected, and moved on the windmill. At the same time two armed steamers, the *Experiment* and the *Queen Victoria*, opened fire from the river. But even with all this power they could not dislodge the invaders, and in an exchange of fire many of the British were killed.

For the next two days fighting ceased while both sides tended their casualties under a flag of truce. Meanwhile, the besiegers waited the arrival of heavy artillery from Kingston. When the guns arrived, the British opened fire on the windmill and other buildings. After a bombardment of one and a half hours that cost them several casualties, the invaders were forced to surrender.

Subsequently, the repentant Von Schoultz was tried in Kingston and defended by John A. Macdonald, then a rising young lawyer. The trial helped to build the future Prime Minister's reputation for sound legal principles and ability, although he lost the case and Von Schoultz was hanged.

On another occasion my wife and I drove from Prescott, which is the beginning of the St. Lawrence Park System, to Iroquois, where we watched the big ships ease their way downriver through the first of the Seaway locks into Lake St. Lawrence. Iroquois has a bright new look with well-paved streets and flat green lawns and new buildings; even the old buildings look new. This is because many of them were moved from the river bank by the Ontario Hydro when their locations were to be flooded by the new lake. The buildings were picked up and transported, we were told, with such skill and care that the owners did not even have to remove dishes from cupboards.

A sign on the highway at the entrance to Iroquois advertises it as "The Best Dam Town On The Seaway."

The whole St. Lawrence Park area is a good example of what government can do when it really wants to and is able to acquire the necessary land. Determined to help this somewhat depressed area and at the same time provide unusual recreational facilities, the Government of Ontario has spent a great deal of money on parks along this section of the St. Lawrence.

Altogether in the park system, from Adolphustown to Glengarry, there are 18 recreational areas, 18 public campsites, 16 sandy beaches, 11 picnic grounds, an airport for light planes so that visitors from afar can drop in as they please, an excellent 18-hole golf course, a marina where international water-ski events are held, a riding stable, a migratory bird sanctuary, and, most spectacular of all, Upper Canada Village.

When we drove up to the marina along a road winding between clipped green grass and trees and ponds, about a couple of hundred Canada geese were strolling about, stretching their necks, riding majestically on the water, and nibbling away at the fresh clover. Tourists were busy taking pictures, kneeling within a few feet of the birds. The geese seem to know they are protected, for they have come from the sanctuary where during migration times thousands are fed daily.

Next to the marina, the main park, which is near the site of the Battle of Crysler's Farm, contains a monument to the men who fought and died there, and a museum where regularly this historic battle is recreated with a stirring sound-and-light presentation. Tourists, many of them Americans, sit in comfortable seats in front of a huge mural depicting the battle. Then, as lights flash and men shout and yell, comes the Canadian version of the actual fighting. On Thursday, November 11, 1813, a force of almost four thousand crack American troops was stopped and defeated by 800 "disciplined" British troops. It was a hard-fought, bloody battle, which CBC actors re-enact on tape, describing how the "thin red line" held and turned back the Americans. As a result, the whole American campaign aimed at the siege of Montreal was abandoned, and the invaders went home, shaking their heads at the stupidity of Canadians who eschewed glorious republicanism and fought like fiends for a "tyrannical" monarch.

It is a good show, with enough anti-Americanism to satisfy the most rabid patriot, and enough glorification of war to send the red blood coursing through the veins.

We then went next door into Upper Canada Village. Here, in an area comprising many acres, is gathered together a satisfying display of pioneer life. All the old tools, furnishings, vehicles, factories, shops, fences, boats, mills, machinery, costumes, houses, barns, and utensils of almost two hundred years ago are assembled here. It does not pretend to be a facsimile of any actual town. Rather, the buildings have been selected from various sites along the river and moved here for display. A one-room, log schoolhouse has been brought from Glengarry, for instance; Ralph Connor later wrote about his experiences in just such surroundings in *Glengarry School Days*.

I liked best the old water-powered sawmill which has been moved from Grenville County; it works away making lumber that is used in the village. The sawyer, a short, leathery-faced man dressed in homemade trousers and a coarse linen shirt (made from flax grown, retted, spun, woven, and sewn in the village), explained how the old "muley saw" worked. Then he pulled a long lever that opened the sluice gates; the water came in to move the eight-foot long saw up and down so that it chewed its way along an immense white pine log that was inched forward on a carriage pulled by a logging chain using the same water power. Up and down went the saw at about the same rate that two men would move it; slowly the log inched forward, until a plank an inch thick and 12 inches wide had been taken from the side of it.

Nothing is used in the operation but the tools, materials, and methods that were common 130 years ago. Grease for the saw and gears comes from the fat of pigs butchered in the village. Water power comes from a mill pond, which also provides power for the textile mill next door. We stood beside the labouring saw with thoughtful expressions, seeing, smelling, hearing, and, if we had reached out, feeling, how it was then. For just a moment we were living exactly as our great-grandfathers had lived.

The blacksmith shop is the same: the glowing forge, the anvil; the sturdy smith (recruited from England) pumping the bellows, turning the iron in the fire, and pounding the white hot iron to shape it. So it is with the quilt-making, weaving, spinning, cheese-making, and corn-husking. And when our feet were killing us, there was a 40-foot long, 12-foot wide bateau to carry us along the canal with the old horse pulling it along the bank, and a helmsman in a red toque telling us about the uses of this handy river craft.

The river here, between the Iroquois dam and the great power dam at Cornwall, has been transformed from wild rapids into tranquil Lake St. Lawrence. The Long Sault Rapids, once the despair of rivermen, are no more. Five years (1954-9) and $1,060 million were needed for this major change to the river and the building of power stations. All of the town of Iroquois was moved and much of the town of Morrisburg. Seven small riverbank communities disappeared altogether, and two new ones, Ingleside and Long Sault, were created. Old roads were flooded out of existence and new ones were built. Twenty-two locks that once lifted small craft up the river through canals on the Canadian side gave way to seven big locks, two of which are on the American side.

As a result of all this, a great inland seaway was created, capable of carrying ocean-going ships to Great Lakes ports; a marvelous recreational area was born; and Ontario Hydro got close to a million new kilowatts of electricity from the Robert H. Saunders generating stations at the Cornwall dam.

Cornwall has greatly benefited from the new power developments, with immense pulp and paper mills, chemical plants, and textile plants. It has the look and feel, and especially the smell, of a busy industrial centre. We crossed the International Bridge at Cornwall to Cornwall Island, where we visited the world's only lacrosse stick factory, in the Mohawk Indian Reserve. A little way on we came to the Snell Lock, where we were lucky enough to see a huge laker being lifted 47 feet into Lake St. Francis. Farther up stream it was lifted another 42 feet by the Dwight D. Eisenhower Lock into Lake St. Lawrence, a total lift of 89 feet from below Cornwall to above it.

After Cornwall, the St. Lawrence River becomes itself once more, as it was when the first explorers sailed up it 400 years ago. The road runs close to the river again and, as we drove along through an early morning mist, we could just barely make out fishermen among the reeds and, beyond them, the grey outlines of an immense ore carrier steaming upstream towards the Snell Lock.

At last I began to get the feel of this great river and its place in all our lives: always there, always pouring its immense volume of water into the gulf. A people's river, a trade river, a romantic river. A river which once frustrated navigators with its rapids and cataracts now provides easy access to the heart of a continent.

We sat on a wharf in the small town of Lancaster and watched three men and a boy fishing for pike in Lake St. Francis. No fuss, no fancy equipment. They sat on the dock eating sandwiches and plums while the boy, as 12-year-olds will, assessed their chances of getting a good catch.

Then one man got a strike, and the others gathered around with nets and advice. "Keep the line tight! That's it. He's a big one. Here . . . my net is bigger."

Then the disappointed cry went up, "Eel!" They pulled the long, snake-like fish close enough to cut the line and let it swim away. "It'll die anyway, with that hook in its mouth."

"Third one this morning," the boy said. "Maybe we've got them all." Then an afterthought. "Maybe this is an eel day. Like at the baseball games they have Ladies' Day . . . maybe this is Eel Day."

Highway 34 leads north from Lancaster into the heart of Glengarry County. We had to follow the road. We just could not leave this area without at least a look at the Ralph Connor country. Those great Scots he wrote about, were they really so great? Being of Irish descent, I had always rather resented them. Well, now I would see.

I am glad we took that trip because we encountered a most fascinating family.

On the road, I am an inveterate historical site visitor. One of those shield-shaped brown signs can bring me to a halt as a railway barrier would. As we followed the highway through the pleasant

Ottawa-Valley-type country with good farms on either side, so flat that most of the land must be underdrained with tile, we came upon a plaque. John Sandfield Macdonald's birthplace, it said, and for a moment I did not know who he was. Ah yes, Ontario's forgotten politician, first premier of the province—no relation to Sir John A. of the same last name. I had to follow that sign.

It took us along a road that led west to the tiny village of St. Raphael, consisting of a tiny store and post office, a couple of houses, and beyond that a big, handsome, limestone Catholic church. Presbyterians?

The plaque in front of the church read:

The Glengarry Immigration of 1786. Early in September of 1786, a group of some 500 Scottish highlanders, the majority of whom were Macdonells, arrived at Quebec. They were led by their parish priest from Knoydart, Glengarry, the Reverend Alexander Macdonell (Scotus). Forced to emigrate because of the depressed economic conditions of the highlands, they had been encouraged to come to Canada and settle among their fellow countrymen in what is now Glengarry County. Despite initial hardships, most of these Scottish pioneers settled successfully in this region where their loyalty and military prowess were frequently demonstrated. Father Macdonell founded the parish of St. Raphael, one of the province's earliest Roman Catholic congregations.

Aha. So there were two groups of Scots in Glengarry: the Loyalist Scots, mostly Protestant, and the Knoydart Scots, Catholic, and maybe a lot more since.

We drove on and came to the plaque we were seeking. It was at the entrance to a long lane, at the other end of which stood a neat, insul-brick farmhouse. This, the plaque said, was where John Sandfield Macdonald was born in the year 1812. The daughter of the house answered the door. The family living there was French and had been there for 21 years and, yes, they did have quite a number of curious callers knocking at their door.

Then we really struck it rich. At the post office we got a line on Willa Macdonald, who put me in touch with Mrs. Alec Maclaren who lives in Alexandria, and who is the granddaughter of Donald Alexander Macdonald, brother of John Sandfield Macdonald.

Alexandria is just about in the centre of Glengarry County, and in the centre of Alexandria on a small square we found the

Maclarens living in a very old house beside a very old mill. So we sat on the wide veranda overlooking the square and sipped lemonade and talked to Alec, a smiling, humourous, story-telling Maclaren, and his wife Hilda.

Hilda Maclaren, gracious and friendly, told us that, yes, this was the house where she had been born and grew up and where her father before her had been born. Her grandfather, Donald Alexander Macdonald (hereinafter referred to as D.A.), was a minister in Sir Wilfrid Laurier's government, and Sir Wilfrid used to have lunch there whenever he passed that way. Later D.A. became the Lieutenant-Governor of Ontario, and Hilda took us into the beautiful old living-room to show us his uniform, sword and cocked hat, that was kept in a metal box under a sofa.

"We had great times in this room," she said. "There were eleven of us, seven boys and four girls. The dances we had! Of course the house was much bigger then. All the back part's been torn down; and there were many acres along the Garry River here. This house is called Garry Fen. Fen means "home." The priest, Father Macdonell, helped D.A. get his education. He said he could tell the boy would amount to something by the shape of his head."

What about D.A.'s brother, John Sandfield? "No, he never lived in this house. He went away to school in Cornwall. That's where he's buried." And so the life of Ontario's first premier remained a mystery, at least to us.

As for Glengarry County, it was as friendly a place as we would want to find. In the restaurant beside the old mill a man sat down and told us stories of the Macdonalds. At one time there were 500 of that name getting their mail from the post office, and the postmaster insisted some of them spell it differently to make his job just a little less bewildering. They are further identified by nicknames according to physical attributes, occupations, hobbies, and the like. There was Foghorn Macdonald, for instance, and Piper Macdonald, Black Macdonald, and Scholar Macdonald, to name a few. I asked him his name, and he said, "Macdonald." He had three more Macdonalds working for him in the restaurant.

And so we left Alexandria, but first I must pass on a story that we heard. It is the kind of story that crops up in many Ontario towns, always with a local flavour. It seems an Alexandrian named Fobby Macdonald for the first time in his life went down to the "Front"—that's what they call Cornwall—where there is a hotel called the King George. (The story works just as well with names like the Lord Elgin, or the Duke of Connaught, or the Prince of Wales, or any hotel named after a famous man.) Anyway, when Fobby got off the train and was gaping bewilderedly about him, a taxi drove up and the driver enquired, "King George?"

Fobby shook his head. "Oh no . . . Fobby Macdonald."

CHAPTER IX

Up the Ottawa River

The Ottawa River is the oldest transportation route into the interior of Ontario. Algonquin Indians, and Hurons too, brought their canoe-loads of furs by this route to trade at Montreal. They carried their loads on their backs on long portages past the Long Sault and other rapids, and their moccasins wore a hard trail, traces of which can still be found. Champlain entered Ontario via the Ottawa. For 200 years fur traders used the river as the first leg of their trip to western Canada. Today the Trans-Canada Highway runs along the bank, taking tourists westward. The Ottawa and its valley have been an integral part of Canada since the beginning.

Some geography. After the last great glacier finally melted away from Ontario about eleven thousand years ago, the land along the Ottawa was depressed by the weight of the ice and flooded by an arm of the sea which geologists call the Champlain Sea.

For hundreds of years the rivers and streams flowed into the sea, bringing with them good clay soil that gradually built up on the bottom. When the sea had finally gone and the land had lifted up again, this good soil remained, covering the rocks and providing flat land for farming. Thus the Ottawa Valley stretches like a long finger deep into the Canadian Shield.

The Ottawa River has its source in a chain of lakes in the Laurentian Highlands, drains into Lake Timiskaming, and then runs southeast to join the St. Lawrence River. The total length is about seven hundred miles. The river is actually a series of long, narrow lakes, some natural and some man-made by dams, joined together by narrow channels. The total drop from the Mattawa River to the St. Lawrence is 500 feet in a series of rapids, but there are no high waterfalls. There are many islands in the river and innumerable secondary channels around them. From Lake Timiskaming east, the Ottawa forms the boundary between Ontario and Quebec.

The first settler to come up the Ottawa was an enterprising Yankee named Philemon Wright. He explored the river and saw its possibilities. In the winter of 1800, together with his wife Abigail, Wright brought five families up the river and settled them near where the Gatineau River runs into the Ottawa from the north. He called his town Wrightstown, and later Hull, after the birthplace of his parents in England. Mrs. Wright decided that the beautiful waterfall on the south side of the river looked like a curtain, and so she named it the Rideau, the French word for curtain.

As I said, Wright was an enterprising man. He built grist mills and sawmills, using the rivers for power, and he brought in more settlers. But farming was slow, tedious work, and Wright conceived another and quicker way to get rich. All about him, and as far back from the south bank of the river as anyone could see, were great stands of white pines, tall trees stretching up straight as a ruler. There was a great demand for white pine in Europe, Wright knew, but the problem was how to get the pine from the Ottawa River to where it was needed.

The answer was obvious. Since Biblical times men have been floating logs in streams, lakes, and oceans. Why not float them down the Ottawa? There were several bad spots, it was true, but maybe chutes could be built to carry the log rafts past them. It was worth a try. So he cut the logs, squared them, tied them together into rafts with logging chains and, in the year 1807, took his first raft down the river. From then on Wright's prime interest in the area was in timber, and the great logging days of the Ottawa began.

In 1809 Ira Honeywell settled on the south side of the river, somewhere between the Chaudière Falls and Lake Deschênes, and later Braddish Billings established a farm on the Rideau where Billings Bridge is. Other settlers followed, many of them retired soldiers, and one of them, Nicholas Sparks, established a farm in what is now the centre of Ottawa where the new National Arts Centre and the Sparks Street Mall are.

It was not until 1826, however, that much building was done on the south side, when it was decided that the St. Lawrence was too dangerous for settlers coming into Ontario. An alternate route was needed. So the British government undertook to build a ship canal from the Ottawa River up the Rideau River, and overland through a chain of rivers, lakes, and canals to Kingston. The canal was completed by Colonel By and his men in 1832.

Great romantic stories are told of the shanty Irish, the Scots, the French, and assorted others who worked on the canal and made Bytown (now Ottawa) their headquarters. Most of the pick and shovel men on the canal were Irishmen, while most of the lumbermen were Scots and French. Regardless of how they made their money, they mostly agreed on how to spend it—on booze in the taverns of Bytown. Words would be passed about French peasoupers and Irish bogtrotters, and fists would begin to fly. Many a man woke up in the jailhouse next morning, dead broke with nothing to show for it but a broken head, broken teeth, and a devastating hangover. Bytown acquired a reputation as the roughest town in the country.

As the trees were cut down, settlers moved in to clear away stumps and farm the land. Mostly they worked the land in the summer and cut trees in the bush during the winter. They were the steadier, more reliable types and, as colonisation roads were built, towns grew up to supply the settlers who were using them.

To get the feel of the river and the smell of it and the sense of past adventure that lingers over it, we left the highway and took the river road. Since there are places where no road of any kind runs along the river, it is necessary to drive down to the water.

This first stretch of river, from the Quebec border to Hawkesbury, is loaded with history. The river here is narrow and swift and deep, and between Hawkesbury and Carillon drops 60 feet, causing the famous Long Sault Rapids, the Chute à Blondeau Rapids, and the Carillon Rapids. But these rapids are gone now and so are the portages along the bank, covered by the waters of a lake held back by the power dam at Carillon.

This was the worst part of the river in fur trading times, for here the Indians and the *coureurs de bois* had to carry their big canoes and packs of furs over three long portages. And it was at this vulnerable spot that the Iroquois often lay in wait for them, killed the canoemen, and made off with the furs.

It was here, too, as every schoolboy should know, that Adam Dollard and 16 gallant Frenchmen, with the help of 4 Algonquins and 40 Hurons, fought a force of more than three hundred Iroquois and, protected by only a flimsy log palisade, held them off for over a week. The exact location of the encounter is just below the present town of Hawkesbury, Ontario, where the determined stand of the Frenchmen so impressed the Iroquois that they abandoned their plans for a full-scale attack on the little settlement of Montreal.

Canals were built around these rapids at the time of the building of the Rideau Canal, and were used by settlers and lumbermen whose only means of access to the Ottawa Valley was by way of the river.

Within the capital, the Ottawa River runs true to form. Leaving Lake Deschênes at the west side of the city, it roars through a narrow gap and tumbles over the Deschênes Rapids. Farther downstream it runs over the Remic Rapids, then the Chaudière Rapids, and at the Chaudière Bridge the famous Chaudière Falls. The French word *chaudière* means "boiler" and was so named because spray and mist caused by the falls resembled a boiling pot. From there on the river is reasonably peaceful with two large islands, Kettle and Duck, forming green parks.

Everything about this river in the city is a reminder of the past. We watched a log boom being towed to Eddy's pulp and paper mills, whose conglomeration of buildings and great piles of logs has for years completely dominated the river across from the parliament buildings.

Ezra Butler Eddy was one of the great "lumber kings" in the days when large fortunes were made from the forest along the river. He arrived in Hull in 1851, when the city was still predominantly English and Philemon Wright's heirs were the great lumber powers.

Young Eddy, already married at the age of 24, had $100 in his pocket and the formula for making matches. In rented rooms he and his wife set about dipping hand-cut splinters of wood into a mixture of phosphorus and sulphur. By working long hours they could make up to five hundred matches in a day, which Eddy would peddle himself to local dealers in Hull and Ottawa, and ship by boat to towns and cities as far away as Hamilton.

They were very fine, those first matches that Eddy made, striking almost every time you scratched them. They had one slight defect; when children sucked the mixture from the end, as they often did, they were likely to die of phosphorus poisoning. Eddy took care of this by inventing an even better match which would not actually poison anybody and which had no after-glow.

But Eddy had much more going for him than determination and energy and a devotion to hard work; he was a financial genius. Ploughing all his profits back into the firm, he quickly branched out into the lumber business, acquiring the rights to thousands of acres of timber and producing a variety of wood products.

A firm non-believer in insurance, Eddy twice lost his factory to fire, once in 1882, and again when most of Hull and much of Ottawa burned down in 1900. Each time he went to the bank and borrowed the money to rebuild, and went ahead harder and faster than ever.

These were the days before unions, and Eddy got along by paying his workers a dollar a day. If they complained, he fired them. Despite that, his workers were so loyal that they once barricaded the plant against a bailiff and drove the rascal off with revolver fire.

By the time of his death, Eddy had amassed a fortune in the wood and pulp and paper business of an estimated $100 million which he left to his second wife, who, in turn, left most of it to the Calgary lawyer R.B. Bennett, who for a while was Prime Minister of Canada.

Another great lumber tycoon of the era was John Rudolphus Booth, who was born the same year as Eddy and came to Bytown one year later. He even matched Eddy for humble beginnings by first painstakingly splitting shingles by hand in his back yard. By incredible hard work and devotion to making and saving money, he soon had a mill of his own and was on his way to owning or controlling a goodly share of the Ottawa Valley. It was Booth who supplied the lumber for the first parliament buildings; it was Booth who purchased from John Egan the Madawaska lumber limits for $45,000, who built the Ottawa–Arnprior–Parry Sound Railway, and who is still a legend throughout the entire upper Ottawa Valley.

We found that the most satisfying way to see Ottawa is to walk, because many of the best sights are within easy walking distance of the parliament buildings. This part of the city alone had enough to keep us busy for a week. We did the best we could in a couple of days.

The parliament buildings, for instance, standing on a limestone cliff overlooking the Ottawa River, are far more majestic than any picture can show. We joined the throng of tourists that filled the street and covered the lawns to watch the changing of the guard. A marching band followed by soldiers in kilts swung along Wellington Street, turned the corner, and marched down Rideau Street.

But we were more interested in the parliament buildings themselves, where our laws are made and remade. A guide explained that the first parliament building was built in 1865 and on the bitterly cold night of February 3, 1916, it caught fire and burned to the ground. "The big bell up in the tower struck midnight and then crashed through to the basement. You can see if it you want, out behind the library."

Then he showed us the Commons chamber and pointed out where the Speaker sits, and the Prime Minister and his cabinet in the front benches on the government side, and the leader of the opposition and his top men across the aisle from him in the front benches of the other side. Everybody was away right then, trying to persuade voters to send them back to fill those seats again. But just seeing the place where our law-makers work gave me a different impression from listening to or reading the abuse and ridicule which are constantly heaped on them by the media.

Then the guide showed us where to get the elevator to the top of the Peace Tower, from which we got a magnificent view of Ottawa and Hull and the Laurentian Hills across the river where the highest and the lowliest civil servants join hundreds of others to ski on weekends.

There is no doubt but that the best place to learn about the history of our country is in the location where much of that history has been and will continue to be made. Each year more and more Canadians find their way to Ottawa. The streets are filled with parents and their children enjoying the action where the action is.

There are many unattended young people in Ottawa, too, for each year more and more highschool and university students from both ends of the country hitchhike to the capital. Our son, Colin, and a friend hit the road, and the first word we got was a phone call from Ottawa.

"How do you like it?"

"Cool."

"Where are you staying?"

"Oh, we're staying at Lisgar Collegiate, right near the centre of town . . . yeah. We sleep in the gym, and we can eat here, too, if we want. Doesn't cost us anything at all."

So they, as they say, butted around Ottawa for a few days, using the washrooms and showers of Lisgar Collegiate. It seems that the Ottawa Mayor's Committee on Youth decided that since the young people were going to come to Ottawa anyway, and since they would have no place to stay, it was more hospitable to put them up in decent hostels than to throw them in jail, and it would probably cost them less in the long run.

Beside the parliament buildings are the locks of the Rideau Canal, very much as Thomas Mackay built them. There are eight of them, made of concrete with a total drop of 80 feet. Each is a miniature waterfall. If you stay there long enough, you are sure to see a motor boat of some size going up or down, because close to ten thousand boats use the locks each season.

And beside the locks in a very old limestone building is the Bytown Museum. The building, which was built by Colonel John By's Royal Engineers when the canal was being built, was originally used as his office, treasury, and stores. It was in this building then that the dynamite was stored in casks. Casks that had to be carried over rough trails by men who knew that if they dropped them they would be blown to pieces. And it was from here that the Irish bogtrotters received their few shillings per day for breaking their backs with pick and shovel for 16 hours or more.

Today it is filled with all sorts of military and civilian objects that were used by the people in the surrounding countryside. Old farm implements and furniture and tools and innumerable pictures of times gone by.

On the other side of the locks from the parliament buildings stands the Chateau Laurier, which is certainly one of the most handsome hotels in Canada. So we had a drink in the bar where members of parliament often entertain, and went down to the basement cafeteria where members of parliament eat and discuss business. But we didn't see anyone we recognized.

In front of the locks is the famous Confederation Square and War Memorial, which is often referred to by Ottawans as "confusion square" because of the traffic snarls it causes in the centre of the city.

The canal goes under the street here, and there are beautiful green lawns on either side of the canal with a spiral stairway leading down to them. And on the banks of the canal in the best possible setting are the fine buildings of the National Arts Centre, which was opened in 1969.

The Arts Centre, which stands on six and a half acres in the heart of Ottawa and cost $46.4 million, is just what the capital of Canada has needed all along. The grey, concrete architecture blends perfectly into its surroundings, and there are plenty of open spaces. Montreal architect Fred Lebensold, who designed the buildings, has described it as "Not a series of buildings, but a series of spaces."

Regularly, at least during the tourist season, there are conducted tours through the centre. With about a hundred other people, my wife and I jammed into the foyer of the centre through glass doors on the ground floor facing the canal. Then we waited and waited, until a guide in the form of a beautiful girl with a bull horn in her hand appeared. She instructed us in a strange metallic voice to divide into two groups: "English speaking on the right and French speaking on the left." We lined up with the English speaking.

Then she ordered us to follow her, and we went through some more glass doors into an attractive, deep-carpeted lobby. She told us to stop and to gather around her while she told us about the opera house, which seats 2,300. The farthest seat from the stage is 115 feet away, so that everyone can hear perfectly. Backstage there is more room for a large-scale production than in any other theatre on the continent, except the Metropolitan Opera.

Our feet were beginning to hurt.

"Follow me this way, please," she bellowed at us, and we trooped after her into the theatre. "You may sit down, if you wish," the bull horn announced, and we did, in the comfortable plush seats that are arranged in a semi-circle facing the stage. Then she told us that the theatre will seat 800 and "is very adaptable according to the type of performance being, uh, performed. It has a thrust stage to thrust drama into the heart of the auditorium. Actors can even mingle with the audience, and the audience can on occasion sit right up on the stage beside the actors." This, she explained, "reduces traditional barriers and heightens involvement between performer and patron."

We went into the studio next, which is hexagonal in shape. The guide explained that the studio was "built for tomorrow. An experimental theatrical laboratory where small groups can present their works. The radical design is a challenge to both director and actor."

After the Arts Centre we went to Sparks Street, which has been converted to a mall with attractive booths and fountains and shady resting places along the centre of the street.

But Sparks Street made me a little sad, for I remembered that it was here that on April 7, 1868, a very fine Irish gentleman was murdered. It is all the sadder, perhaps, because there have been so few political assassinations in Canada and this man, Thomas D'Arcy McGee, was one of the more colourful Fathers of Confederation.

Before becoming a member of parliament for a Montreal riding, McGee, who was 42 when he was killed, had worked mostly as a newspaperman in the United States. At one time while back in the old country he had become associated with Irish rebels and had been forced to flee the country disguised as a priest.

But by the time he settled in Canada, McGee had become a staunch British Empire advocate and an impassioned pleader for Canadian unity. And for this he drew the ire of the notorious Fenians, a group of Irish expatriates living in the United States and Canada who hated Britain and made several attempts to conquer Canada. Their abortive attacks on the border were partly responsible for Canadians wanting to join together for reasons of defence. Naturally the Fenians hated McGee.

A poet as well as a journalist and politician, McGee was perhaps the finest speaker of all the members of John A. Macdonald's government working for union. He travelled widely, swaying people with his fine oratory and intense devotion to the cause. In the famous picture of the Fathers of Confederation, he is seated next to his chief, who is standing.

On April 6, 1868, with the federal union still on shaky ground because of Nova Scotia's threat to pull out, McGee made one of his best speeches. Again he was pleading the cause of national unity, and he used all his powers of wit, scholarship, and passion to sway his listeners. There was one man, however, sitting in the gallery who became more angry with every word McGee spoke. When the house adjourned at 2 a.m., this man followed McGee through the muddy streets to his lodgings on Sparks Street. His name was John Whelan, a Fenian who had sworn to kill McGee, and now he was very drunk.

Along with some other members of parliament, McGee lived at the boarding house of a Mrs. Trotter, and as he was often late he carried his own key. At the corner of Metcalfe and Sparks Street, McGee parted from a companion and walked on alone to the door of the Trotter house with Whelan, like an evil shadow, following behind. McGee was in high spirits after his triumph and had just lit a good cigar. As he put his key into the lock, Whelan stepped up behind him, placed the gun against the back of his head, and blew his brains out.

The shot attracted Mrs. Trotter, who thought it was youths with firecrackers. However her son Willie, who was a page in the House of Commons, arrived home shortly after, saw the bloodied figure slumped on the doorstep, and raised the alarm. It was Sir John A. Macdonald himself who helped carry the dead man into the Trotter house.

Thus died D'Arcy McGee, a true martyr to the cause of union. His murderer was soon caught, tried, convicted, and publicly hanged, the last public execution ever to take place in Canada.

We went to see the statue of McGee on Parliament Hill. It is a fine likeness, they say, and at the feet of the great orator, who was only five feet, three inches in height, sits the muse of poetry. It gave me a warm feeling to think of McGee, the one poet among all those stern politicians who founded this country . . . and him an Irishman.

On Sparks Street we learned something of the present and future, too, by visiting the offices of the National Capital Commission, which for many years has had the task of making the National Capital Region something all Canadians can be proud of. There we met the Commission's information officer, who told us that the National Capital Region is twice as big as the whole country of Luxemburg, comprising as it does 1,800 square miles in the provinces of Ontario and Quebec. It is estimated that by 1986 it will have a population of close to a million people.

On the map he showed us the 41,500-acre green belt that surrounds Ottawa on the three sides not bounded by the river, and explained that this will effectively "prevent the terrible urban sprawl that is the bane of so many cities." On the other side of the river, extending right through Hull to the river's edge, is the 88,000-acre Gatineau Park. An excellent road leads right into the heart of this wilderness area, and in no time at all harried civil servants and parliamentarians alike can be out there skiing, hiking, swimming, boating, riding, or doing whatever else their physical conditions and the season permit.

The information officer pointed out, also, that the railway has been removed from the centre of the city, providing an example that has since been followed by many other cities. Where the unsightly railway tracks once blighted the area, the attractive Colonel By Drive now runs beside the Rideau Canal. Along the Ottawa River, old buildings, factories, and dumps have been removed to make green lawns stretching down to the water, and here a four-lane parkway gives an excellent view of the river.

There are, of course, many other places to visit in Ottawa. The National Gallery, for instance (just down the street from the Arts Centre), the National Library, the Royal Canadian Mint, the Museum of Science and Technology, and the Canadian War Museum, to name a few. And if you want to look and not visit, there is the Prime Minister's residence at 24 Sussex Drive, across from it Rideau Hall where the Governor General lives, and the various foreign embassies.

Another time that we went to Ottawa it was early May, and we went just to see the flowers. They are everywhere, crocuses, daffodils and, of course, the tulips. Red tulips, yellow tulips, white tulips, mahogany-coloured tulips, and multi-coloured blooms. The parks, the grounds of the parliament buildings, the green swards along the canal and the river, all have their multitudes of tulips.

Tulips have always been popular in the city, but this great plethora of bloom began in 1946 when Queen Juliana of the Netherlands presented the city with a gift of 100,000 choice Holland bulbs. And every year since then, she has sent over 14,000 more.

Queen Juliana spent the dark days of the war as a refugee in Ottawa when her own country was overrun by the Nazi hordes. She fell in love with the city and has been back many times to visit and see her tulips.

I think the most colourful display is that along the driveway near Dow's Lake. They are arranged in groups of carmine reds, yellows, whites, and pinks, a mass of blooms that attracts camera bugs from far and wide. Without doubt, Ottawa is the tulip capital of Canada.

We left Ottawa by Highway 17, cutting across country instead of following the river which bends sharply northward and southward again to the town of Arnprior, which sits on the bank just where the Madawaska River flows into the Ottawa.

We were in Renfrew County, a farming and lumbering county whose past goes back to the days of the great lumber drives on the Ottawa. In each of the principal towns there was a museum in which we saw the tools and equipment of the great lumber days, pictures and models of camboose camps, and even great pieces of squared white pine that made up the rafts that went down the river.

So the people never forget those great days. Back then, men went into the bush for the entire winter, living in big, square, windowless camboose lodges, eating beans and salt pork and blackstrap molasses and game. Working hard in the bush, chopping at first and later sawing down the huge trees, squaring the big logs with the broad axe, and hauling them with horses to stream or lake or river.

And then in the spring the famous log drives and the making of rafts and the long, long trips down to Quebec City. Then, so the story goes, most of the men, let loose after their long abstinence of the winter and spring, went on one long, glorious extended drunk until their money was all gone.

It is a story told many times and so it will not be repeated here. But you cannot travel along the Ottawa without being infected by it. And the lumber museums and even some old-timers are there to tell you all about it.

The beginnings of the town of Arnprior give some idea of the nature of Scottish immigration. In 1823 a crotchety, dictatorial laird by the name of Archibald MacNab was granted 1,200 acres in the area, and given the task of supervising the settlement of almost an entire township.

But the laird let his enthusiasm run away with him and tried to run the area as a complete oligarchy. He looked upon the settlers as his vassals who owed him absolute fealty and service, and proceeded to treat them as such.

The settlers, on the other hand, many of whom had come to Canada in the first place to escape just such treatment, began to mutter and then to protest loudly. It got them nowhere with the laird. The land was his by rights, he said, and they had better do as he directed.

The laird built himself a great mansion on his place and called it Kinnell Lodge. He also built a mill and a store and a blacksmith shop, and required that all his clansmen should deal only with him. Then he encountered two more Scottish gentlemen by the name of Buchanan, Andrew and George, who were descendants of the Laird of Arnpryor in Scotland. The three lairds got roaring drunk one New Year's Eve and decided then and there to name their settlement after the one in the auld countree.

Things went from bad to worse after that. MacNab not only fought with the settlers, but developed a feud with the Buchanans. The town he had begun did not prosper and, finally, the settlers were able to get rid of MacNab, who left the country and finally died in poverty.

Then there showed up another Scotsman, a good one this time, who bought the water rights to the Madawaska, built a sawmill, hired hundreds of men, and laid out the town in lots, which he sold cheaply or gave away. After that, Arnprior has more or less prospered as a lumbering and manufacturing community.

Farther upstream from Arnprior, on the Bonnechère River which flows into the Ottawa, is the town of Renfrew, famous for its Stanley Cup finalists of 1910, the Renfrew Millionaires. Like Arnprior, Renfrew began as a lumbering town, and the first settlers that stayed there called the community Second Chute. A chute was the wooden slide built beside a waterfall, down which a 24-foot wide section of raft called a "crib" could be slid. Each raft was made up of 100 cribs which could be separated when necessary to get through dicey parts of the river.

But what made Renfrew was the famous old Opeongo Road, which was built to encourage farmers to come and try their luck on the rock soil of the area. The government sent posters to Britain and other countries extolling the beauties of the landscape and the fertility of the soil. They were mainly truthful about the landscape, but not quite so truthful about the shallow soil, as abandoned farmsteads and rocky fields still indicate.

The Opeongo was a corduroy road over the worst spots, and some of that can still be found by the explorer willing to take the time, for the stretch of road between Dacre and Barry's Bay is still used. As a result of the road and the settlers, Renfrew developed as a distribution centre and later, as some of the European artisans gave up on their farms and turned to their trades in town, something of a manufacturing centre. It still is.

Travellers in the upper Ottawa Valley will sometimes stop a farmer on the road to ask directions just to hear him say "It's not very fair down the road, just a wee distance from that fairthest tree. Ye'll make it in no time in a cair such as this one." The Ottawa Valley dialect, a favourite with some comedians, is made up of Gaelic, Polish, Indian, and French which became mixed when the men worked together in the bush. They will talk of a "snye," meaning a narrow channel in the river, and a good guess is that it started out as the French word "chenal." Oiseau Rock has become "Weesa Rock," and the local pronunciation for the Des Joachims Dam is Deswisha.

Farther upriver is the largest town of the upper Ottawa Valley, Pembroke. It is situated on the shore of Allumette Lake, which is where the Ottawa River divides to run around Allumette Island, the largest island in the river.

In Champlain's diary, the great French explorer and coloniser tells how in 1613, with a party of four Frenchmen and an Indian, he paddled up the river to the rapids at Portage du Fort. There they left the Ottawa and travelled overland to the foot of Muskrat Lake, paddled the length of the lake, and then walked along what is now known as the Stoqua Trail to the shore of Lower Allumette Lake.

And of course the same route was used for years by missionaries, traders, and explorers on their way west. They never settled there but, in 1828, Colonel Peter White did, and built a cabin in a clearing. That was the beginning of Pembroke.

During the great lumber raft period Pembroke was a thriving, bustling community. In the local museum we saw an excellent collection of reminders of that time. Today it is still a lumbering town, and most of its industries are connected with wood products of one kind or another.

We crossed a bridge to Allumette Island to visit the "digs" where by painstaking work archeologists have unearthed the remains of a paleolithic Indian culture that goes back to a time thousands of years before the Algonquins lived along the river. These were copper-using people who made fish hooks, spear heads, knives, adzes, and awls from pure copper which was probably brought from Lake Superior locations. Made us feel a bit insignificant to stand there and think of those people who lived there so long before white men came to North America.

We felt even more insignificant at Chalk River, the site of Canada's largest nuclear reactor. It is possible to visit the establishment there, they say, if you make an appointment ahead of time, but we didn't want to go in.

Deep River, so named because the river is very deep at that point, is upriver about eight miles and is the town where the people who work at Chalk River have their homes. It is a relatively new community with good houses, schools, and shopping centres. We picked up a teenaged hitchhiker going to his home there, and he told us that it was the "most organized" town he had ever heard of. "There are about 6,400 people in Deep River and there are 64 different clubs—music clubs, bowling, rowing, tennis, etc.—which makes a club for every 100 people."

Upstream from Deep River, the Ottawa is wider, and the long section beginning at Deux Rivières goes by the name of Holden

Lake. There is a turn in the river at Mattawa, and this is where the *voyageurs* left it to continue west. Highway 17 leaves the river there too, and we followed the highway to North Bay.

Before we got to North Bay, we took a wee jog south on Highway 94 to the site of one of the most bizarre stories in Ontario's history. It is the village of Callander, which was once as internationally known as any city in the world. In a poor farmhouse near Callander, on the evening of May 28, 1934, a plump French-Canadian farm woman, Elzire Dionne, wife of Oliva, who already had several children, gave birth to five girl babies who altogether weighed barely more than ten pounds.

Quintuplets have been born since and have caused no more than a paragraph or two on the back pages of newspapers. What made the Dionne Quintuplets front-page news from New York to Hong Kong was that up to that time in the whole history of the world no five children born at the same time had ever lived more than a few days.

It certainly looked for a while as though the Dionne quintuplets would not live either, but Dr. Allan Roy Dafoe, a general practitioner who served a large community, managed to keep them alive with the help of the now famous "few drops of rum." Then an improvised incubator was provided and a nurse and help from many quarters arrived, and the babies actually lived. Not only that but, because of the hard times, perhaps, and the sorrow in the world, they became symbols of hope and joy and good simple values, and incidentally made millions for themselves and the Ontario government which appointed itself official guardian.

We drove down the neglected road from Callander, where gas pumps were once named Annette, Emilie, Yvonne, Cecile, and Marie, to the tiny farmhouse where the Quints were born and the hospital across the road where they were cared for as babies and toddlers, and the immense home that was later built for the Dionne family. It is difficult to believe that every summer for years this road was packed with tourists from all over North America (some people came many times) who would stand for hours outside the fence waiting for the nurse to come out and hold the babies up to be seen.

Millions came and oh-ed and ah-ed at the sight of the cute little tykes. And they bought souvenirs of all kinds, including "fertility stones" that were supposed to have been picked up on the Dionne farm, but were actually imported. Every move the babies made was front-page news—their first steps, first words, progress as reported by eminent child care specialist Dr. William Blatz, squabbles, preferences and, most especially, their first trip away from Callander when they went to see the King and Queen of the British Commonwealth at the time of the 1939 Royal Tour.

Only the buildings remain now. The Quints have long gone and have tried to forget all this hoopla and nonsense and live normal lives. Only three of them are alive now, Annette, Cecile, and Yvonne, and it is hoped they are finding some peace away from the cruel glare of publicity.

North Bay could be called the dividing point between southern and northern Ontario. Situated on the north shore of Lake Nipissing, it is the southern terminus of the Ontario Northland Railway, and the gateway to the French River summer resort area.

It was along this same French River that the *coureurs de bois* and the *voyageurs* paddled their canoes towards Georgian Bay. The 60-mile stretch of the French River, containing as it does some fifteen rapids, was one of the most hazardous sections of the entire journey. It was always a temptation for the more rambunctious of the canoe-men to run the rapids instead of making the long portages. As a result, many big canoes were overturned and many cargoes lost.

Historians knew this must have been so, but they had no actual proof. There were few diaries left by these busy adventurers, and there was no solid evidence of all this history except for a few hardworn paths along the side of the river.

So it was natural that someone should search the bottom of the river for the artifacts. This was first done by a group led by John Macfie, a conservation officer of the Ontario government. He enlisted the help of two scuba divers, Don Hughson and Jim Sheppard, who on October 17, 1961, made their first search of the bottom of this historic river.

At Double Rapids, 12 miles below Lake Nipissing, the two divers disappeared below water while Macfie and Carman Douglas sat on the bank and waited. Would there be anything there or not? There was. In a surprisingly short time the divers were up and piling stuff on the bank. There were hatchets and axe heads, copper and iron kettles, and the biggest find of all, a flint-lock gun of the *voyageur* period, badly eroded but still a gun. There were many other articles, some of which are now in the Royal Ontario Museum for anyone to see.

The long stretches of the French River look exactly as they did

200 years ago. The forest is little changed, the rocks are still there, and the boiling, rushing rapids still present their challenge. But anyone planning to take up the challenge had better be very handy with a canoe. Some good men have lost their lives in these same waters.

But even the soft tourist in his car can still enjoy this trip along the Ottawa and part of the French, especially if he is willing to get out of the car once in a while and go down to the riverbank and sit and let his imagination range back over the centuries before the days of aircraft or trains or automobiles, or even roads, when the *voyageur* canoe was king.

If his ear is keen enough, he may even hear the rhythmical chant of those squat, powerful men as they dig their paddles into the water.

Trans Canada Highway near Agawa Bay in Lake Superior Provincial Park. Nowhere in Northern Ontario is the road far from water.

Left: Lake of the Woods near Kenora in Northern Ontario rivals Muskoka in beauty.

Right: Good fishing in Northern Ontario. Pike and maskinonge (shown here), lake trout, bass and others are taken with rod and line. Professional guide cooks breakfast.

Top Left: Black spruce logs on the way to a pulp mill in Fort Francis. One of Northern Ontario's principal industries.

Lower Left: Family of wolves in Algonquin Park. Protected and studied, their night choruses provide thrills for nature lovers.

Right: Not all the Bruce Trail is as rugged as this section near the tip of the Bruce Peninsula. Much of its 400 miles is through rolling farm country.

Left: Abandoned hydro plant at Cataract on the Credit River once produced electricity for surrounding communities.

Right: Swans nesting on the Avon River at Stratford, Ontario, with the Shakespearean Festival Theatre in the background. Tourists come to feed the swans and watch the plays.

Top: Ontario farm house with attached driving shed and shops.

Bottom Left: Anxious parents, tough judge, cool calf and handler at fall fair.

Lower Right: Mennonite cook and produce at Kitchener market.

Top: Spacious limestone houses on a shady street in Kingston, Ontario.

Bottom Left: Main street of Port Hope, sixty miles east of Toronto.

Bottom Right: Town house with "gingerbread" trimming in Belfountain on Credit River.

Left: Commerce Court at King and Bay in Toronto. Canada's highest office building in 1974.

Right: Bay Street with rush hour traffic, looking north to Queen Street and old city hall.

Top Left: Carabana parade down University Avenue, Toronto.

Bottom Left: Ferry bound for Toronto Island and Mariposa Music Festival.

Top Right: Hockey is a rough game at Kew Beach in Toronto.

Bottom Right: This is Yonge Street in Toronto? The summer mall with trees and music and outdoor beer gardens.

Skating on the Rideau Canal near Parliament Buildings, Ottawa.

CHAPTER X

Huronia

Whenever I drive north from Toronto through that area northwest of Barrie, I think of the great people who lived and loved and worked there for thousands of years before the white man came. They were the Hurons (or, more properly, Ouendats), and the area between Lake Simcoe and Georgian Bay is known as Huronia. The northern boundary is the Canadian Shield which begins at the Severn River, and the southern boundary is an imaginary line drawn between Collingwood and Barrie.

Before the white man came with his great need for lumber and his metal saws and axes, the entire region was covered with heavy forests of pine and hardwood.

Here the Hurons, who had no metal tools of any kind, hunted and farmed for a living. They were a well-organized nation of 30,000 people who lived in villages surrounded by wooden palisades. Their lives were busy, interesting, and relatively peaceful. At least they were, until the Europeans came and instituted a fierce rivalry between the Hurons and the Iroquois who lived south of Lake Ontario and were farmers of the same linguistic group as the Hurons.

The route we decided to take to Huronia was straight north from the west end of Toronto on Highway 400. The old route is up Yonge

Street and along John Graves Simcoe's old road, now called Highway 11, which goes through the towns of Richmond Hill, Aurora, and Newmarket. This is the route that the early traders, soldiers, and settlers used, and their destination was Holland Landing on the east branch of the Holland River, south of Cook Bay on Lake Simcoe.

Holland Landing is not much today, but in the early 1800s it was a busy shipping point. Goods, military equipment, and people were unloaded from carts, wagons, and coaches; they were placed on shallow draft boats that could navigate the stream and then went across Lake Simcoe and Kempenfelt Bay to the Nine-Mile Portage.

For many years this was a most important portage in Upper Canada, because it was part of the route from Lake Simcoe and all points east and south, including Toronto, to Lake Huron via the Nottawasaga River. Enterprising men dwelt in the area and made their living hauling supplies over the nine-mile-long portage. The rate in 1815 was, we are told, £3, 15 shillings a trip.

Just west of Holland Landing, on the main branch of the river, is the Holland Marsh which now produces many of the vegetables consumed in Toronto and other centres. The marsh is a good example of how something can be made from nothing. For centuries it was a mucky swamp which was in prehistoric times an extension of Lake Simcoe.

It was the home of frogs and snakes and turtles and muskrats and billions of mosquitoes. The only crop to amount to anything in the 1800s was marsh hay that was harvested with horses wearing a special kind of snowshoe so that they would not sink in the muck. The hay was used to stuff mattresses.

Then William Henry Day, one-time professor of physics at the Ontario Agricultural College, became convinced that the swamp could be drained and made into a productive market gardening region. He harvested his first crop in 1920 and proved his point. After that, canals were dug around the entire marsh with smaller connecting canals to drain off the water. What was left was the blackest, flattest, most productive 7,500 acres in southern Ontario. Each time we drive through it we are struck by the straight, straight rows of carrots and onions and celery and lettuce, and the rapidity with which everything grows. The town of Bradford is the marketing centre for the Holland Marsh.

The first railway north of Toronto was built to the town of Barrie in 1853, and later extended, following the same route as the old portage trail to Collingwood.

As a result, the town of Barrie, already a transshipment point, grew and spread itself around the end of Kempenfelt Bay. As more and more settlers and lumbermen came into Huronia, Barrie, the gateway from the south, continued to grow. In 1871, Barrie was incorporated as a town, and today it is a busy manufacturing city, well-known for its hockey teams.

Different people find different qualities which are attractive in a town or city: with members of the board of trade it's the factories and shopping centres; with historians it's statues and plaques; with educationalists it's schools. With me it's libraries. I have always loved libraries. When I was a kid in Saskatoon and summer holidays came along, other kids went to camp, but I went to the library. I carted home armfuls of books and read them and went back for more. I still love libraries, because now they contain my own books, and I like to go in and ask, "Do you happen to have any books by Max Braithwaite?" Usually they do, and usually they recognize me. And library people are such gentle, refined, helpful, literary people who make you feel at home.

Barrie has a great library, on which the town obviously spends some money (you can gauge the worth of a town by the condition of its library). The chief librarian and her assistant spent a good deal of time getting us books about Huronia and advising us on where to go for more information. "Visit all the towns and the museums," they said, and we took their advice.

First, we drove along the northwest shore of Lake Simcoe. This enormous lake, which covers 280 square miles, was described by Stephen Leacock, who spent his boyhood on a farm near the south shore:

> To my way of thinking, nothing will stand comparison with the smiling beauty of the waters, shores and bays of Lake Simcoe and its sister lake, Couchiching. Here the blue of the deeper water rivals that of the Aegean; the sunlight flashes back in lighter colour from the sandbar on the shoals; the passing clouds of summer throw moving shadows as over a ripening field, and the mimic gales that play over the surface send curling caps of foam as white as ever broke under the bow of the Aegean galley.

Some of the many cottagers on Lake Simcoe might question the "mimic gales." Storms on Simcoe are far from mimic, and every boatsman knows that it can be disastrous to get caught on the lake in a sudden storm. The waves can run to eight feet, swamping unwary lake boats.

At the point where Lake Simcoe runs into Lake Couchiching (an Indian word meaning "water squeezed out"), is the town of Orillia, which has been made famous by the writings of Stephen Leacock who lived there in 1912, when it was much smaller than it is now. The town was the model for Mariposa in his wonderful comic novel *Sunshine Sketches of a Little Town.* Although the town is surrounded by thriving new subdivisions, many old buildings are still standing on its main street. And the atmosphere of the Ontario small town still lurks in the old brick and stone structures.

There is a bust of Leacock in the excellent public library, and a collection of his books. There is no statue of Leacock in the town, but there is a magnificent one of Samuel de Champlain, who was the first white man ever to see this area, for he spent a winter with his Huron friends there in 1615. The statue stands in beautiful Couchiching Beach Park amid rolling lawns and great maple trees overlooking the lake. Designed by Vernon March of Farnborough, England, who also designed the Ottawa War Memorial, the statue was erected in 1925 and has been Orillia's pride and joy ever since.

The Stephen Leacock Memorial Home on Old Brewery Bay is a beautiful big white stucco house with a full-length front veranda, surrounded by fine trees and great lawns overlooking the still-quiet waters of the lake where Leacock used to fish. He built the house in 1929, when he was a professor of economics at McGill University and had already become world famous as a writer of very funny pieces and books.

Leacock did much of his writing in this house. You can walk along the spacious front veranda where he used to walk, sit in the leather chair in his office where he used to sit, and visit the large living room where he loved to entertain his friends with parties and stage plays written by himself and acted out by his son Stevie and the neighbours' children.

It is all there, his favourite books, his desk, his letters. And in the back garden there is a sundial made by Leacock himself, on the cement base of which he inscribed "HORAS BREVIS ANNOS LONGOS ... SHORT HOURS MAKE LONG YEARS." We drove northwest to the town at the end of Matchedash Bay, a long inlet of Georgian Bay,

with the beautiful name of Waubaushene. The name is purported
to mean "meeting of the rocks," and this is most appropriate
because Waubaushene is on the bottom edge of the Canadian
Shield. On either side of Highway 103 which runs north from
Waubaushene are the jagged, dynamited chunks of precambrian
rock through which the highway has been cut.

Waubaushene has largely been taken over by cottagers and those
who serve them. Motor boats tied up at the piers in the harbour are
owned by people who live on islands that can be seen in the bay.
But it is the story of what happened near Waubaushene that is of
the greatest interest.

My wife and I went a few miles west from Waubaushene along
Highway 12 which runs close to the water, and we came upon one
of those green signs with "Historic Site" printed on it. We made a
left turn and followed a deserted gravel road through the bush,
wondering where this historic site could be. Finally, we came to
another sign that pointed into the bush and had St. Ignace II
printed on it. In front of us, as soon as we made the turn, was an
old, rusty iron farm-yard gate with a rusty chain and padlock holding it shut. Beside this was a small opening and a footpath.

We walked for about a hundred yards along a rutted road
through poplar and young oak trees. Then we came into a clearing
of sandy soil covered with tufted grass, ragweed, pigweed, and
mullein. Grasshoppers leaped beneath our feet. In the middle of the
clearing stood a stone and concrete altar that obviously had not
been there very many years. Near it was a rough wooden cross about
twelve feet high, with a plaque on it and, beyond that again, the
outline of a building marked out with cement blocks in the grass.
At the far side of the clearing stood a tiny one-room shack, obviously
deserted. In fact the whole place looked as though nobody had been
there in some time. Save for the grasshoppers and the birds, there
was no sound.

I read the plaque.

St. Ignace II. Here in 1648 on a site chosen by Jesuit missionaries
the Hurons from Taenhatentaron (St. Ignace I) built a new
palisaded village. Bounded on two sides by the Sturgeon River
it offered greater protection against the invading Iroquois.
However on March 16th in 1649 it was captured together with
the neighbouring St. Louis where Jean de Brébeuf and Gabriel

Lâlemant were seized. They were brought here and after suffering horrible tortures Father Brébeuf died the afternoon of March 16th and Father Lâlemant the following morning.

This, then, was the actual place! This was where the deed was done, the one we had learned about in our Grade Five history lessons. How the "savages" tortured the brave priests who had come to help the red men to salvation. A picture from the old history text popped into my mind. The two expressionless priests stood straight, with their hands bound around a post. The Iroquois looked like long-haired actors in a nudie production. One Indian was casually slicing the flesh off a priest's arm, another was pouring boiling water over the second priest's shoulders, and still another was kneeling by a fire heating knives and axe heads to a red-hot glow.

We were to learn more details later but, as we stood pensively on the hot sandy ground, we wondered why the place was so deserted, so desolate.

To satisfy our curiosity, we went on to where there was a sign designating another historical site a mile ahead. We turned left off the highway and followed a second gravel road, until a beat-up sign instructed us to turn left again. A short way along this road we came to a point where a sign had been half shot away by a happy hunter, and it directed us to turn in at a gate. We drove past some new pine trees in straight rows into a clearing with a stone cairn and a plaque which stated that this was the location of Fort St. Louis where Fathers Brébeuf and Lâlemant had been captured by the Iroquois on a cold winter day more than three hundred years ago. A goodly supply of empty beer bottles and other trash under the pine trees indicated at least one use that the place was being put to these days.

We left the spot feeling depressed, not just because of what had happened there, but because nobody seemed to care very much. From the unkempt condition of the place, it was obvious that official care and money were being spent elsewhere.

A few miles farther along Highway 12, after passing the towns of Port McNicoll and Victoria Harbour, we came to the spot where the attention and money is being lavished. This is the Martyrs' Shrine, a magnificent two-steepled church standing on a beautifully landscaped hill. Across the highway from it is the reconstructed Jesuit mission centre which has been named Ste. Marie Among the Hurons.

We left our car in the immense parking lot, paid our admittance fee, and entered the large glass and brick orientation centre. Here we were welcomed by a girl in uniform who gave us a brochure containing diagrams and information, and told us when the next film showing sould be.

We looked at large blow-ups and the C.W. Jeffreys paintings on the walls showing Champlain, torture scenes, and Indians playing lacrosse. We also bought some books at the book stand and some post cards.

Along with about thirty other tourists, we were shown into an attractive little theatre with leather-padded seats, tastefully decorated walls, and lighting that seemed to come from nowhere. We watched a 20-minute colour film depicting the building of the original Ste. Marie, the daily life of the Frenchmen and Hurons who had lived there, and the final burning of the fort by the Jesuits themselves on June 14, 1649.

The film had barely finished and the flames were still lapping around the carved IHS above the door of the mission, when the entire screen swung upward like a barn door, and we were invited to walk through into the open air. There, right before us, was the same door we had seen being burned.

We walked through the doorway and entered the past. Here were the buildings, made of wood or stone with bark shingles on the roofs, in their original positions. Archaeologist Kenneth Kidd and later Indian expert Walter Jury had, by long and patient excavation, found their outlines in the ground. As the handy brochure which we had been handed at the ticket wicket stated: "Today you can walk where saints and Indians walked side by side; through Jesuit residence, churches and granary; through blacksmith and carpenter shops, hospital and Indian longhouse. You can heft tools and artifacts of the pioneer."

Gradually, as we listened to the girls in blue who were stationed in every abode, we pieced together the story of how this establishment was born, thrived for ten years, and died. Father Brébeuf and the Jesuits, along with priests of the Recollet and Franciscan orders, had followed Champlain's route up the Ottawa, along the Mattawa River into Lake Nipissing, and hence by the French River into Georgian Bay. Then they had gone south through the Thirty Thousand Islands into Huron country.

They went to the Indian villages and lived there through the beautiful summers and horrible winters. Father Jerome Lâlemant (uncle of Gabriel, who was martyred with Brébeuf), wrote in the famous Jesuit *Relations*, a diary from which all our detailed information of these events has come:

> If you go to visit them in their cabins—and you must go there oftener than once a day if you would perform your duty as you ought—you will find there a little picture of hell. You will see nothing, as a rule, but fire and smoke and on every side naked bodies, black and half roasted, mingled pell-mell with the dogs, which are held as dear as the children of the house, and share beds, plates and food with their masters. Everything is in a cloud of dust, and you will not reach the end of the cabin before you are completely befouled with soot, filth and dirt.

About all the missionaries could do during their first 12 years in the area was to explore the country, get to know the Indians, learn their language and, most important of all, gain their trust. For these Hurons, always industrious traders, had already learned from dealings with the Frenchmen of Quebec that the white man could not be trusted, that he would take much and give nothing in return. However, they slowly discovered that the "black robes," as they called the missionaries, were men of a different stamp. They gave much and asked for nothing in return.

It was extremely difficult to bring the Indians to Christ while depending on their hospitality. A guest cannot forever be telling his host what he is doing wrong, and how he should be living. Besides, since there was absolutely no privacy among the Hurons, it was almost impossible for a man to become a Christian. Nowhere could he escape the gibes and scorn of his fellow villagers, and there was always the medicine man who had a vested interest, naturally enough, in preserving the established order. "Don't trust these strange calm men," they whispered. "They bring nothing but disease and trouble. You will see."

Sure enough, in 1636-7, the plague did come; first influenza, and then the horrible smallpox. The Hurons, with no natural immunity and weakened by a hard winter, died by the thousands. Desperately the Jesuits ministered to them as best they could, and baptised the dying who would permit it. At least they would save the soul, if they could not do anything for the body. It was hard and perilous work. Because so many whom the priests ministered to later died, some Indians concluded the priests had caused the deaths. The Jesuits were threatened and even molested, but they kept to their task. When the smallpox finally burned itself out, almost two-thirds of the Hurons were gone. What had been a fairly constant population of 30,000 was reduced to about 10,000.

In the 12 years that they lived with the Indians, Father Brébeuf and his associates made very few converts. And the ones they did make could never be relied upon to stay long in a state of grace. So in the summer of 1639, when the Hurons were too busy with their hunting and trading to be preached to, the good fathers held a meeting. What the Jesuits needed, they decided, was a place of their own. A place where they would be in charge, where they could establish their own rules and routines, and live as civilised people should live. It would be permanent, and not like the Huron villages which were subject to being torn down and carted off to fresh ground. From such a well-ordered place the fathers could go forth in pairs to teach the Indians. What was more important, the converted Indians could come to them and have their own chapel and worship free of the harassment of their unregenerate brothers. In the settlement they could learn the ways of civilisation and decency and peace.

They chose the location of their mission with great care, on the bank of the Wye River a few miles from where the town of Midland now stands. As described in the *Relations* of May 27, 1640, it was:

> . . . a place situated in the middle of a country, on the shore of a beautiful river, not more than a quarter of a league in length, which joins together two lakes. One extending to the West and verging a little towards the North, might pass for a fresh-water sea; the other lies toward the South and has a contour of hardly less than two leagues.

The mission was of necessity a self-contained town. There were carpenters, blacksmiths, shoemakers, and tailors. Boys were brought from France to act as servants, and some of the converted Hurons learned trades. Together they built the sleeping quarters, cook house, churches (one for the whites and another for the Indians). Barns were also built to house the cattle, pigs and chickens transported 800 miles from Quebec by canoe through the rapids and around portages. As the mission grew, a gate was cut through the palisade fence and a new fence was built to enclose the addition.

The mission had many firsts for what is now Ontario; the first church, first school, and first hospital. The first organized white settlement, in fact. The first white man's farm, too, for outside the palisade the settlers grew corn, sunflowers, pumpkins, and squash that were native to the area. Within the mission itself was Ontario's first canal, a three-foot wide waterway with sides made of poles, through which canoes could enter the fort with loads of provisions from Quebec. Ontario's first locks were there, too, to lift the canoes from the level of the river to the level of the fort floor.

The missionaries went out from the settlement in pairs to live and teach in the many Huron villages about the area. And Indians came to the mission: some out of curiosity, others from a sincere desire to learn of the one God, and still others because they were hungry.

Thus it was necessary to add a third section to the fort, to separate Christian Indians from the hangers-on. There is a tiny graveyard in this section where lie the remains of the 20 Christian Indians buried there. In the middle of the little wooden crosses stands a bigger monument, which is to the only white man who died at the mission. He was 22-year old Jacques Douart, who was whacked over the head by recalcitrant Hurons egged on by their medicine men. "They also broke his ankles," the girl in blue explained, "so that he couldn't walk to the happy hunting grounds, you see."

Inside the Indian chapel, which has only a hard-packed earthen floor ("The Indians were afraid of evil spirits that hid under planks"), is the original grave of Father Brébeuf. He was buried in Ste. Marie after his martyrdom in St. Louis. When the Jesuits left their beloved St. Marie, they unearthed Father Brébeuf's remains, boiled them in lye to remove the flesh from the bones, wrapped the bones in little silk bags, and put them in a wooden treasure box which they carried to Christian Island. After spending only one winter there, they went back to Quebec, taking Father Brébeuf's remains with them and carried them to Quebec where they rest now, with the Ursuline nuns.

In 1954, Father Haegerty from the Martyrs' Shrine discovered Father Brébeuf's grave in the remains of the Indian church. The outlines of his coffin were indicated by dark stains in the soil, and there was also a plaque on which was written in very old French: "Father Jean Brébeuf killed by the Iroquois on the 16th of March in the year 1649."

As for Father Lâlemant's remains, it is thought that they were carried back to Ste. Marie as well, though nothing has been found to really prove this. But we do know from the Jesuit *Relations* that Father Lâlemant's remains were finally taken back to France and given to his parents there.

It is plain to see that Ste. Marie was a successful, well-run mission doing the job it was established to do. In a letter to Rome, the superior, Father Ragueneau, reported that there was plenty of food on hand, that 1,700 persons had been baptized during the year, that another mission was being established on Manitoulin Island, and that "vice finds no place here, virtue rules, and the place is a home of holiness."

By this time we were so keen to learn exactly how the Hurons had lived that we went to the reconstructed Huron village in Midland. The Huron village is all there: palisades, longhouses, pottery sheds, storage pits, drying racks, grinding stones, lookout posts, and all the rest of it. From this reconstruction it is plain to see that these earliest Ontario residents were stone-age people of considerable organization and skill. They were reasonably good agriculturalists, cunning traders, and fierce fighters. Although it has been the custom in our history to class them as "good Indians," as opposed to the Iroquois who are classed as "bad Indians," they were as cruel in their torture of captives as were their enemies. The Indians were almost as cruel, probably, as the white mercenaries who killed, degraded, cheated, and destroyed them with no consideration for their rights or feelings.

Midland itself is a pleasant shipping and holiday centre, with a fine public library. The building itself is impressive: a converted post office and customs building made of limestone blocks, with a clock tower and a magnificent oak stairway. We got a splendid reception and all the help we needed.

Farther up the peninsula near the end of a five-mile-long finger of water, we came to a town with the most beautiful name and, they say, the tastiest water in Ontario—Penetanguishene. Like the other towns in the area, its principal industry, since shipping has all but ended, is tourism. To further this, the Ontario government has reconstructed the old naval establishment at the edge of town. Here you can see where the officers lived during the War of 1812 and after, and the hulls of two American ships, the *Tecumseh* and the *Tigress*, which were captured by the British during that unpleasantness.

As for the water, well, it's from an artesian well and it tastes like pure water, right enough, but it fell somewhat short of teaching us "the true meaning of enjoyment," as the tourist brochure promised it would.

A short drive from Penetanguishene across the peninsula brought us to the shore of Nottawasaga Bay and the great sand beaches. The action of currents in the bay over the centuries has deposited fine white sand along this shore for many miles. The best known of these is Wasaga Beach, whose ten-mile stretch has been called the "longest freshwater beach in the world." Certainly it is the longest and best sand beach in Ontario. The water is clear and shallow for long distances out into the bay, so that the smallest child can play safely, except near the mouth of the Nottawasaga River where signs warn of dangerous currents.

There are cottages all along the beach and on both sides of the Nottawasaga River which, because of ancient sand dunes, parallels the bay for four miles before emptying into it. There is also an amusement park with rides for the children, and hotels with beer parlours for the adults. And there is Wasaga Beach Provincial Park, with plenty of facilities for tent and trailer dwellers.

We visited the Ontario Zoological Park, a 55-acre wooded area where we saw lions, tigers, bears, bison, hippopotami, rhinos, and dozens of other animals both foreign and domestic. The curator, who looks upon his superb collection of animals as much more than something for the tourist to gape at, told us that a lot of research is carried on in the park. For instance, there is the question of keeping tigers, cheetahs and other tropical cats in central Ontario in winter. Actually the big cats feel fine in the cold weather, the curator has found, as long as their diet is supplemented with carbohydrates and fats to provide the extra body heat needed.

The Nottawasaga is of great interest, both as a site of important historic events and for itself. Near the mouth of the river is Nancy Island, on which has been built a fine museum. The island is named after the British supply ship *Nancy*, whose job in 1814 was to carry supplies to the beleaguered British fort at Michilimackinac, which commanded the narrows between Lakes Huron and Michigan.

On August 14 the *Nancy* had been caught by three American warships, the *Niagara*, and *Scorpion* and the *Tigress*. The little supply ship scurried into the mouth of the Nottawasaga, where there was a blockhouse filled with supplies. But the guns of the American ships could still reach her, and she was sunk by their fire. Fortunately, the British managed to escape from the ship and the block-house with their supplies, which they later loaded onto bateaux and a canoe, and transported the 360 miles to Michilimackinac.

The burned hull of the *Nancy* sank into the waters of the Notta-wasaga and was apparently lost forever. However, the waters of the river at this point are filled with fine sand, which over the years built up around the sunken hull to form a small island. Naturally it was called Nancy Island.

The hull has since been dug up and we saw it in the museum, along with a 12-foot rigged model of the *Nancy*, a replica of her figurehead, besides carronades, anchors, windlasses, and other relics of early Great Lakes naval battles. A sound and light presentation in the modern theatre of the museum tells the story of the gallant *Nancy*, and how she was later avenged when the ships that had sunk her were captured by the British.

For anyone with a canoe or other light boat and an urge to explore, the Nottawasaga is great fun. The name comes from the Indian *noahdoway*, which means Iroquois, and *saga*, which means "outlet of a river."

Four miles upstream is the site of Fort Nottawasaga, or Schooner Town as it was originally called, which was the winter quarters of the Royal Navy in this area from 1814 to 1817. Farther upstream, where the river is still wide and navigable and cuts through a moraine, is Glengarry Landing, where in the winter of 1813-14 Colonel Robert McDouall of the Glengarry Light Infantry had his men construct 29 bateaux to be used in transporting supplies to British forts. You can pull ashore here and camp on the grassy bank in the shade of huge maple trees. But be careful of your fires because this is part of the 14-acre Edenvale Conservation Area.

Not far from here we found a couple of heronries with dozens of nests in them. This is a colony of Great Blue Herons, those big wading birds who build their nests in groups in the topmost branches of high trees. The young were still in the huge nests, and as the big birds came squawking in from nearby Minesing Swamp with fish or frogs or even young muskrat, the fledglings opened their mouths and screeched with ecstasy.

The 13,000-acre Minesing Swamp itself is an adventure for any naturalist. Muskrat, beaver, and mink swim in its waters, and many species of water and shore birds nest in its rushes and reeds.

Farther along the Georgian Bay shore at the mouth of the Pretty

River is the town of Collingwood, a town long important for its harbour and shipbuilding. At one time much of the grain shipped from the prairies came through Collingwood and was transshipped by rail from there. Today Collingwood is more of a tourist town and a manufacturing centre. Situated on a low, flat plain, it has for a backdrop the famous Blue Mountain, noted for its ski runs, pottery manufacture, and caves.

From Collingwood, also, tourists with a rock-collecting bent find their way farther along the coast to Craigleith Provincial Park. No place in Ontario can equal this stretch of rocky shore as a hunting ground for fossils of the ordovician period. These fossils, not only of the ordovician but of other periods as well, are found in the lime-stone, shale, and sandstone of river beds, road cuts, and gravel pits in many parts of southern Ontario. They are usually scarce, but at Craigleith they are so plentiful that even the most inexperienced rock hound can pick up all he can carry.

Highway 24 south from Collingwood took us abruptly from the lakeshore plain up onto the escarpment, and provided a magnificent view of much of the Georgian Bay shoreline. We passed Devil's Glen where the Pretty River has cut a deep gorge through the limestone, and where there is yet another provincial park.

We kept on travelling south and east along a river valley through rugged scenery and little hamlets to Angus, where we stopped in at the Ontario Department of Lands and Forests' seed collection plant. Hundreds of pickers collect cones, from pine and spruce mostly, and in the seed collecting establishment the seeds are extracted and sent to the reforestation station at Midhurst, where they are planted and grow into seedlings for distribution throughout the province.

Actually, Huronia is one of the areas in southern Ontario where reforestation has been most successful. When the Hurons lived here, the predominantly sandy terrain was clothed with huge pine trees. The early settlers and lumbermen soon took care of that. Trees were felled by the millions to clear farm land and to provide lumber for the growing towns and cities. As a result, the land was denuded and left prey to water and wind erosion.

This led to an aggressive tree planting program begun in the early 1920s under the Drury administration and gradually expanded. As you drive through Huronia today, you pass stand after stand of white and red pines planted in nice straight rows. The wealth of potential lumber in these stands is inestimable. And, incidentally, they add greatly to the stability of the soil and the natural beauty of the area.

The pines look especially attractive in winter, when the deciduous trees are bare, and Huronia has become a favourite playground for skiers and snowmobilers. The Simcoe Highlands, which lie along the west side of Lake Simcoe, are characterized by steep hills and deep valleys excellent for ski runs. (In prehistoric times they were islands in Lake Algonquin.) In the area west of Barrie and Orillia, there are no less than four excellent ski resorts.

More spectacular is the skiing at Blue Mountain and Beaver Valley, both of which are part of the Niagara Escarpment. Blue Mountain is the highest and perhaps the most popular, with international ski meets, sensational hotdogging competitions during which skiers turn flips and perform all sorts of other tricks in the air.

Snowmobiling, since it requires no skill or training, is even more popular. Every Friday evening in winter the main highways leading north from Toronto are jammed with cars hauling trailers with one or more snowmobiles loaded on them. Most snowmobilers belong to well-organized clubs, and the great complaint of local residents that snowmobilers are ruining the country is largely dying down. Instead of roaring about on back roads and over private property as they once did, the snowmobiles are largely confined to marked trails through the woods, up and down the hills, and over frozen lakes.

Ice fishing is also popular in winter, especially on Lake Simcoe which, after the ice has become thick enough, is dotted with huts. Some are fairly crude, but others are fitted out like miniature modern bungalows with comfortable furniture, refrigerators, cooking facilities, plumbing, and many of the comforts of home.

So that's Huronia, one of our favourite parts of southern Ontario. It has just about everything: rivers, large lakes, small lakes, marshes, hills, a "mountain," beautiful villages, prosperous cities, and close ties with the past.

CHAPTER XI

Lake Country

No part of southern Ontario, except the central southwestern highlands, is far from a lake. But when a citizen of the Golden Horseshoe says he is "going up to the Lake Country," he means the Muskoka Lakes or the lakes in Algonquin Park or the islands of Georgian Bay or the Haliburton Lakes or the Kawartha Lakes. The first four groups are wholly within the Canadian Shield and are unbelievably beautiful, even with the thousands of cottages that surround them and the millions of motor boats that roar over their surfaces.

The lake country is southern Ontario's principal playground. The swimming is great, the water skiing is perfect, the fishing is fair, and there are still many canoe routes for the hardy who prefer the open campfire to the four-burner electric stove. The most recent trend is to winterize cottages, so that the harassed city dweller can escape to the lakes to ski or roar over the frozen lakes and through the bush on a snowmobile.

And this, too, is the land of lodges. Many lakes have them, large and small. Some are as posh as big city hotels, with golf courses, heated swimming pools, riding stables, tennis courts, liquor licences, and spacious ballrooms. Others are smaller and slightly more primitive, but then they cost less. However, there has been an alarming swing away from the lodge to the cottage, and more than a few problems have resulted.

By Georgian Bay, I mean that portion of the bay north of the mouth of the Severn River. The Severn, the last leg of the Trent Waterway, is wide and deep, with cottages along its banks. Rocky little waterfalls are by-passed by locks.

North of Port Severn, a side road winds through rock and bush to Honey Harbour, one of the hundreds of inlets of Georgian Bay. Here there are good marinas and first-rate lodges that offer all the comforts that lodges can offer.

We travelled by boat out to the islands of Georgian Bay Islands National Park, of which Beausoleil Island is the best. The waters of Georgian Bay are crystal clear; the little islands we passed, with moss-covered rocky shores and giant pines and hardwoods mirrored in the water made us realize why devotees drive many hundreds of miles from deep in the United States every year to enjoy them. There are, in fact, a large number of Americans who have built and maintain summer homes in the lake country.

Most of the Thirty Thousand Islands along the east shore of Georgian Bay are privately owned. Many have been in the possession of the same families for years, having first been obtained for practically nothing as Crown property. Some families own several small islands, with different members visiting back and forth.

Another jumping-off place for many of these islands is Parry Sound on Highway 69. Situated on a deep bay, Parry Sound is a city of boats. All summer long, boats are coming and going, taking passengers and supplies to the islands.

Owning an island in Georgian Bay or, in fact, on any of the lakes, is the ultimate in summer living. Completely isolated from everybody else, you can do what you like: swim in the buff, fish, sunbathe on the big rounded rocks, explore, water ski, and entertain.

The part of this area that I know best, since we live there and I have done the most research about it, is Muskoka. There are three big lakes in Muskoka—Joseph, Rosseau and Muskoka—and scattered in among them are hundreds of smaller lakes. Ours is one of these, about a stone's throw from Lake Rosseau at one end and about the same distance from Muskoka at the other. It is called Brandy Lake and, if it were not for blackflies and mosquitoes, it would be a perfect place to live.

What I have to say about the early development of the Muskoka area applies pretty generally to the Lake of Bays region, the Haliburton Highlands, and the Madawaska Valley.

The main road leading into the Muskoka region is Highway 11 north from Barrie. At the north end of Lake Couchiching is the tiny settlement of Washago, which few motorists even notice as they roar by. But in the mid-nineteenth century, when the Muskoka area was first being settled, Washago was a most important town. It was the southern terminus of the Muskoka Road, the first of the "settlement roads" into the region.

When most of the timber in the south had been cut, lumbermen looked farther north for new supplies. The Muskoka area had it: towering white pines four feet thick at the base, hemlock, oak, maple, and yellow birch, they were all there, just waiting to be cut down and sawed up into lumber.

In 1853 a railroad was built to Barrie, but that was as far as it went. From there on it was water and road. The first settlers crossed Lake Simcoe in sailboats or paddle steamers and then went across Lake Couchiching. This was the easy part of the journey.

Driving along four-lane Highway 11 at 70 miles an hour, it is hard to imagine the trip on the Muskoka Road over a hundred years ago. It was terrible. The road ran over rocks, through swamps, around hills, and across rivers. The first of these was the Severn and, according to the report on the inspection of surveys in 1861:

> The piers are weak and ill founded—the king posts and brace beams too ponderous for the foundation—the result is the swerved and sunken condition of the bridge. The abutments are likewise very poor—the approaches are not carried out far enough to admit of an easy ascent so that in its present condition a short, abrupt hill with a mud hole at its base has to be overcome from each side in order to ascend the bridge. . . .

And this was just the beginning. Coach travellers have written about being bounced around like butter in a churn. The coach springs were nearly always broken, and each time one of the big wheels hit a rock, the passenger was pitched up to the ceiling, only to meet the seat coming up as he came down. More often than not, the travellers got out and walked. Then their problem was getting too far ahead of the coach and having to sit down amid the black-flies or mosquitoes to wait for it.

The northern end of the road was a tiny lumbering community called McCabe's Bay (now Gravenhurst) at the south end of a long inlet of Lake Muskoka. Here the traveller could get a good meal at a log shack known as McCabe's Tavern and, if he were lucky, a job in the tiny sawmill. Otherwise he would have to go farther north.

From here on the trip was by water: some went by sailboat, others rowed or paddled. One enterprising man built a flat-bottomed scow that was powered by a horse on a treadmill. But it was geared up wrong, so that the horse had to gallop in order to turn the paddle wheels fast enough to make the boat go. And the resulting vibrations jarred all the caulking loose from the seams so that, on its maiden voyage, the boat sank and the horse drowned.

The next stop was North Falls (now Bracebridge), a tiny settlement a few miles up the Muskoka River, where a waterfall put an end to further navigation. Here there was another sawmill and a shingle mill, a few Indian shacks, and nothing more.

At the north end of Lake Muskoka the pioneer entered Indian River, which took him upstream to Lake Rosseau. But Lake Rosseau is a few feet higher in elevation than Muskoka, resulting in some rapids and necessitating a portage. At this meeting place of the lakes there had always been an Indian village, and so the small community growing up around a sawmill there was naturally enough called Indian Village (now Port Carling).

Once on Lake Rosseau the newcomer could travel many more miles by water, and with one more short portage could get into Lake Joseph. Thus a large area was opened up to lumbering, and settlers soon followed the lumbermen. Although this is rock country, there are pockets of good clay and loam soils deposited there by glacial lakes that have, over the years, been filled in with debris and sphagnum moss and willow and ultimately big trees. Hundreds of optimistic individuals from the southern plains came and tried to farm this land. After all, it was free.

The homesteader and his wife received 200 acres of land free, with an extra 100 acres for each child over 18. For $5 he could get another 100 acres. All of this was contingent upon his clearing two acres of land per year, constructing a house, keeping up the roads, and living on the place at least six months out of every year.

The Crown reserved rights to all the white pine on his land and granted rights to lumber companies, but the settler could have the remaining timber for his own use. But since it was the land he really wanted, the homesteader often hurried the clearing process by setting fire to his bush and burning up the white pine along with all the rest.

The greatest period of settlement was between 1869 and 1873, and then it slacked off. Gold was discovered in the Gravenhurst area in 1877, and that brought another rush of people. By 1881, there were no less than 27,000 settlers, lumbermen, and others in the Muskoka area.

At that time the chief means of transportation for people and supplies was lake steamer. The first of these was the paddle-steamer *Wenonah*, 80.5 feet long, 15.9 feet wide, with a gross tonnage of 83. She was followed by dozens of others—*Waubamic, Nipissing, Simcoe, Muskoka, Ahmic, and Cherokee*, to name a few—that busily carried passengers and freight over the lakes for almost a hundred years. A canal big enough to accommodate the steamers was built at Point Sandfield in 1870, joining Lake Rosseau and Lake Joseph, and the following year a canal and locks were installed at Port Carling. In 1875 the railway reached Gravenhurst, so that the long, horrible road trip was eliminated, and passengers could transfer directly from train to ship in Muskoka Bay.

Great tales are told of the sailing days, and any Muskokanite will tell you that it was a sad day when they took the steamers off the lakes. For, besides carrying supplies and passengers, the ships often made pleasure cruises. They were great for Sunday school picnics, Bible class outings, chartered trips by lodges and clubs, and marine excursions of all kinds. There was always an organ on board, and often an orchestra. Bigger and bigger ships were built with lavish dining rooms, salons, and sun decks. The grandest of them all was the 744 ton *Sagamo*, built in Toronto in 1903. It is estimated that the mighty *Sagamo* sailed a total of 305,000 miles on the lakes. She caught fire and was partially destroyed in 1925, but was rebuilt bigger and grander than ever. In 1961 she was decommissioned, but in the very next year she was opened as a floating restaurant. They were going to make a floating hotel of her in 1969, when she caught fire again and her career finally ended.

There is still one of the great lake ships left, the 275-ton *Segwun*, and anyone with a nautical interest can go aboard. For the *Segwun*, painted all shiny new, has become a floating museum tied up at the Gravenhurst wharf. On board, you can see old charts and furniture and compasses and anchors. You can, in fact, learn the whole story of the great days of shipping on the lakes: the fun and the tragedies, the fires and the sinkings, and the colourful captains who navigated the great ships into the bays and up the rivers of the Muskoka lakes.

A natural outgrowth of the lake ships was the development of tourist lodges on the shores and islands. The first of these was the Polar Star, a large, frame structure built by John Thomas in 1869 beside the canal that is now in the centre of Port Carling. Originally it was used as a boarding house for the workmen building the canal and locks and, later, when the big ships began to pass by, became a tourist home. Its name was changed to the Interlaken and later to the Port Carling House, but its glory has gone. In 1973 it was demolished to make room for a shopping mall.

We visited the Port Carling House before it was torn down. It was faded but stately, on the hill overlooking the locks. We peeked through the front window, and there was the long, hardwood bar at which so many weary tourists had slaked their thirst. The floor was littered with papers, bits of boxes, and pieces of furniture. Another room was a mess of empty cans, cookie boxes, and even half-eaten loaves of bread left by a young couple who had lived there that spring and had hoped to be able to open it for trade.

It is a good thing for them that they never got permission to do so. It would have broken their hearts. Like so many others, the old Port Carling House outlived its usefulness. Fifty years ago tourists came by train and boat to this sleepy town, paid a modest board, and sat on the wide veranda to watch the activities on the lake. There was swimming there, and boating, and from this central location a small fee would take them by boat to Bala or Rosseau or Windermere, and then back to the lodge. In the autumn, the trip through the lakes was one of great splendour, with leaves of the hardwoods—red, yellow and bronze—gleaming in the sun against the dark green backdrop of the pines, hemlocks, and spruce.

But there is little demand for that type of accommodation today. The modern lodge must offer every facility that discriminating tourists can get anywhere else. The guests have been around. They compare. Nothing but the best rooms will do now, with lavish bathrooms and colour television in every room. The golf course must be of the best, the tennis courts of championship quality, and the pool big and heated. All of this calls for a tremendous capital investment on the part of the operator and, since his season is four months long at best, he just cannot compete with luxury hotels.

While it is true that the popularity of snowmobiling and other winter sports is lengthening the season somewhat, this adds even more capital expense.   As a result, more and more of the big lodges are finding themselves in financial trouble. Then they are sold, and the land is quickly grabbed by eager cottagers. So where you had perhaps five thousand people vacationing in the season, you have only twenty or so families.

The beauty is still there, though. In the fall the road trip along Highway 118 between Bracebridge and Port Carling can knock your eye out with colour. Green meadows, stark rocks, rustic farmhouses and barns, and the backdrop of the leaves in full colour. Thousands drive the 120 miles from Toronto just to see it.

Farther north along Highway 11 is the town of Huntsville, still a thriving lumbering community and the centre of a smaller group of lakes: Vernon, Fairy, Peninsula, and the much larger Lake of Bays. They follow the same pattern as the Muskoka lakes, with thousands of cottages on their shores and islands, as well as modern lodges that vie with each other for the more casual trade.

By the side of the road just outside of the little town of Dwight, near the entrance to Algonquin Park, stands a garish establishment known as the Indian Trading Post, where in 1956 there occurred a most bizarre accident. At that time the trading post was operated by an Englishman named Earl Boyden. He called himself Indian Joe, dressed in buckskins and the heavy feathered headdress of the plains Indians. Many tourists, particularly Americans, stopped to take pictures of him and his big teepee and maybe buy some of his goods. Earl spent his winters in New York, living well, attending the theatre, and incidentally contracting for some of the authentic Indian ware he sold during the summer. His life was comfortable and uncomplicated.

Then one day a tourist stopped and said he wanted to take some movies of Indian Joe. Fine. Earl posed in front of his tent with a bow and arrow and struck some poses, and smoked his peace pipe, while the delighted tourist's camera whirred. Then the man said to Earl something like: "Say, why don't you go into your teepee and get your rifle, and bring it out and pretend to shoot me. Make a great sequence."

So Earl shrugged and went in and got his rifle, which he always kept unloaded. He came out, pointed it at the tourist's head, pulled the trigger, and shot the man through the forehead.

There was an inquest, of course, but nobody could see that Earl Boyden was really to blame. Somebody else had obviously been fooling around with his gun and had left it loaded. His gun and hunting licence were taken away from him, and he was warned to be a little more careful with kookie tourists in future. But Earl was never quite the same after that. He sold out to his partner, Roger Mitchell, and went away. Shortly after that, Roger heard that Earl had died.

Algonquin Park is by long odds the largest park in southern Ontario, 2,910 square miles of rock hills, ravines, countless lakes, rivers, and streams. A wilderness paradise for campers, naturalists, hikers, fishermen, canoeists, and amateur geologists.

For years, Algonquin Park was famous as the place where you could see deer; does and fawns timidly feeding in among the rocks by the side of the road, and stately bucks standing erect waiting for handouts. Often, driving through the park, cars would be held up for fifteen minutes or half an hour while the cars ahead stopped to let their children feed, pat, and have their pictures taken with the wild deer.

But when we drove through the park recently, there was not a deer to be seen. I went to the research station of the Department of Lands and Forests and asked the ranger why the deer had all disappeared. Had they been shot? I wanted to know. Surely the government was not permitting hunting in the park, along with those dastardly lumbermen who were cutting down the best trees, and according to the Algonquin Wilderness League, ruining the park.

The ranger was very patient with me. Yes, he said, they did allow some shooting in the park in the southern section that juts down into Haliburton. Sixty per cent of the hunt, he said, takes place in the first four days of the season, and if the weather is bad then the hunt is down. No, there weren't necessarily fewer deer in the park than previously, but certainly the tourists were seeing fewer. The reasons? Roads had been widened and the bush cleared back much farther from the sides, and deer are afraid of open country. Besides, many of the deer had hung around the Department's camp at Cache Lake and since the camp had been abandoned the deer had gone back into the bush.

I asked him about the timber wolves. Yes, there were still plenty of timber wolves in the park and they would still howl for the tourists. In recent years "howling parties" have been popular with city dwellers, many of whom suffer the Red Ridinghood syndrome regarding wolves and are titillated by the thought of being near these wild animals.

The rangers take groups of panting would-be naturalists on a trek into the woods at night to where they know there are wolves. (They know because they have carried on extensive research with wolves, involving the placing of a radio transmitter on a collar around a wolf's neck so that his every move can be charted.) Then the rangers either play a record of wolf howls or just let loose howls of their own. If there are wolves in the vicinity, they will howl back. That in turn will stimulate other wolves to howl, until you have wolves howling all about you.

The ranger did not think much of the vigourous campaign continually being waged by some northern sportsmen to convince the government that all timber wolves must be eradicated, by poison if necessary, because they kill deer and thus adversely affect the lucrative hunters' outfitting business. He did not think that wolves actually cut down the deer population at all. Deep snow, he said, was the worst enemy of the deer. They cannot move around enough to browse if the snow is more than 20 inches deep.

But listening to wolves and walking on nature trails are two of the lesser pursuits in the park. Hundreds of thousands of campers come every year to fill up the park's many campgrounds with tents and trailers and to enjoy summer activities.

For the more rugged there is canoeing, and the park is one of the few remaining places in southern Ontario where it is possible to get completely away from motels and automobiles and people. Thousands of acres have no roads within miles and can be reached only by a person in a canoe, and a person strong enough to carry the canoe on his back at that.

The park's official map describes in detail 15 separate canoe routes with all the portages carefully marked and, besides, suggests that: "In addition to the routes listed, there are other less used courses, as well as side trips that can be made by the more experienced trippers who are qualified to lay out their own course and know how to cope with any eventuality that may be met."

It is, in fact, a tradition in southern Ontario to go canoeing in Algonquin Park. A considerable number of boys' and girls' camps are operated there with emphasis on overnight trips. The most outstanding of these are the camps established by the late Taylor Statten. The term "a Taylor Statten boy" is one that many adults use with pride. Pierre Elliot Trudeau attended camp Ahmek as a boy, and developed there his enthusiasm for canoeing and the outdoor life.

The best-known lake for camps is named, naturally enough, Canoe Lake. There is a well-developed landing near Mile 9 off Highway 60, with a huge parking lot, outfitters' stores, and a restaurant. Any day during the summer you can see canoes loaded with kids, with two to twenty-five in a canoe, leaving from or arriving at the landing, paddling like crazy, shouting to each other, and generally having fun. There are as many girls as boys.

Canoe Lake has the added interest of being the place where artist Tom Thomson lived and painted and drowned. A memorial consisting of a huge totem pole marks the location where his body was found. There is an aura of mystery surrounding the location because it has never been definitely established whether the artist died accidentally or from a blow on the head administered by a person or persons unknown.

At the first information centre in the park, we picked up a map of the park and various other pamphlets giving its history, location of campsites, facilities, and information about the museum. We also got for 30 cents a booklet titled *A Geological Guide to Highway 60*. This describes the different kinds of precambrian rock found in the park and tells how they formed. A detailed map shows exactly where good examples of the different kinds and formations may be seen.

After visiting the park many enthusiasts join the Algonquin Wilderness League, a group of naturalists and wilderness buffs dedicated to the task of ensuring "that the wilderness areas of Ontario will be maintained and held intact for succeeding generations." Their biggest battle is to prevent logging in the park, a battle that they are losing.

South of Algonquin Park is that great area of eastern Ontario which, excluding the Ottawa and St. Lawrence Valleys, lies within the Canadian Shield. It is sparsely populated and well supplied with rivers and lakes along with deep, scenic valleys and high hills from the tops of which you can see for miles.

The rivers of this region—South Nation, Rideau, Mississippi, Madawaska, Bonnechère and Petawawa—all drain into the Ottawa River, rather than south into Lake Ontario or the St. Lawrence, and they provide outstanding scenery. The Madawaska and Bonnechère Valleys are especially spectacular. My favourite view is the one on Highway 60 leading into the little lumbering town of Barry's Bay.

This is hunting and fishing country. The people we met talked of the great deer hunting and bear hunting of the distict. In most back yards there are kennels with brown and black hounds baying away at the visitor. The dogs have nothing to do but wait for the deer hunting season when they come into their own.

We took a trip through some of this country, and the first place we stopped was the town of Winchester, which is in flat farm land that was once the bottom of the Champlain Sea. Why Winchester? Well, it is not the biggest or most historic town in the area, but it has special significance for me because of a girl named Arabel Timmins who lived there more than a hundred years ago. She was my grandmother.

The town remembers the Timmins family. An old stone building on the main street is called the Timmins Block. And in the United Church, there is a picture of a woman whom everyone called Grandma Timmins (not mine), who was a devoted church worker and supporter. I met a most charming Helen Timmins who is also Mrs. Hitsman; she looked a lot like my sister Doris, but she never heard of Arabel Timmins. I never saw Arabel because she died before I was born, and I have only one picture of her taken when she was a very old woman. All I know is that young Jim Copeland came to Winchester and courted her and married her, and carried her off to Saskatchewan where they raised a big family, one of whom was my mother.

From Winchester we drove west through more flat country and then into rocky country, for it is here that the Canadian Shield extends south to the St. Lawrence and beyond.

Now we were in the area of the Rideau Waterway which extends 125 miles through rivers and lakes from Ottawa to Kingston. The little town of Merrickville is right on the waterway. There are big locks there, and an historic plaque that tells how William Merrick came in 1793 after leaving his home in Massachusetts because he wanted to remain British. He got a grant of land from the British government and built a mill and started a community.

Right beside the lock in Merrickville there was the kind of thing that makes me mad when I'm travelling. All the way into town were signs advertising the Blockhouse Museum and telling us to be sure and visit it. Sure enough there it was, big and square and made of stone with holes in the walls through which to shoot at enemies. A sign said it was built in 1832 to protect the Rideau Waterway from the Americans. Great. So we rushed up to the front door to go inside and see all this historic stuff and the place was closed.

A tiny sign told us that this museum was open on certain days and at certain times and, of course, if you just happened to be there then you could get in. Now what I want to know is why in hell go to the expense of having a museum and advertising it—and we ran into this situation everywhere—if it is not kept open. Tourists are not going to arrange their trips to suit the museums' times. Surely somebody could be available to let travellers in, even if they had to go and fetch him. But there it sat, big and solid and intriguing and closed.

So we did not hang around Merrickville, but pressed on to Smiths Falls. Now there is a town for which I have the fondest feelings. We got there about seven in the evening, pulling our house trailer. We were tired and hungry and thirsty. The problem was where to find a place to park and unwind. So we stopped and asked a lady in a store and she said, "Oh yes, the Victoria Park Campground is open. Just go across the new bridge and turn right on Lombard Street. You can't miss it."

Now if I were in the business of giving advice to towns who want tourists, I would suggest having a campground right in the middle of town and keep it open from early spring until late fall.

We went to the campground, and it was great, right on the canal that takes the waterway around the falls for which Smiths Falls is named. Boats can tie up there as well as trailers, and there are electric outlets and water taps right along the canal wall for the convenience of both. We decided to stay a while in Smiths Falls.

The next morning the library was not open but the Chamber of Commerce office was, and they gave me a pamphlet about the person who founded the town. It was a man named Smyth, and he had a mill which used the water from the falls. Then I went to talk to a lock master who was sitting in a little white house beside one of the locks. He told me that the lock was operated by hand, and that all sorts of boats come through during the summer months and this lock, like the other 48 on the waterways, was absolutely free.

"Why?" I asked. He didn't know, but was sure that if they did charge a fee, the boaters would gladly pay it. Waterways, I learned, are under the federal Department of Indian Affairs, and are damned expensive to keep up. They are always being repaired and rebuilt and "grouted" so they will not leak, and it costs a lot of money which comes out of federal taxes which are paid by every-body in Canada. We agreed that it didn't seem fair for sodbusters in Saskatchewan, for instance, to have to help maintain a lock for a few boaters, most of whom are Americans who have lots of money.

The biggest boat to go through his lock, he said, was 109 feet long. He also said the total lift at Smiths Falls with its five locks is 51 feet, which is not the greatest on the waterways. While we were there a tall boat came along, and the bridge had to be lifted and the locks operated and the railway spur line cranked up to let it go through.

My wife and I got the feeling that we wouldn't mind living in Smiths Falls. It is just the right size to be manageable, and all around are lakes that can be reached by road or water. But we had to press on down the road to Perth.

We liked Perth, too; not a large town, but a lively one. As we drove into the town from the east, we just naturally stopped at the attractive tourist information centre, beside which is a life-size model of the largest cheese ever made in Ontario. This succulent hunk of mouse bait was manufactured in the Perth cheese factory of the late Hon. A.J. Matheson in 1892, to be sent to the Chicago World's Fair as an example of Canadian ingenuity and skill.

The big, round cheese weighed 22,000 pounds, stood 6 feet high, and had a circumference of 28 feet. The 207,000 pounds of milk needed came from 12 cheese factories in the Perth area, who each contributed a three days' supply. When the big cheese was finished and pressed and aged, it was shipped to Chicago on a flat car. As it was being placed in position at the fair, it broke through the floor of the space allotted for it. According to the report, the cheese was the sensation of the Fair, with thousands coming to see and taste it. Finally it was broken up and shipped to a Tooley Street cheese merchant in London, England.

Inside the tourist centre is a picture of the largest lake trout ever caught in the area, a 36 pound, 2 ounce monster hooked in 1950 by one D.W. Cockfield. Each year Perth runs a biggest fish contest, and anglers from far and wide come to try their luck in the 100 lakes that lie within a radius of 50 miles of Perth.

The biggest Perth story, however, even bigger than the fish story, is the one about the last fatal duel ever to be fought in Canada. It

took place between two young Perth law students on a rainy afternoon of June, 1833.

This true story is like something right out of a novel by Thomas
Hardy. We have a village, settled by retired army officers and thus
most strict in its social structure and code of behaviour. We have
two law students, handsome, debonair young gentlemen represent-
ing the cream of eligible bachelors; a beautiful "unprotected lady";
and even a heartless villain bent on destroying one of the law
students, whom he considered to be his rival.

To make the melodrama more melodramatic, the two young law
students, Robert Lyon and John Wilson, were fast friends and
drinking companions. They both were acquainted with a school
teacher, Miss Elizabeth Hughes, who, according to reports, tended
to be just a trifle flirtatious. Wilson had been courting Miss Hughes,
but had switched his affections to another, and really wanted out
of the situation.

He got his chance one day when he and Lyon were in Bytown
(now Ottawa) on business and having a couple in a fashionable
drinking spot. Lyon, who was quite the tease, made some joking
remark about how Miss Hughes permitted their mutual friend,
Henry Lelievre (the villain of the piece) to put his arm around her
in public.

So Wilson got busy and wrote a letter to Miss Hughes's guardian
saying, in effect, that because the beauteous lady was getting herself
talked about, he no longer wished to be considered a suitor. Well,
saying a thing and writing it, as both youths were to discover, were
two different things.

In less than no time it was all over town that Lyon had made
insulting remarks about a lady. When that young man returned to
Perth he discovered that he had been branded a scoundrel, and the
doors of high Perth society were resolutely closed to him. Even the
girl he loved slammed her door in his face.

So Lyon sought out his friend Wilson, encountered him in front
of the courthouse, knocked him down with one sturdy blow, and
called him, publicly mind you, a "damned lying scoundrel."

Well, it could have ended there with both sides cooling off
gradually, and the town finding something else to talk about. But
it did not. In the first place, Wilson was only the son of a farmer
and therefore overly sensitive about his place in society. In the
second place, there was the villain Lelievre, who kept the hate pot

bubbling in the hope that Wilson, whom he considered as a rival for Miss Hughes's affections, might be killed or disgraced.

A challenge was issued and accepted and on the afternoon of June 13, 1833, the two men and their seconds met in a field just out of town. Lelievre was Lyon's second, of course, and was urging his principal, an excellent shot, to kill his opponent.

Wilson, who couldn't hit the broad side of a barn with a pistol, was confident right up to the last that he and Lyon would both intentionally shoot wide, and that would be the end of it. As it turned out they did both miss with the first shot, Wilson by a country mile, and Lyon just barely. In fact Lyon's shot grazed Wilson's temple and scared him silly.

Both combatants probably would have let it go at that but Lelievre insisted that honour demanded they take another shot and, before they realized it, they were pointing the pistols at each other again. As he testified later, Wilson was sure he would be shot but, to his surprise, when the smoke had cleared it was Lyon who lay on the ground, shot plumb through the lung and soon very dead.

There was a trial, of course, with Wilson charged with murder. But he made such a strong appeal to the jury, and his second made an even stronger appeal, that the jury decided Lelievre was the real cause of the trouble and acquitted Wilson. Lelievre, who had left as soon as Lyon fell, was never again seen in the district.

Unlike a Hardy story, the ending was relatively happy. Wilson did the decent thing and married Miss Hughes, became a lawyer, a member of parliament, and finally a judge of the Supreme Court of Ontario.

And that is the way it was in the Perth area when Ontario was very young.

From Perth we drove west to Madoc, and then we were in eastern Ontario's principal rockhound country. In fact, this is where Ontario mining had some of its beginning. As early as 1837, a gentleman by the name of Uriah Seymour opened an iron mine near Madoc and built a blast furnace for smelting iron. Hematite was mined in the area at about the same time.

Then in 1866, a few miles north of Madoc, gold was discovered by Marcus Herbert Powell, a clerk of the Division Court, who was also something of an amateur geologist. While poking about in a pasture he found "gold in the form of leaves and nuggets . . . the largest nuggets about the size of a butternut." The resulting development was the first gold mine in southern Ontario.

Gold fever was in the air then because of the findings in British Columbia and California, and for a while the area had a goldrush. Hopeful people came from all over by boat or by coach or on foot, and began digging up the countryside. The nearby settlement, naturally enough, was named Eldorado. A number of small gold mines were established, but the ore soon petered out and the countryside went back to farming. The weed- and shrub-infested openings of the old mines are still there for anyone who wants to walk a few miles from the highway to find them.

Highway 62 north from Eldorado is great. Not only does it pass close to many lakes, but there are frequent picnic spots along the road where a car and trailer can pull off to rest and enjoy the scenery. Parallel to the highway is a hiking trail which has been cut through the bush all the way from Lake Ontario to Bancroft. The whole of Hastings County is also criss-crossed with well-marked snowmobile trails.

The town of Bancroft itself is having a minor boom these days. Between 1956 and 1964 it was noted as the uranium centre of southern Ontario, with three major mines producing over $100 million worth of ore during the eight year period. But the mines are all closed down and only one, the Faraday Mine, has any chance of re-opening. So Bancroft is pretty well forgetting about uranium and concentrating on the other minerals found in the area.

The town now calls itself "The Mineral Centre of North America" and claims there are 68 collectable minerals in the area. Each year the Chamber of Commerce stages a giant Rockhound Gemboree which attracts thousands of collectors from far and near. One year no fewer than 22,000 rockhounds came and scoured the countryside for soladite, star sapphires, garnets, zircons, and the rest.

And the minerals are not hard to find. At one rock cut on Highway 62 just north of town, collectors have hacked away so much from the usually high sides of the road as to almost level them. The local bookstore keeps on hand a supply of an excellent book published by the Ontario Department of Mines, entitled *Geology and Scenery of the Peterborough, Bancroft and Madoc Area*, which tells the rockhound exactly where to go and how to find the stones.

We got a good feeling in Bancroft and thought it would be a fine spot in which to live. The people are pretty happy about their place. So much so that one man who had a good job and a lot of seniority quit cold when his employers tried to move him to a city farther south.

We decided that we might move to Bancroft instead of to Smiths Falls.

West of Bancroft, we were in the Highlands of Haliburton which are very rocky, very hilly, very wild, and very beautiful. The village of Haliburton, like all communities in the lake country, has the net out for tourists, and advertises a School of Fine Arts, a hockey school where kids can learn to play like professionals, and various winter, fall and summer festivals.

South of Haliburton, we drove along close to the shore of a lake with the utterly preposterous name of Kashagawigamog. Kash, as it is locally referred to, is one of the largest lakes in the Haliburton region and the most developed. On its wooded shores are lodges, camps, schools, resorts, and trailer parks.

We drove down a steep, winding road to one of these and registered for a space with electricity and sewers and good clean washrooms. This park had everything a family would need; play yards, recreation hall, laundromat, tennis, horseshoes, shuffleboard, and lending library, with excellent beaches and a golf course and riding stables nearby. All for a few bucks a day.

When we drove in and were going through the horror of parking, we noticed that there were at least fifty trailers and tents parked in the open and under trees. A crowded place, we decided. But all the time we were there we did not see one person or a car. It gave us an uneasy feeling. Where was everybody? Then we realized that this was a Wednesday, and that this place was mostly used on weekends. People brought their trailers and tents to the park and left them there all summer, visiting them during their weekends and two-week holidays. Some had little flower gardens around them, and others had built-on porches and outdoor eating shelters. Much cheaper than owning a cottage, and almost as satisfactory.

The town of Minden farther south is about the same size and puts on much the same kind of show for the tourists. All of this lake country, in fact, which once was supported largely by lumbering, now depends upon its recreational value for its economic support. And it really is a great place to be, with plenty of space and beauty and things to do.

Another route home from Madoc would have taken us southwest to the city of Peterborough, where we have driven many times before. This is scenic country of another type, for it is southern Ontario's largest drumlin field.

The Trent Waterway runs through Peterborough, and right in town is "the world's highest lift lock." This is a different lock from the ones in Smiths Falls where water is let in and out to raise or lower boats.

These locks operate on hydraulic lifts like two immense bathtubs; each is 140 feet long, 33 feet wide, and 9 feet 10 inches deep. As one goes up, taking a boat or two with it, the other comes down bringing boats to the lower level. The principle is simple. They fill the top tub a little fuller than the bottom one, 100 tons more, and the extra weight and force of gravity take care of the descent. The extra water is then released into the canal and the lift is ready to go up again.

This part of Ontario was settled first in the early 1820s by a man named Adam Scott, who built a grist mill on the Otonabee River. A few years later, a British official named Peter Robinson brought 1,900 settlers from southern Ireland, and established them in the surrounding country. Subsequently, the town and county were named after him.

At first the principal export from the area was timber, which was rafted down to Lake Ontario and thence to Quebec. Then a man named John Stevenson began making canoes out of basswood, and the famous Peterborough Canoe was born. He later switched to cedar ribs; today many canoes made in Peterborough are of fibreglass. The Edison Electric Company was established in Peterborough in 1892, and is still there under the name of Canadian General Electric.

There are many things to see in Peterborough, but perhaps the most interesting of them all is Trent University, built on the banks of the Otonabee River at the site of the Champlain Trail. There are no old buildings (the university was founded in 1963) and the architecture of Champlain College is striking, to say the least.

The lakes of the Peterborough region are different from the lakes farther north, since they lie south of the Canadian Shield. Although they lack the splendid rock scenery of the shield lakes, they are easier to get to and the fishing is good.

Rice Lake is less than ten miles north of Lake Ontario, and is joined to it by the Trent Waterway. The Indians used this route for thousands of years before the white man came, and at the northeast end of Rice Lake there is a burial site that is more than 1,800 years old. It was built by the Hopewellian people who, it is estimated, go back more than five thousand years. The serpent shaped mounds contain, besides bones, fragments of pipes and pottery as well as adzes and gouges.

Rice Lake receives its water through the Otonabee River from the Kawartha Lakes northwest of Peterborough, by way of Little Lake which is right in the city. These long, narrow lakes—Katchiwano, Clear, Stony, Lovesick, Buckhorn, Deer, Little Mud, Chemong, Sandy, Pigeon, Sturgeon, Cameron, and Balsam—stretch north like fingers to the very edge of the Shield. Since this region was once covered by prehistoric seas, the sedimentary rocks contain numerous fossils such as trilobites, gastropods, nautiloids, and the like. Abandoned cement quarries, like the one at Lakefield, are good places to find fossils.

Lake Scugog, which is south of Sturgeon Lake and drains into it, has a large island in the middle which is actually a township of Ontario County. Scugog, shallow and muddy, would still be little more than a marsh if a man named Purdy had not built a dam across the Scugog River in 1837, raising the lake level by four feet. The City of Lindsay at the location of the dam was originally called Purdy's Mills.

The entire lake region of southern Ontario, especially the portion lying within the Canadian Shield, is still sparsely populated. So it has become a haven of relative solitude and fresh air for the harassed citizens of Ontario's large cities. Every Friday afternoon, summer and winter, hundreds of thousands of Torontonians get off work early, pack up their cars, hitch up their trailers to carry boats or snowmobiles, and join the stream of vehicles heading north to the lake country. On the rare occasions that I am crazy enough to travel on weekends, I get the impression from the number of cars roaring along the highways that the lake country will be jammed to overflowing and be as crowded as Toronto itself. No such thing. All of those cars are swallowed up by the forests and lakes, and there is little evidence of them until Sunday night when they all hit the highways again and crawl, bumper to bumper, along the routes leading into the city. Evidently the fresh air and the space and the water are worth all the effort it takes to get a couple of days in the lake country.

CHAPTER XII

Rock, Water and Forest

Northern Ontario is full of surprises. Our initial surprise was its size. When we crossed the border from Manitoba into Ontario for the very first time in 1944, we had some kind of crazy notion we were in the land of the big cities, the Toronto Maple Leafs, and Niagara Falls. It was something of a shock to learn that there were at least two days of travelling by train through wilderness such as we had never seen, before we would reach the heavily-settled area of the province.

All of northern Ontario, except for a few thousand acres of low muskeg around Hudson and James Bays, is part of the Canadian Shield. It is rock country with a vengeance. This means countless glacial lakes ranging in size from the 1,870-square-mile Lake Nipigon to little McCoy Lake, and thousands of others too small to have names. It means great forests of spruce, balsam, hemlock, birch, and pine. It means mines so deep that it is hot near the bottom of them. It means fish and moose and deer and bear and geese and ducks for the hunter. It means Indians travelling by snowmobile over their traplines in winter. It means people as different from the people of southern Ontario as Newfoundlanders are from Albertans.

It is still a land for the adventurous: for the man who wants to get away from crowded cities, for prospectors who still search for the big strike and, especially if he has an aircraft to take him to remote lakes and forests, for the sportsman.

No one, no matter where he lives in northern Ontario, is more than a mile or so away from the wilderness. It is an easy country to get lost in.

North Bay on Highway 11 is the beginning of Northern Ontario. Not far north of that the scenery suddenly dramatically changes from rock and trees to fertile fields, fences, big barns with silos beside them, and good farm homes. This is the area known as the Little Clay Belt around Lake Timiskaming, and it is one of the several pockets of good clay soil found in northern Ontario, old lake beds which provide some twenty million acres of fertile farmland. Much of it so far unused.

The first town of any size is Cobalt, built on rocks, with all the characteristics of a typical mining town. It was at Cobalt that the great mining boom that extended north to the Porcupine district really began.

At the beginning of the twentieth century this area was practically unsettled except for an occasional Hudson's Bay trading post, a few lumbermen, and some farmers who had made the arduous trip north by way of the Ottawa River and Lake Timiskaming. To encourage more people to go north, the Ontario government decided to build a railroad into the wilderness. And this disturbance of the ancient hard rock by dynamite and pick had a tremendous effect on the future of Ontario.

At Mile 103, when the rock was shattered by a blast of dynamite, the workmen saw bright streaks of metal in the chunks of rock. The contractors sent samples to Montreal for assay, and the assay was good—4,000 ounces of silver to the ton.

The history of this mining area is full of stories of men who found by accident, or else barely missed, fabulous veins of rich metal. One of the best stories is that of Fred LaRose, a blacksmith with the railway crew. One evening while working away, LaRose saw a fox poking around the camp and threw his hammer at it. He missed, of course, but where the hammer landed it broke off a hunk of rock. And there it was, almost pure silver. LaRose promptly gave up blacksmithing in favour of mining, and established the rich mine that is named after him.

Even with these rich finds, however, and the enthusiastic report of the government geologist, Dr. Willet Green Miller, there was no great rush to the Cobalt camp. Then some enterprising men, notably the brothers Noah and Jules Timmins, became interested in the area, and the mines began to pay big profits. In just about no time Cobalt had a population of 7,000. After that the fortunes of the mining town fluctuated wildly as the price of silver went up and down on the world market.

Today the town is making a big comeback with the renewed activity in silver mining in adjacent townships. There is a fine mining museum where we learned about the early days of mining. And there is a plan to bring back those days by making the centre of the town into a living museum with saloons, eating places, stores, dance halls, and even the old Classic Vaudeville Theatre in full swing again. The promoters of the scheme argue that, since Cobalt is within easy range of southern Ontario and since the whole mining thing began here, tourists will come by the millions to relive the old days. Maybe they will, at that.

As it is tourists come by the tens of thousands in early August for the annual Miners' Festival which features competition in all manner of mining skills. And a well-organized mine tour takes visitors around to working mines to see how it is being done today.

Farther north on Highway 11 is the great gold mining region surrounding Kirkland Lake. South of the city, near the junction of Highways 11 and 66, is a small community with the opprobrious name of Swastika. No, it was not named after Hitler's notorious symbol; rather, one story states that Hitler got the idea for his emblem from this northern Ontario town.

There was this British peer, Baron Redesdale, a powerful believer in the Nazi idea and a pal of Hitler. In 1920 this chap purchased mining claims between Swastika and Kirkland Lake and, along with his daughters, sometimes came to vacation on the property. The baron was quite taken with the swastika sign or "lucky cross," the pattern for which had been an Indian good luck charm. So, the story goes, he showed it to Hitler who thought it would be fine for the symbol of his rotten movement.

During the war, as always happens, somebody wanted to change the name of Swastika to something more patriotic, like Winston, for instance, but the movement never got off the ground. The feeling of the residents was well expressed by the sign on the Swastika Drug

Company which stated: "Hitler be damned. This is our sign since 1922."

Kirkland Lake itself is perhaps the most interesting of all the mining towns. It is built on top of an ore body, and the main street is actually paved with gold. This is because the construction crew that was building the street mistakenly took the rock for its foundation from a pile of gold ore. By the time the mistake was discovered, the asphalt was already laid, and, what the heck, there was plenty more gold ore where that came from.

There are headframes of mines right within the town. Together, the mines of Kirkland Lake—Lake Shore, Kirkland Minerals, Macassa, Sylvanite, Teck-Hughes, Toburn and Wright-Hargreaves—have produced over a billion dollars in gold.

A few years ago I had the good luck to go down one of the largest gold mines in the Kirkland Lake area. About six o'clock in the morning I caught a bus along with about fifty miners going out for their shift. This mine employed some eight hundred men underground. They were a taciturn group, but when I got them to talk they told me what a hard life mining is and the danger of "bumps." A bump is when the rock shifts, and you have a cave-in; often men get killed.

At the mine office I was met by a public relations man who took me to the pit-head. The headframe is a high structure that looks something like a prairie grain elevator and contains the motor and cables and immense pulleys of the hoist that carries miners' equipment and ore. First we went into a change room where the miners dress for underground. When the men come up out of the mine, they take off all their mining clothes and leave the change room stark naked to go into the showers before they dress in their street clothes. This is to discourage high-grading, which means having your pockets full of high-grade ore that can be sold outside. Despite every precaution, high-grading is still a flourishing business.

I was outfitted with a pair of coveralls, a hard hat, and a miner's lamp that fits onto it. Then we went into the cage with a group of miners and sank into the ground at the rate of 2,000 feet a minute. We got off at the 2,000-foot level, though the mine was actually more than five thousand feet deep. Then we walked along the shaft dug through the hard rock, which is lighted by electricity. Along the ceiling were pipes carrying water and cement—they use a lot of both in a mine—and in gutters along the side of the shaft there was a stream of water from underground sources. If this is not continually pumped out, the mine will soon flood.

We came to a drift, which is like a cross street, and walked along it until we came to a manway, which was a hole with a ladder down it, and then I began to feel a bit like a gopher. We climbed down the ladder into a big cave called a stope, which is the real business part of the mine. The shafts are built to cut across the ore bodies which slant in seams down into the rock, and the stopes cut into it at different places.

Here I saw actual mining. The miners were using diamond drills to make deep, thin holes in the face of the ore body into which they put dynamite. The PR man picked up a piece of black rock about the size of a hockey puck from the floor and handed it to me. "Ore," he said. "See those little specks? That's gold. Every day we take about four thousand tons of it out of this mine. It takes more than four tons of ore to yield 100 pounds of gold."

The big scraper was pushing ore that had been blasted loose down a hole in the floor. It went down a chute and was loaded into small railway cars that carried it to another chute that led to the crusher. Then the crushed ore was hoisted to the surface for refining.

The PR man told me I could keep that piece of ore, and I still have it. High-grade ore. The stuff of dreams: stuff that is worth a couple of hundred bucks an ounce on the open market. The stuff that for centuries men have slaved and schemed and worked and even murdered for. And yet, except for making watches that will not rust and rings and fillings for teeth, it is practically useless.

It is still possible to find old-timers in Kirkland Lake who will tell stories of the great mining men who have become legends in the area. There was William Wright, for instance, and Edward Hargreaves, who in 1911 were part of a larger prospecting party looking for gold. Bill and Ed got into an argument with the others about the best place to look and finally left the party. They scraped away at moss and debris and chipped away at rocks, but found nothing. Finally, after they had looked everywhere else, they sawed in half an immense fallen tree and labouriously heaved the pieces aside. Underneath, they found the vein of gold they were after.

That was on the shore of a lake that used to be where Kirkland Lake is now, but the tailings from the Wright-Hargreaves mine gradually filled in the lake. There was no railway in the area then, and the ore had to be back-packed to Amikougami Creek, which ran through the railway town of Swastika.

There was Sir Harry Oakes, whose chateau still stands in Kirkland Lake. He was once kicked off the train in Swastika because he could not pay the fare. He tried to get credit from a grocer and failed. Later, when he became a millionaire, he deliberately put the grocer out of business by financing a competing business. Restaurant owner Charlie Chow, who still runs Charlie's Hotel in Kirkland Lake, was wiser and luckier. He loaned money to Oakes and later, in lieu of cash, accepted shares in the Lake Shore Mine which were then selling for less than a dollar each. Oakes made enemies as well as friends, and his murder in the Bahamas in 1943 has never been solved.

Kirkland Lake produces another kind of gold: hockey players. Since the winters of northern Ontario are on the average several degrees colder than those in southern Ontario, the abundance of natural ice has always produced a good crop of skaters. Add to this the fact that mining is a hard life with low pay, and the incentive to make it big in the National or World Hockey Leagues is great.

The boys of Kirkland Lake have before them the example of Dick Duff, for instance; because he could skate like the wind and stick-handle and put the puck in the net, he never went down the mine as his father did, but lived well in Toronto, Montreal, Los Angeles, and New York instead of Kirkland Lake. Ted Lindsay, who is in the Hockey Hall of Fame, Ralph Backstrom, Gus Mortson, and the three Hillman brothers are some of the other heroes the kids can look to.

When I was in Kirkland Lake in the winter, I watched the kids practising on the open-air rinks. I remember two boys in particular, one below-zero night when all the other kids had quit, going from one end of the ice to the other, just the two of them, their breath like smoke in the frosty air, passing the puck back and forth, back and forth, practising the rudiments of the game. Those kids had ambition and drive. They knew what they wanted and what they had to do to get it.

Another night, I watched a game between two teams in one of the many leagues sponsored by the town. It was good hockey, taken seriously by the players and spectators alike. "You know, that young Tom skates a lot like Lindsay used to," I heard a spectator say. And then the next day the hockey buffs gathered in Arthur Hillman's restaurant to perch on stools, drink coffee, and talk about how the Hillman boys and the other graduates from their local leagues were doing in the big time.

Farther north on Highway 11, and a jog west on High 101, is the rich Porcupine mining district. The towns of South Porcupine and Schumacher, and the city of Timmins have long been famous on the stock exchanges of the world. In April 1964, the city of Timmins went crazy with one of the biggest speculation booms in history when the Texas Gulf Sulphur Company was opening up a major copper and zinc ore body in Kidd Township, 15 miles north of the city.

But it all began in the summer of 1909 with the discovery of the ore body that led to the Dome Mine. The story is typical of the way many great finds are made. Three prospectors were fighting black-flies and mosquitoes near the southwest shore of Porcupine Lake. They were tired and frustrated and ready to quit when one of them, Harry Preston, stepped on some moss on a slope and slipped. When he got up he soon quit cursing, for there under the moss was a vein of almost pure gold. They followed this ledge of ore, scraping moss and debris away furiously, until it ended in a dome of the richest ore they had ever seen.

That is the way it always happened; some prospectors made fabulous finds by accident, while others missed because they made a wrong turn at the wrong time. Benny Hollinger and Alex Gillies were cutting posts to stake a claim when they discovered a vein of quartz that "looked as though someone had dripped a candle along it, but instead of wax it was gold." Result, the great Hollinger Mine.

The Porcupine area was just nicely getting established when it was hit by one of the worst fires in Ontario's history. The spring of 1911 was a dry one. As early as May small fires were burning, and one wiped out the surface plant of the Hollinger Mine. Bush fires flared up here and there all spring until July 11, when they all seemed to come together and hit with the fury of a thousand devils.

There was no way to cope with the fire. As it grew, its own wind developed to hurricane proportions. Roaring through the woods with the speed of a freight train, it produced such unbelievable heat that horses standing in the lake had their backs baked. The citizens of South Porcupine had never seen such a fire, and many waited too long to escape.

The lake was the only refuge. Men, women, and children stood neck deep, ducking their heads regularly to keep from roasting. Then the wind of the fire whipped the waves to such a height that a great number were carried out into the lake and drowned.

Nothing was spared. Even valuables buried underground were burned to a crisp. One mine manager took his family and some workers underground for what he thought was certain safety. The roaring fire burned the headframe in minutes and sucked the air from the shaft; all were suffocated.

When the fire finally burned itself out, three townsites had been destroyed, along with 11 mining properties. Seventy-three persons were known to have perished, but nobody knew how many prospectors, trappers, and others without relatives to investigate their fates also perished in the fire.

Five years later another fire struck, this time farther north around the town of Cochrane. In some ways this one was even worse, covering 49 townships and completely devastating 20 of them. The official death toll this time was 224, but old-timers know that many more lost their lives. One of the ironic sidelights of that fire was that a freight train with 20 empty cars left Cochrane when the fire was threatening, and the conductor offered to take anyone who wished to go, free. Only a few took up his offer; a short time later many of those who did not were dead.

Much of the glamour of the old free-wheeling gold rush days is gone, but the communities of Kirkland Lake and Timmins continue to prosper. Today it is iron, lead, zinc, and copper for which the prospectors search, and it is these finds which cause the greatest flurry on Bay Street.

But there is still gold in the rocks that has never been found and this, along with the base metals awaiting discovery, makes it a good gamble for prospectors. And more than one vacationing camper carries along the prospector's short pick and chemicals for testing, with a good book on minerals and rocks. You never know when you might stumble on something. There is still wealth in the rocks.

A favourite trip of many Ontarians is to the seaside. Not the sea proper, but the shore of James Bay where the ancient town of Moosonee and its sister community, Moose Factory, give them a real sense of Ontario's fur-trading days. The most fascinating part of the trip for many is the long train ride through unsettled wilderness aboard the Polar Bear Express, which is the community's lifeline.

Passengers board the train at Toronto or North Bay or Cochrane, which is as far as the good road goes in that direction. The express is a great mixture of the old and the new. Her equipment is modern and the seats are comfortable, but she acts like one of the first chuggers that ever rode a track. Riding the Polar Bear Express can give you an idea of what the railway meant to all parts of the country before the advent of the car.

The express carries everything that the communities along the way need. Besides food and mail and equipment, it has supplies for the lonely trappers, hunters, and prospectors living in the vast wilderness. There is a stop at Mile 56, for instance, to drop off a piece for an outboard motor; a delivery of a small package at Mile 67 containing false teeth for a trapper. And so on.

Big game hunters and anglers use the Express to take them to where the fish and moose are. Indians use it for visiting relatives a mile or so up the line. For missionaries, teachers, and lumberjacks it is the only means of getting to where they are going. They will talk to the tourists, of course, and tell them anything they want to know. Often when they do not know the answer to a silly question they make one up.

The entire trip has a decidedly carnival tone. A beaming, loquacious man whom everybody knows as Gino prances up and down the aisles of the cars dressed in funny costumes, laughing and joking and playing requests on the accordion. When he plays "The Irish Washerwoman," for instance, he wears a cap that is supposed to be Irish, and a French toque for French songs, and so on. His biggest success, especially with the kids, is when he dresses up in his polar bear costume.

Besides the fascinating people, there is a variety of fascinating sights. There is the endless bush, streams, lakes, beaver dams and, when the rivers tumble from the shield down onto the Hudson Bay Lowlands, waterfalls. At Mile 93, the train stops to permit camera bugs to shoot pictures of Ontario Hydro's Otter Rapids Dam.

The part I liked best about the trip was the big black ravens that came to visit the train at every stop. They perch on poles, roofs, and trees. When the cook throws out some food to them, they swoop like huge black gulls to gobble it up. Ravens are beautiful birds and are rarely seen south of North Bay. Now they have become a tourist attraction.

At the end of the line, the traveller can either catch the next train back after a six-hour visit, or he can stay there and poke around

Moosonee and Moose Factory for as long as he wants. There is moderately good accommodation, but in summer it is well to book it ahead of time.

The Moosonee–Moose Factory complex (the latter is an island in the river) contains a contrast in living. The Hudson's Bay Company people and the government people live in good homes and send their children to a good school and attend pleasant churches. The 2,000 Cree Indians on the other hand, live—as do Indians in most other parts of Canada—in shacks.

An old blacksmith shop built in 1740 is still in operation, and there is a small stone magazine that has been there since the mid-eighteenth century. In the autumn, when geese gather in the bay preparatory to their long migration flight, the railway runs the Blue Goose Special to carry hunters. For the big game hunters, there are numerous outfitters' camps where the nimrod can rent everything from a pair of boots to an aircraft to take him to remote areas where he can shoot polar bears, timber wolves or moose.

If you have the money and feel up to it, you might hire a pilot to fly you to Polar Bear Provincial Park at the north end of James Bay. Covering an area of 7,100 square miles, Polar Bear is one of the newest and by long odds the largest park in the province. If you go you must take everything you will need, for there are no services of any kind in the park. But the park is there, a wilderness area which the greedy hand of man cannot tear apart and devastate. Remote and forbidding now, who knows but that within a few years it may see thousands of visitors every summer. For such is the expanding population of Ontario that soon these northern regions will be populated, too.

Another interesting trip for the camper, fisherman, history buff, or just plain sightseer is the one that leads from Parry Sound more or less along the north shore of Lakes Huron and Superior to Thunder Bay, the modern name for the lakehead cities of Fort William and Port Arthur.

We made our first stop at Grundy Lake Provincial Park where, on the shore of a lovely little glacial lake amid forests of pine and birch and poplar, were good campgrounds. The swimming was great, with a beach and a diving raft and lifeguards on duty. It cost a couple of dollars to pitch a tent and there were tables and fireplaces and good washrooms. All of the other campgrounds we stopped at were much the same: a good lake for swimming, fishing, or water skiing for those pulling a boat, and adequate facilities.

Then came Sudbury, the largest city in the district of the same name. To Ontarians, Sudbury means nickel. It also means the city of the north and devastation. One resident who had moved away described Sudbury as "the town that sits on a rock and stinks." The first impression of the city is immense black heaps of slag from the mines, with houses and stores huddled in their shadow, and an almost complete lack of vegetation. A closer look reveals many attractive features of this modern active, multi-lingual city.

Sudbury is on the edge of the famous Sudbury Basin, 37 miles long and 17 miles wide. There are two different theories about the origins of this freak of nature.

Both theories agree that whatever happened it was a long time ago, something like 1,700 million years. They also agree that the formation of the Sudbury Basin was an extremely violent and rapid event. One theory says that a volcanic eruption formed the basin, a great volcanic explosion that caused "multitudes of tension fractures to open and close like giant jaws." The minerals were thrust up from deep in the earth to fill these cracks, and that is where they are today.

The other theory says that the Sudbury Basin is the result of a giant meteor that struck the earth many millions of years ago, and that the force of the impact had much the same effect as a volcanic eruption would have had.

Whatever the origin, the Sudbury Basin is one of the richest deposits of nickel on the surface of the earth. The nickel and copper ore was first discovered when the CPR was being blasted through this region in 1880. At first it was the copper ore that mining magnates were after, and there was plenty of it. Later, however, as the world needed more and more hard steel, and nickel became the principal alloy in its manufacture, that metal became the more valuable. Now some twenty mines in the Sudbury area produce nickel, copper, iron, platinum, and a variety of other minerals.

Sudbury seems very remote from southern Ontario. In the first place, the population of this fast-growing city does not come from southern Ontario, but from Quebec, western Canada, eastern Canada, and Europe. About 53 per cent of the population is French speaking; there are bilingual schools, and the only bilingual university in Ontario, Laurentian University. Besides the French, there are large numbers of Italians, Poles, Ukrainians, Finns, and many others. In a "country and western" bar a singer sadly croons a song called "Farewell to Nova Scotia" while some of the patrons weep into their beer. In another eating place, the Caruso Club, the waiters all speak Italian.

West from Sudbury is one of the most remarkable communities in all Ontario, Elliot Lake. In many ways it is typical of the new north. It did not begin as a rough and ready mining camp where the search for riches was the only concern, and the problem of how people would live was secondary. No, Elliot Lake was planned from the beginning. It began with the raw bush of the Canadian Shield, and in a few short years became a model community of new homes, paved streets, green lawns, shopping centres, churches, schools, parks, and recreation centres—everything that people need.

The development of the region was fast and efficient. It began with the famous "backdoor staking bee," in which mining promoters who had investigated the wealth of the uranium discoveries hired hundreds of men who, with the greatest of secrecy, staked out the 80-mile stretch of the uranium field, and in one fell swoop filed title to 1,400 claims.

Then, when the mines were begun and accommodation was needed for the miners and all the camp followers who make up a mining community, the federal and provincial governments stepped in with the money for highways, streets, services, and houses.

The whole operation was based on United States Atomic Energy Commission and Canadian government contracts to buy $1,500 million worth of uranium by 1963. When the contract was not renewed and some uranium mines closed down, it looked as though Elliot Lake might become the most beautiful ghost town in the world. But the Ontario and federal governments again came to the rescue and located establishments there, while the discovery of other metals and the improvement of the uranium market have helped to sustain the economy.

Highway 17 runs along the North Channel of Lake Huron, in some places so close to the water that you can see the ferries that run from Manitoulin Island to Blind River and Thessalon. Both towns were once big in the lumber trade, but in recent years have done most of their business with fishermen, hunters, and tourists.

Sault Ste. Marie, on the St. Mary's River which flows from Lake Superior to Lake Huron and drops 20 feet on the way, is one of Ontario's more historic cities and the oldest community in northern Ontario. Etienne Brulé was probably the first white man to see the beautiful falls. The early explorers and fur traders also went upriver on their way west. The Ojibwa tribes that lived there were called Sauteurs, or "people of the falls," and the name gradually became Salteux.

Ever since the canal was opened on the Canadian side of the river in 1895, the city of Sault Ste. Marie has prospered. The Americans had built their canal 40 years earlier and when they refused permission for General Garnet Wolseley's expedition to the west to pass through it in 1870, the Canadian government realized it must have a canal of its own. This marked the end of the fur trade era and the beginning of industrial growth. Along with the trade that naturally came with the canal, one of the busiest in the world, there was an abundance of pulpwood forest in the area, and iron mines to the north. Today the Sault is the second largest producer of steel in the province.

The Sault also does a big business with American tourists, who like to cross the International Bridge and then make the grand circle around Lake Superior.

Just north of the Sault is the immense Lake Superior Provincial Park, with some sixty miles of Superior shoreline and over a thousand inland lakes. There are good campgrounds, picnic areas, scenic lookouts, and hiking trails. A tourist pulling his own motor boat and willing to live in a tent can spend weeks in the park and never fish the same lake twice.

North of the park is the lively little town of Wawa (Indian for goose), which owes its existence to the iron mines on its mountain. At the point on the Trans-Canada Highway where the road branches off to the town is an immense statue of a Canada goose that most tourists stop to take pictures of.

An attempt was made after the last war to change the name of the town to Jamestown, after the mining magnate Sir James Dunn, but the townspeople would have none of it. They simply took down the Jamestown signs from station and post office and replaced them with Wawa signs. As one resident put it, "We had nothing against his lordship, you understand. It's just that Wawa is a hell of a lot better name for a town."

Between Wawa and Nipigon there are three provincial parks along the highway, with accommodation for campers. We stopped at Rainbow Falls, which is close to Lake Superior but on pretty, little White Sands Lake. The waterfalls are beautiful, spilling down over granite shelves in a clear, sparkling spray.

The country here is more rugged than that we had passed through before, with big hills and cliffs near the shore, the famous "north shore" of Lake Superior which has attracted so many landscape painters.

Nipigon, at the mouth of the river that flows from Lake Nipigon into Lake Superior, is a typical northern pulpwood town. The river is usually full of logs, and there is a huge pulp and paper mill in the town. I had a haircut there, and the barber told me that when he came to Nipigon 30 years before there was not a Frenchman in the town. Now more of the inhabitants speak French than English.

The city of Thunder Bay is next, Ontario's newest city, made up of the two cities of Port Arthur and Fort William, which have been competing with each other for industry and business and attention since both settlements began. Fort William began as a trading post for the North West Company, and Port Arthur began as a silver-mining camp. Thunder Bay is just about in the geographical centre of Canada from east to west, and it is an ocean port. It is much closer to Winnipeg than to any of the large cities of southern Ontario, and Thunder Bay citizens refer to themselves as westerners.

The best place from which to see the city and the lake and the harbour is Hillcrest Park at the top of Mount McKay. Looking east you see the bay (Animikie Wekwed, the Ojibwas called it, which means Thunderbird Bay), protected from the storms of Lake Superior by Pie Island and a great rock formation called "the sleeping giant" because from the shore it looks like a giant lying on his back.

There is the breakwater that the citizens of Port Arthur fought so hard to get from the government, while the citizens of Fort William argued that the best harbour could be made by dredging the Kaministikwia River. In the end, both jobs were done to make Thunder Bay the best and busiest inland port in Canada.

And there are the grain elevators, the biggest in the world. More than two dozen of them tower high above the flat town, with the great grain ships busily loading for the long trip across the lakes and down through the seaway to the Atlantic and to other countries. Most of the grain from the prairies passes through the Thunder Bay harbour, and much of it must be stored there.

The ore-loading docks can be plainly seen, too. In some ways they are even more impressive than the grain elevators. Millions of tons of iron ore from the great Steep Rock mines are loaded into ore boats to be carried to the steel milling centres of the Great Lakes: Gary, Indiana; Hamilton, Ontario; and Cleveland, Ohio.

And there is always a great boom of logs in the bay, being shipped away to be made into paper or lumber. Wheat, iron ore, wood products, and package freight all pass through the port of Thunder Bay.

You can see the railway terminals, too. The best story of the Lakehead has to do with the early days of the railway. Fort William worked very hard to get the railway terminal there, because the people knew that if it went to Nipigon, their community would never grow the way they wanted it to. They got the railroad, all right, but the company decided to build its freight sheds and offices in Port Arthur, and the rivalry between the two cities was more intense than ever.

The arrangement was certainly not a happy one. The Port Arthur city fathers considered that the railway should pay taxes on its property there, while the railway company, considering the great benefits they were bringing to the town, refused to pay a nickel. So, the city fathers got a court order and actually seized one of the CPR trains for back taxes.

The wheat was in the fan then for sure. Sir William Cornelius Van Horne, who was not accustomed to taking any guff from anybody, was so provoked that he moved the freight sheds and offices from Port Arthur to Fort William. "For this act, the grass will grow in the streets of Port Arthur," he predicted. It almost did, too, until the Canadian Northern Railway was built and Port Arthur gradually caught up to its rival again.

The rivalry between the two cities was probably a good thing in many ways, becaust it kept each working hard to outdo the other. When the poet Rudyard Kipling visited the cities, he wrote that "The twin cities hate each other with the pure, passionate, poisonous hatred that makes cities grow. If Providence wiped out one of them, the other would pine away and die . . . a matchless hate bird."

All that animosity is gone now, however, or at least most of it. On the first day of January, 1970, the two cities were joined together under their new name of Thunder Bay. Most of the citizens interviewed for television agreed grudgingly that it was probably a good thing. Some did not like the new name, but since it was chosen by a vote of the citizens of both cities, there was nothing to be done about it. It remains to be seen if the wedding can produce the same vigour and activity as the rivalry did.

The huge section west of Thunder Bay can be travelled by Highways 11 and 17. There is camping at Kakabeka Falls, where the water drops 150 feet over a granite shelf, and a plaque tells you that an Indian maiden once plunged into the falls to save her tribe from its enemies. There are great stretches of wilderness which can be reached only by canoe or aircraft; there are no towns at all, and no roads.

This is hunting and fishing country with moose, deer, and bear being the principal animals the hunters seek. Numerous outfitters will provide guides, food, equipment, transportation, and other hunters' requirements, and in many places this is the only industry.

Quetico Provincial Park, which can be reached by Highway 11, is more than a million acres of wilderness. There are no roads, and aircraft are permitted to land at only a few designated lakes. The interior is reserved entirely for the rugged. You can travel for days without seeing anything but the occasional deer or moose or bear. Immense blue herons lift ponderously from the shore as you round a bend in a river. Mink or otter splash in the water, and there is a long chance that your canoe may be tipped over by a moose who has submerged to reach the succulent water plants. You pitch your tent on a huge rounded rock and watch that the chipmunks do not steal your bread in broad daylight, and that 'coons don't stage a midnight raid. The swimming is good, the fishing is wonderful, and never a motor boat roars past to smash the silence.

For anyone addicted to scuba diving, there is a special attraction in the lakes and rivers along the south boundary of Quetico Park, which is also the boundary between Canada and the United States. It was along here that for over a hundred years hardy *voyageurs* freighted their furs and supplies in huge birchbark canoes. Spills into the river were frequent, and divers have brought up a variety of articles which date back to the mid-eighteenth century.

It was the Sieur de la Vérendrye, the great French trader and explorer, who first travelled these waters in 1731. An Indian named Ochagach drew him a map showing the rivers that flow into Lake Superior from the west: the St. Louis, the Kaministikwia, and the Pigeon. La Vérendrye chose the Pigeon River route, which became known as the Grand Portage or "great carrying place." The French traders used the route extensively, and later it was used by the North West Company which, at the height of its activities, employed more than five hundred men to transport its furs.

A company's bill of lading tells what was carried by one canoe: "1 Keg Spirits, 3 Kegs High Wines, 1 Bale Twist Tobacco, 1 Keg

Powder, 1 Case Guns, 2 Bags Shot, 2 Bags Balls, ½ Keg Grease, 1 Keg Butter, 3 Bushels Corn, 2 Cases of Iron Goods [axes, etc.], etc., etc." The canoe also carried spruce gum and sheets of bark for making repairs along the way and, of course, trade goods for the Indians. The commonest of these were the nested iron kettles which fitted inside each other and hence were easier to carry. Some have been recovered by divers, and dated by experts as having been manufactured about 1790.

All the goods were packed with the greatest of care to keep them dry and intact. As nearly as possible, each "piece" weighed 90 pounds, which was a handy bundle for a man to carry on portages. Some of the *voyageurs* would carry three or four at the same time, loaded on their backs and held in place by a strap that came around the forehead. On the Grand Portage route there were over forty carrying places.

A well-known fur trader, Alexander Henry, has left this account of an accident on the river:

> I perceived the canoe on the north side coming off to sault [shoot] the rapids. She had not gone many yards when, by some misman-agement of the foreman, the current bore down her bow full upon the shore against a rock. The canoe was found flat upon the water, broken in many places. The loss amounted to five bales of merchandise, two bales new tobacco, one bale canal tobacco, one bale kettles, one bale balls, one bale shot, one case guns. I was surprised that a keg of sugar drifted down about half a mile below the rapid as its weight was 87 pounds; it proved to be but little damaged. The kegs of gunpowder also floated a great distance and did not leak.

Back on Highway 11, you will pass Atikokan, near which is the famous Steep Rock Mine, worth a visit even if just to learn to what lengths and expense mining companies will go to get valuable ore. Early discoveries and later exploration showed that the main iron ore body lay at the bottom of the lake. So the river was diverted, part of the lake was dammed off, and 100 billion gallons of water were pumped out. Then a layer of silt, in some places 100 feet thick, was bulldozed off, and the open-pit mining began. Today the tourist can still see some of the lake bottom 300 feet below the surface.

The usual route, and the best, across northwestern Ontario is

Highway 17 which follows the line of the CPR. It is a long, long road with little to see but a wall of black spruce forest along either side of the highway and the occasional glimpse of a lake. The settlements are small and far apart. English River, for instance, is one we looked forward to as a break in the monotony. When we got there, a sign told us: "You are looking for English River? This was it."

North of the highway is a vast area, stretching to Hudson Bay, filled with muskeg, forests, lakes, and rivers. This is as wild country as can be found anywhere in Canada, and it is inhabited mostly by Indian and Métis hunters, trappers, and fishermen. There are, of course, many minerals in the rock, as the mines at Red Lake indicate, and anyone with strength, determination, and hardiness can get plenty of co-operation to go prospecting.

The bush plane, that hardy little aircraft that lands on lakes and rivers, is still the principal means of transportation and travel in this part of the country. And in communities such as Sioux Lookout, you can hire a free-lance bush pilot to take you anywhere you have the nerve to go. That is, except during fall freeze-up and spring break-up, when floating chunks of ice make the water unfit for landing.

Dryden is a fair-sized pulp manufacturing town on the highway that also caters to hunters and fishermen who fly up from the States to make use of the northern wilderness. Unfortunately, many of them bring everything they need for the entire stay, and return home with their fish or moose without leaving a dime in Dryden.

I have always had a bad feeling about Dryden since reading an article about its vigourous campaign to stamp out timber wolves. Shooting them in winter from aircraft was popular, the article explained. The pilot harasses the poor animals until they run out onto a lake and, then the plane swoops low so that the "sportsman," who is paying well for the privilege, can pick them off. Fortunately, all this has had little effect on the wolf population.

We always get pretty tired travelling along this stretch of road, and last time we were also unbearably hot. Then we got into the Lake of the Woods region, which is as beautiful as Muskoka. It was getting late and we had to camp soon, and at the junction of Highways 17 and 71 we saw a sign that pointed south to Rushing River Park. We went to have a look.

Well, Rushing River turned out to be one of the most attractive, the most convenient, and the best-run parks we have ever been in.

A small river slides over precambrian rock into a sand-bottom pool that is clear and cool and sparkling. I stopped the car in a camping space and, without pausing, jumped out and headed for that pond, kicked off my sandals, and dove in. Few things I have ever done have felt better.

The hot weather continued, and so we just stayed there, swimming and hiking and picking berries, for three whole days. Then we felt able to face the road again and drove on to the town of Kenora.

Kenora is the largest town in the more than three hundred miles from Thunder Bay to the Ontario–Manitoba border. It is a lumbering, tourist-outfitting, and mining community which was established as a trading post in 1790. Because of the thousands of muskrats, it was first called Rat Portage.

During the building of the Canadian Pacific Railway, it was a divisional centre and had the reputation of being one of the roughest, bawdiest, drinkingest, hell-raisingest towns along the whole line. Innumerable stories are told of the escapades of the booze peddlers and the speculators and just plain roughnecks and, allowing for the fact that probably half of them are apocryphal, it adds up to a pretty randy place. Today, Kenora is as quiet and peaceful as any Ontario town.

Twenty miles farther on, we were at the Manitoba border, having travelled well over a thousand miles from North Bay. Ontario is a mighty big province.

CHAPTER XIII

Last Word

This is Ontario as I see it. Many people see it differently. The miner sees it as a hole in the ground from which he emerges periodically into the sunlight. The socialite sees it as mink stoles, opening night at the O'Keefe Centre, and shaking the hand of the Lieutenant-Governor. The immigrant sees it as a rickety upstairs flat on Euclid Street in Toronto, or a tiny restaurant on Mill Street in Orangeville. The advertising executive sees it as the largest and richest market in Canada. The Grey County farmer sees it as a nice, safe, conservative province.

One thing that I am sure of, after 30 years in Ontario, is that generalizations are rarely true. When you speak of the Ontario character to me, you must define your terms. Which Ontario citizen do you mean? The one whose family has been here since 1780, or the one who just arrived from Ireland last year?

Is it Bert Davies, who came from Wales a few years ago and sounds like it? A lean, handsome young man, with a hungry look in his eye, who is trying to make it selling insurance weekdays and nights, and spends his weekends playing rugger at an Aurora pitch with a group of other newcomers from Britain.

Is it Olan Pernowsky, who came to Streetsville from Poland in the early Fifties, with no money and unable to speak the language?

He lived in the barn of a friend of mine and picked up odd jobs around town. He would do anything, paint a house, fix an eaves-trough, dig a ditch, or buy scrap iron from you for a few cents. He bought my old furnace when I had a new oil-burning one installed, and carted it off down the road in a rickety wagon. The next time I saw him he had replaced the rickety wagon with a rickety truck, and was hauling bigger loads. He had moved out of the barn into a shack. Six months later I saw him again, and he had a better truck with his name painted on the side. Shortly after that, he made a payment on a rundown piece of land that was there for anyone to buy, and when the big real estate boom hit Streetsville, he sold it at a good profit. When I last saw Olan Pernowsky, he looked very happy indeed. He had managed to bring his wife and family from Poland, and was building a fine house. He had more money in the bank than I had, and when I first knew him he could not even speak English.

Ontario is the lonely prospector searching the hard rock of the Canadian Shield for the big strike. It is the young man from Estevan living in a cold-water flat on Parliament Street and showing his radio plays to the CBC. It is the actress from Red Deer, the sports editor from Cypress River, and the script girl from Oxbow.

Ontario is the dozens of descendants of Featherstone Osler, who came to Bond Head from Cornwall in 1837. He worked in that tiny forest community building churches, burying the dead, teaching the ignorant, marrying the hopeful, scolding the sinful, and riding hundreds of miles every month to do what he knew must be done if a community was to fulfil itself. And he raised eight children, one of whom was to become one of the most important medical men of the century.

Ontario is also university students. Thousands of them: arguing, debating, protesting, and studying. Some are idealistic, some cynical, but all are determined that things have got to change.

Ontario is the headquarters of banks and insurance companies, and the throngs of people who work in them. It is the men who run the factories, and the men who work in them, each convinced that he should have more of the profits. It is a province where governments do not interfere too much with a man's right to exploit his neighbour, whether it be by selling him a phony chrome cleaner at the door, or a worthless mining moose pasture over the telephone.

And most of the people who live in Ontario know, just as people in many other provinces do, that they live in the best part of Canada. They have the lakes and hills and forests at their doorsteps, and they make full use of them. They travel and they camp and they ski, and they go to Florida in the winter, and have never been to Saskatchewan. When they get back from their travels they say, "I didn't see any place as good as this."

That is Ontario, or at least a part of it.

Index